9.95

FORGOTTEN EMPRESS

The Tragedy of the Empress of Ireland

by

David Zeni

Avid Publications
Garth Boulevard
Bebington, Wirral,
Merseyside.
CH63 5LS
Telephone / Fax: (44) 0151 645 2047
e-mail info @ AvidPublications.co.uk
website http//www.AvidPublications.co.uk

THE FORGOTTEN EMPRESS
-The Tragedy of the Empress of Ireland
by David Zeni

ISBN 1 902964 15 2

**Editing, Typeset and cover design by William David
Roberts MA, Avid Publications.**

Front cover: 'Sunset over the Empress of Ireland' from a
painting by Yves Bérubé (Courtesy of the
artist) and stark piles of the bodies of some of the victims.
Rear cover: A Dying Ship. The *Empress of Ireland* sinking
fast, lifeboats pulling away and the collier *Storstad*.From a
painting by William Wheeler 1964. Courtesy of the
Salvation Army Heritage Museum, Toronto.

Acknowledgements

Special thanks to the following individuals whose extra effort made this Avid Edition possible:

Geoffrey E. Whitfield and Craig Stringer for revisions to the Passenger Manifest and for preparation of the never-before-published crew list;

Michel T. Prévost and Alain Vézina of Merlin Films, Montreal, for their assistance in providing images;

Bernard Reischl and Prometheus Graphics, Montreal, for digital restoration of images;

and to Dolores and Mark Fallon for their skilled crafting of the index.

David Zeni 2001

The *Empress of Ireland* leaving Liverpool.
A Mersey Ferry can be seen in the background as can
one of Cunard's massive four funnelers, perhaps
Mauretania or *Lusitania.*
In the foreground hundreds of people stroll along the
promenade at New Brighton

Contents

The Author.
David Zeni pictured in
Govan, Glasgow UK.

Forgotten Empress

The Tragedy of the Empress of Ireland

David Zeni

'...dubbed 'The 'Forgotten Empress'...the second in a shocking trio of tragedies at sea...sandwiched in between the disasters of the Titanic and the Lusitania ... and it was a sudden death... that sent Liverpool into mourning...'

Liverpool Echo

'It grips the reader in such a way as to make it hard to put aside...it is excellent'

Sea Lines

' Zeni brings a fresh, moment by moment urgency to this real life tragic drama'

Winnipeg Free Press

Introduction

Ariveting story of collision at sea, the *Empress of Ireland* should be remembered as number two in a triumvirate of Atlantic liner losses beginning with *Titanic* and ending with *Lusitania* — all lost within three years of each other. More importantly, the *Empress* should be remembered for having a higher fatality of passengers (840) in one calamity than either *Titanic* (832) or *Lusitania* (791). Many passengers on the lower decks never had a chance as volumes of frigid water burst into cabins late at night. These victims awakened just in time to experience the final seconds of life. Water soon overcame their resistance, invaded their lungs, and ended their prayers. Other passengers, who believed they had successfully escaped when they reached the top deck, discovered the horror of an ocean liner about to capsize.

My goal in writing Forgotten Empress was to learn about the Empress of Ireland. The more I learned, the more I became hooked on the story. Unlike Titanic, the Empress of Ireland holds the interest of a small number of historians and enthusiasts. This makes the story ideal for the discovery of new, instead of rehashed, information. The Empress of Ireland story is intriguing to me because it involves the puzzle of how two ships initially in sight of one another managed to collide in the fog. I also find the death-throes of a capsized ocean liner to be far more graphic than a gradual settling by the head.

The *Empress*'s maiden voyage, from Liverpool to Quebec, took place during the summer of 1906. She instantly set new standards for speed, reliability, and comfort on the high seas. Today, an unrecognised stepchild in the family of maritime tragedies with less than a handful of books published to tell her story, she is the *Forgotten Empress.*

A work of this scope on events which took place over eighty years ago is bound to have errors in it. Many details remain hopelessly irreconcilable. An extensive variety of sources was used to help ferret out inaccuracies. There are no fictitious or composite characters. To the extent I have misspelled or misreported any information, I apologize.

The history of Canadian Pacific Railway is drawn from *The Last Spike*, by Pierre Berton; *History of the Canadian Pacific Line* by Frank C. Bowen; and *The Romantic History of the Canadian Pacific* by John Murray Gibbon. The true crime story of Dr. Crippen is based on two definitive sources: *The Mild Murderer* by Tom A. Cullen; and Captain Henry G. Kendall's autobiography *Adventures on the High Seas.* The stories of passengers come from contemporary newspaper accounts and from information provided by descendants of survivors. Information about the wreck is from interviews with divers. Monetary amounts which are mentioned are unadjusted from their original value in sterling or Canadian dollars.

No finer compliment could be paid to this author than to have others improve and build upon this research. I hope that readers will find the *Empress of Ireland* saga as compelling as I do. The next time someone shares a word in the never ending story of *Titanic*, you might mix it up a bit with an *Empress of Ireland* story from *Forgotten Empress.* Bon Voyage!

David Zeni - Author

Marvels of an Edwardian age — the *Empress of Ireland* and the automobile.
(Maritime Museum of British Columbia, Victoria)

1 Auspicious Beginnings

The *Empress of Ireland* was owned and operated by the Canadian Pacific Railway (CPR). The origins of this company date back to the second half of the nineteenth century. Four men of means met during the summer of 1880 in Ottawa to discuss the terms of a contract for construction of a trans-Canadian railroad which would link the Eastern Maritime Provinces to the Pacific Ocean. These entrepreneurs, who together became known as the Syndicate, were James Jerome Hill, railway builder, Donald Smith, Commissioner of the Hudson Bay Company, Duncan McIntyre, dominant investor in the Canada Central Railway, and George Stephen, President of the Bank of Montreal. This historic meeting was not about the design of colossal new ships, as would later predominate a similar dinner engagement between J. Bruce Ismay and Lord Pirrie giving birth to *Titanic* and her sisters. The focus of the Ottawa gathering was how to finesse support from Parliament for construction of a mammoth transcontinental railway run by private enterprise. It was as ambitious in the 1880s as landing a man on the moon would be in the next century.

The Syndicate chose one of its own, George Stephen, to lead their colossal venture. Stephen, born in the Highlands of Scotland, moved from Aberdeen to Montreal at the age of 21 in 1850. Thirty years later he was champion of the Syndicate's vision — an intermodal transportation system of steamships and rolling stock stretching from Europe, across Canada, all the way to Japan. Stephen was not alone in his vision. What many authors describe as the romance of the Canadian Pacific Railway is best illustrated by this excerpt from a speech by the Marquis of Lorne, Governor General of Canada, who travelled west with his daughter, Princess Louise, to view the Pacific railway under construction:

> *Affording the best and safest highway between Asia and Europe, she will see traffic from both directed to her coasts. With a hand upon either ocean, she will gather from each for the benefit of her hardy millions a share of the commerce of the world, To the East and to the West she will pour forth of her abundance, her treasures of food and the riches of her mines and of her forests, demanded of her by the less fortunate of mankind.*

Syndicate entrepreneurs were motivated by the financial success of the first American transcontinental line completed in 1869. Their challenge would be to convince Parliament and investors that the Syndicate could deliver similar success with a trans-Canadian rail network. George Stephen, like all product champions, had the requisite drive, tenacity, passion, and power of persuasion. In addition, Stephen and Syndicate members had solid financial backgrounds which included rescuing a failing rail company from bankruptcy and returning it to profitability as the St Paul, Minneapolis, and Manitoba Railway. Prime Minister Sir John A. Macdonald and the Syndicate's McIntyre reached an agreement with Parliament in September 1880. They were triumphant, having obtained extremely favourable terms for Canadian Pacific.

The ink was hardly dry on the contract before Stephen sailed for London to line up an international group of financiers. Personally, Stephen had misgivings, thinking the whole project wrung with folly. Would the Rocky Mountains present elevations too formidable for locomotives to climb? Would the surveyors locate a pass through the Selkirk Mountains in British Columbia? Once completed, would the line attract settlement and freight or would it be a railroad to nowhere? Stephen's uncertainty was closely held, shared only with the closest confidants.

Stephen's Canadian Pacific Railway Company contract was ratified by an Act of Parliament on 15 February 1881. The contract required construction of 2540 miles of track from Bonfield, Ontario, in the east to Port Moody, British Columbia—Pacific terminus in the west. The Government was constructing 700 of the 2540 miles in three separate pieces. The balance, a little over 1800 miles, was CPR's to build. Completion was to take no longer than ten years, subject to penalty if not finished by May 1891. The agreement also required that a majority of board members be British citizens. The Government backed the enterprise with a $25 million subsidy, land grants, exemption from taxes on imported materials, and a prohibition against construction of rival lines south of Canadian Pacific's for a period of 20 years. The cash subsidy was payable based on progress for each 20 miles of track laid.

Land on either side of the proposed track was divided into a patchwork of large square blocks. These blocks appeared as alternating red-and white-coloured squares on charter maps. The red blocks denoted areas retained by the Canadian Government. The white blocks represented grants of land to Canadian Pacific. This simple pattern may have inspired the design of CPR's house flag which is a traditional red and white checkerboard.

The Canadian Pacific contract also reveals that the company was both a railroad and steamship company from the beginning. The company was chartered to purchase or lease any rail lines necessary to connect with deep water Atlantic ports. Further, CPR was authorized to:

> *maintain docks, dockyards, wharves, ships and piers at any point, and at all the termini... and to acquire, own, hold, charter and run steam and other vessels for cargo and passengers upon any navigable water, which the Canadian Pacific Railway may reach or connect with.*

Canadian Pacific Railway Company held its first meeting on 17 February 1881. By the end of that year, James Hill, one of the founding four, was not satisfied with the progress of construction. The cash subsidy was but a trickle into company coffers. To speed things up, CPR hired the aggressive American engineer William Cornelius Van Horne, former boss of the Chicago, Milwaukee and St Paul Railroad.

Van Horne, ten months later, lured another American away from Van Horne's former employer. That American was Thomas G. Shaughnessy, a second generation Irish immigrant. The Shaughnessys came to America with literally nothing, having been robbed on the crossing from Ireland. Van Horne was impressed with Shaughnessy's management of dry goods and material at Chicago,

William Cornelius Van Horne, builder of the Canadian Pacific Railway and designer of the red and white checkerboard house flag. Van Horne is often credited as the founder of North American tourism because of his famous statement: 'If we can't export the scenery, we'll import the tourist'. (Canadian Pacific Archives).

Milwaukee, and St Paul. Van Horne took Shaughnessy to lunch and recruited him over a mug or two of Milwaukee beer. Shaughnessy was enticed by the challenge of working on the most extensive rail project ever built. He accepted the position of Purchasing Agent at CPR.

Construction continued until January 1885, when a cash crunch combined with labour strikes brought the great railroad to its knees. The collapse of CPR was imminent. Founders Stephen and Smith used their personal assets as collateral to meet payroll and pay creditors. At the final hour, Prime Minister Macdonald, arranged a temporary Government loan which was used to pay back wages. Construction resumed at a frenetic pace. The Pacific end of the line from Port Moody eastward, constructed as part of the 700 miles of public work, was completed to a point known as Eagle Pass by the end of September 1885. The other end of the line from Ontario westward reached Eagle Pass during the first week in November 1885.

Eagle Pass represented a southern route through the infamous, once thought insurmountable, elevated ranges of British Columbia. It is here on 7 November 1885, at a spot called Craigellachie, where the last spike was driven home to mark completion of the trans-Canadian railway. As historical events go, it was not without its moments.

To commemorate the occasion, a silver spike was purchased for the ceremony by then Governor General of Canada, Lord Lansdowne. Van Horne objected to the use of this glittering spike, seeing it as bad luck and presumptuous of prosperity not yet achieved. Instead, Van Horne preferred to have one of his labourers drive home a standard spike just like the thousands which went before it. Van Horne also discouraged non-employees from attending the ceremony. Apparently, Van Horne was not in a celebratory mood. One of the 'employees', Donald Smith, of the founding four, was among attendees and he was in the mood to be part of the festivities. As ranking company man, he chose to drive home the last spike. In accordance with Van Horne's wishes, 65-year-old Smith prepared to hammer down the ordinary spike rather than the silver one.

Arthur Piers, manager of Canadian Pacific Railway steamships. (Canadian Pacific Archives).

Hearts stopped and lumps grew in the throats of those assembled as Smith raised the sledge hammer high above his head. To everyone's horror, Smith struck an uneven blow and bent the spike in half. A quick acting trackmaster, named Brothers, pried the disfigured spike out and replaced it with a fresh one, sparing Smith prolonged embarrassment. Brothers tossed the fallen soldier aside where it caught the eye of Arthur Piers, administrative assistant to Van Horne, who later became head of CPR steamships.

On the second try before a greatly relieved assembly, Smith used a series of short blows to gradually tap the spike into place. The first element of the greatest transportation system in the world was completed. Those assembled cheered. The story of the last spike, however, does not end here. This continuing saga should be especially amusing to souvenir hounds and collectors.

The disfigured spike which Brothers had casually tossed clear of the track was surreptitiously snatched from the ground by Arthur Piers. As CPR managers boarded the company coach, Smith noticed a bulge in the overcoat Piers was wearing. Although we don't know the exact words exchanged, Smith relieved Piers of his burden as only an executive handling an underling knows how. It may have been as unkind as 'Hand it over, office boy,' because Smith wanted to destroy the embarrassing bent spike.

Destroy the spike he did. He had it fractured into many small flat tokens. Diamonds were mounted on these for brooches and other presentation pieces for the wives of dignitaries. These historic gifts were so highly prized by women associated with CPR that Smith ran out. To avoid slighting anyone, he had another spike broken down and made into similar presentation pieces. The ladies were still not satisfied because the second set of gifts could be distinguished from those cut from the original bent spike. Smith wisely decided to stop, accepting that some of the women would never be content with anything other than a brooch made from the genuine article — a bent railroad spike.

Brothers, afraid that souvenir hounds would destroy his track in search of the last spike actually driven home by Smith, decided to remove it. That spike was given to Sir Edward W. Beatty, who became President of CPR in 1918. The spike was later stolen from his desk. As for the unused silver spike, it was mounted and kept by William Cornelius Van Horne.

Transcontinental passenger service did not commence on a regular basis until 28 June 1886. The first through train left old Dalhousie Station in Montreal at 8:00pm. Enormous fanfare marked the occasion including a fifteen gun salute. The journey west to Port Moody took a little over five days.

Stephen never lost sight of the fact that he would need ships once the two oceans were bridged by rail. As early as October 1884, he and Macdonald sailed for England to begin negotiations for a Pacific Ocean Royal Mail subsidy. Stephen knew that the success of his railroad depended on ships not just for freight but also to land immigrants who could build Canada's economy. The first step in getting those ships was to secure a contract for carriage of mail. Stephen told the Montreal *Daily Star*:

> *I hope that by the time I return to have succeeded in establishing a line of steamers to run in connection with the Canadian Pacific between Port Moody, Japan, and China. These steamers will make the voyage in three days shorter time than between Yokohama and San Francisco, and will be larger and much finer vessels.*

Although Stephen was not successful in obtaining the Pacific mail subsidy, 1884 was noteworthy for another reason. CPR ordered its first new construction ships. These small Great Lakes steamers of about 3,000 tons each were the *Alberta*, *Athabaska*, and *Algoma*. Since the route of the railroad passed by all of Lake Superior to the north, steamers were an ideal way of moving men and material along the northern shore. CPR had good luck with two of their first three ships. The *Alberta* and *Athabaska* would be in service for decades. The *Algoma*, however, was shortlived. After barely a year of service, she succumbed in a violent storm on Lake Superior taking 48 souls out of 63 on board with her.

Stephen, not discouraged by the loss of *Algoma* and lack of Pacific mail subsidy, plunged ahead to fulfil CPR's dream of transoceanic transportation. In 1886, CPR leased its first ship to link Pacific trade with customers in the United States and Canada via trans-Canadian rail. This ship was the *W. B. Flint*, an 800 ton, American-built, wooden barque. She sailed from Yokohama on 19 June, loaded with enough tea for the next millennium (17,430 chests to be exact) and arrived in Port Moody, British Columbia, on 27 July. This voyage, which became known as the 'tea run', proved the wealth in trade of tea leaves and dramatized the need for more vessels to carry more tea and other Oriental freight. CPR chartered six different sailing vessels to make single trips from the Orient to Port Moody. Eight million pounds of tea were landed at Port Moody by the end of 1886.

In 1887, CPR was ready to make the leap to steam on the Pacific run. Port Moody had demonstrated too many disadvantages for continued use as a commercial steamship terminal due to unfavourable tides and a lengthy harbour transit. Fortunately for CPR, British Columbia came to the rescue with a land grant of nine square miles. This gave birth to the port of Vancouver. Port Moody land speculators tried to block the extension of the transcontinental line but it was eventually completed to Coal Harbour, Vancouver, where CPR constructed a 1,000-footlong wharf.

The new wharf became host to three iron-hulled steamships, all added to the tea run within one year of *W. B. Flint's* inaugural voyage. These ships were the former Cunarders, *Parthia* and *Abyssinia*, 3,600 tons each, and *Batavia* of 2,600 tons leased from W. G. Pearce of Glasgow. Built in 1870, the trio was showing its age despite several refits. They had no electric lights. Equipped for sail as well as steam, they served admirably, pulling their weight in cargo many times over. This kept the Orient run viable until that glorious day arrived when the Royal Mail subsidy was secured.

The subsidy was awarded on 15 July 1889. CPR signed a ten-year contract for Pacific mail service from Halifax via rail to Vancouver and onward by ship to Yokohama, Shanghai and finally to Hong Kong. The Postmaster General of Great Britain had negotiated a tough deal which was particularly favourable to the Royal Mail. The contract required delivery from Halifax to Hong Kong within 684 hours. That worked out to 28.5 days or the equivalent of monthly service. The total annual subsidy, 25 per cent of which represented Canada's contribution, amounted to £60,000. A stiff schedule of penalties was included for late departures and arrivals. The contract demanded even more. CPR's mail ships had to have a trial speed of 17.5 knots and be convertible to auxiliary cruisers and meet all Admiralty specifications.

CPR was delighted with the ten-year contract because it catapulted the company into the ocean-going steamship business. CPR wisely agreed to place an order for three new ships with the Naval Construction and Armaments Company of Barrow-in-Furness so that its new ships would comply with Admiralty specifications. Shaughnessy was sent to England to see to the particulars. Naval construction suggests ships totally lacking in aesthetics but this was hardly the result of the work at Barrow. CPR's new vessels, the *Empress of India*, *Empress of China*, and *Empress of Japan* were the most gorgeous steel hulls to ever grace the water.

The description 'yacht-like lines' is frequently used to describe *Titanic* but more aptly fits CPR's first trio of Pacific *Empresses*. Sparkling white hulls, three masts, two raked funnels, clipper ship stem, bowsprits and counter stern combined to boast of speed and elegance. The stern of these *Empresses* tapered upward from the waterline to trail behind the hull. As they glided over the water, white enamel reflected the sheen of their wake like a piece of fine crystal. It is this quality of seemingly effortless movement through the waves, as well as speed, which gave rise to the trio's nickname 'Flying *Empresses*'.

CPR's three new ships were 485 feet long and weighed approximately 6,000 tons. They had twin-screws powered by triple-expansion engines which easily moved them across the Pacific at better than 16 knots. Passenger accommodation was 180 first-class, 32 second-class, and 600 steerage. Comfort was maintained by the wonderful features of electric light and electric heat. They were not designed to carry lots of cargo — about 3,000 tons, because space was needed for the large quantities of coal required for Pacific voyages. The *Empress of India* was the fastest on trials achieving just shy of 20 knots and she was the first placed in service on 8 February 1891. She was distinguished from her sisters by a majestic Queen Victoria figurehead. The *Empress of Japan* and *Empress of China* followed the *India*, commencing service in April and July of the same year respectively.

Baron Thomas George Shaughnessy, President of the Canadian Pacific Railway. He ordered construction of the Atlantic Empresses. (Canadian Pacific Archives).

The 'Flying *Empresses*' were not without their episodes of bad luck. In 1892, the *Empress of Japan*, only two days out of Yokohama, had a serious electrical fire which set off a conflagration in portions of her cargo hold. The Captain ordered the lifeboats swung out but fortunately superhuman effort brought the blaze under control before the boats had to be lowered. In 1903, the *Empress of India* was rammed by the Chinese cruiser *Huang-Tai*. The *India* was slightly damaged while the *Huang-Tai* sank. Culpability was fixed to the India's Captain for crossing the cruiser's course. CPR had to pay damages to the Chinese Government. The third sister, *Empress of China*, was completely wrecked in 1911 on a rocky reef off the coast of Yokohama. Visibility was poor due to fog. Wireless was used to call for rescue and there was no loss of life. A substantial cargo was successfully off-loaded including 150 bars of silver bullion. An inquiry determined that inoperative navigational aids ashore caused the accident. It took five months to free the hull from its high-tide perch. CPR abandoned any claim to the wreck after settling with the insurance underwriters. The Japanese purchased the ship for scrap.

Occasional bad luck aside, CPR's rapid entry into wholly owned steamships was a smashing success. Extremely pleased with revenues from Pacific operations, CPR cast its eye on the pond at the other end of the tracks. An Atlantic steamship service was on Stephen's agenda only weeks after the last spike was hammered home. In January 1886, Stephen wrote to Sir John A. Macdonald:

> *I had a visit from Andrew Allan this morning and gave him roughly my ideas as to what would be necessary to perfect the Liverpool end of CPR. At first he was startled, but breathed easier before he left me and after he understood me better. He now knows that nothing but the very best and fastest ships will be of any use to us, and that whoever owns them the CPR must have a substantial control over them so as to ensure a unity of action. He is to think over what I said and to see me again. He admits Halifax could be made in 5 days from Liverpool; so could Quebec barring fog or ice or both.*

Andrew Allan was one of the brothers in the Allan Steamship Line dynasty which dominated the Canada-to-Europe trade. This memo is curious because Stephen is advising his rival of CPR's intention to compete on the Atlantic run. It was no secret that CPR wanted 'in' on the Atlantic ferry. Perhaps Stephen anticipated a level of service which exceeded that offered by the Allans, creating a new luxury market exclusive to CPR. In any event, both companies needed to fill third-class berths with immigrants to make money.

To get into the Atlantic immigrant business without delay, Shaughnessy, now President of CPR, purchased almost all of Elder Dempster's steamship fleet. This move was made public on 27 March 1903. The price for the 15 vessels, £1,417,500, was very reasonable. Lloyd's insured them for close to CPR's acquisition value at £1,200,000. CPR ran these ships on the Liverpool- to- Canada route via the St Lawrence River. CPR had no mail subsidy.

The Royal Mail subsidy to the St Lawrence was held by the Allan Line. In January 1904 the subsidy was renewed for two years. It was worth from £500 to £2,000 for each round trip depending on the age and speed of the vessel. It appeared that CPR lost a chance for the subsidy due to complacency. The real story was a gentlemen's dispute in the boardroom over the size and quantity of new construction Atlantic ships.

Donald Smith, of last spike fame, held to the romantic notion, as did George Stephen, that CPR should have the best and fastest vessels on both oceans. Smith, now Lord Strathcona, argued for ships which could compete knot-for-knot with existing New York-bound liners and Cunard's planned *Lusitania* and *Mauretania*. This would require 25-knot or better steamers. Shaughnessy was more analytical.

He knew that the increased acquisition and operating cost of a 25-knot ship made them 'commercially impossible'. There was also a great deal of discussion among company officials about the overall dimensions of their Atlantic ships. The concern was to build liners to an optimum size for safe navigation of the St Lawrence. CPR also had to decide if the ships would be designed to transit all the way to Montreal or terminate in Quebec.

The Allan Line was not indecisive. The company was ready to compete and the best way to do so was to build new ships. Allan Line ordered two 10,000 ton, triple-screw, steam turbine, Atlantic liners, each sporting a single funnel. These sister ships, the *Victorian* and the *Virginian*, had a design speed of 19.5 knots. This was a dramatic move on the part of the Allan Line. The new liners would be the first steam turbine powered vessels on the transatlantic run. The decision to use one high-pressure and two low-pressure turbine engines was made shortly after construction had already started. The keels were laid for the *Victorian* and *Virginian* in the summer of 1904 by two different yards — Workman, Clark & Company of Belfast and Alexander Stephen & Sons of Glasgow, respectively.

The publicity attending Allan Line's new construction did not stir CPR's boardroom into immediate action. Months passed before Shaughnessy placed the order for CPR's Atlantic *Empresses* in December 1904. He decided to buy two 20-knot liners of 14,500 tons from CPR's preferred builder — Fairfield Shipbuilding & Engineering Company. Fairfield was a southside River Clyde yard located in Govan about three miles west of Glasgow. Shaughnessy argued that a 20-knot vessel would reach Quebec, a distance of 2,623 miles, sooner than a 25-knot ship could make New York City, a distance of 3,108 miles, if both sailed from Liverpool on the same day.

The fact that westbound ships would reach the Canadian shore sooner than ships crossing to New York was a feather in CPR's cap but it wasn't about to seriously alter travel patterns of New York-bound passengers. CPR did capitalize on one aspect of its geographic advantage. Since rough seas were a concern of many transatlantic travellers, CPR advertised 'ONLY FOUR DAYS — OPEN SEA' as a lure for prospective passengers. The open sea distance was considered a track from Tory Island, off the north coast of Ireland, to Belle Isle, Newfoundland. Another two days were required to complete the voyage to Quebec but this involved sailing through the protected waters of the Gulf of St Lawrence and inland on the St Lawrence River.

Fairfield Shipbuilding, like any good business, was in tune with the needs of its customers. Dr Francis Elgar, the renowned Professor of Naval Architecture at Glasgow University, whose name was synonymous with Fairfield, completed concept drawings for a twin-screw Atlantic steamer in anticipation of CPR's order. An original waterline sketch dated 28 November 1904, signed by Elgar can be seen at the City Archives in Glasgow. There is no doubt that this was the first rendering of what mushroomed into a full set of schematics for Hulls 442 and 443. They were twin sisters by design at 548 feet 9 inches in length overall and 65 feet

7 inches in width. Their height from keel to top deck was 87 feet. They would draw about 27 feet of water fully loaded. CPR would employ the twins in service on the Liverpool-to-Quebec run. Montreal steamship passengers travelled by rail to Quebec for embarkation. Hull 442, constructed in Fairfield's Berth No. 5, would later be named *Empress of Britain*. Hull 443, constructed in Berth No. 4, would be christened *Empress of Ireland*. Her keel was laid on 10 April 1905.

Dr. Francis Elgar, the naval architect who designed the Empress of Ireland. (Keeper of the Records of Scotland).

The agreement between Fairfield and CPR was a fixed-price contract. Fairfield was required to build two, twin-screw steamers at a price of £375,000 each. Delivery was due 18 months after contract execution. The specifications called for each ship to demonstrate a sustained speed of 19.25 knots on trials. To get an idea of what £375,000 could buy in 1906, one can look to two other Fairfield vessels built during the same period. The *Volturno*, a twin-screw, 14-knot, 340-foot steamer, (originally built for Canadian Northern) was priced at £80,000. An armoured cruiser, the *Indomitable*, cost £696,500. The 550-foot-long *Indomitable* was one of three *Invincible* class 25-knot battle cruisers.

It is not unreasonable to suggest that Shaughnessy's ethnic background may have made it easier to settle on the name *Empress of Ireland* for Hull 443. As for Hull 442, *Empress of Britain* was certainly an appropriate name for the company's first new construction ship to connect Canada with the Empire. Other names were considered for these vessels including *Empress of Germany* and *Empress of Austria*. An embroilment prior to World War I would have made the names *Empress of Germany* and *Austria* so unpalatable that CPR would have ordered them scraped off the hulls.

The Germans were angry with Canadian Pacific for encroachment on their shipping and rail interests in Austria. The conflict boiled over when Canadian Pacific ships started calling in the port of Trieste. As far as the Germans were concerned, this was too close for comfort. Charges against CPR were drawn up

for violation of military conscription laws. CPR was alleged to have lured 600,000 potential Austrian soldiers to Canada. The staff of CPR's Vienna office was arrested and detained but then released after diplomatic intervention. A sensational legal battle ensued which eventually vindicated Canadian Pacific. The claim that Canadian Pacific's agents were proselytising hundreds of thousands of Austrian citizens into crossing to Canada fell apart when the prosecution's evidence was examined. The names of 600,000 so-called emigrants were lifted from death records. Many of the deceased had been dead for over a hundred years.

CPR's Atlantic *Empresses* were the largest and most elaborate vessels to be constructed at Fairfield at that time. The history of the shipyard can be traced back to the year 1834 when a millwright shop became established on Centre Street in Glasgow. Doing business as Randolph, Elder & Company, this shop invented the first marine compound engine in 1854. Partners came and went until 1864 when the firm established itself in Govan as a shipbuilding concern. In 1868, John Elder became the sole partner. Following his death a year later, his widow changed the name to John Elder & Company. The Fairfield Shipbuilding & Engineering Company, Ltd, name was finally adopted in 1886 and remained unchanged for the next 84 years.

Fairfield was a full-service shipyard which constructed everything from the keel right up through the superstructure including the engines, boilers, furnaces, turbines, dynamos, hardware, and cabinetry. Very little was subcontracted outside the yard's 85 acres at Govan. Fairfield was also versatile. It built warships, submarines, ocean liners, channel steamers, excursion vessels, river boats, and yachts. Fairfield built several ships for Cunard including the *Umbria* and *Etruria* (1884). These 19-knot sisters held the single screw transatlantic speed record and remained in continuous service for over 24 years. It also built ships for North German Lloyd, Hamburg-American, Union-Castle, Donaldson, Allan, and Orient lines. Famous yachts to Fairfield's credit are the *Giralda* (1884), built for the King of Spain; and the *Livadia* (1880), a radically designed, oval-shaped hull with exceptional seakeeping properties built for the Czar of Russia, Alexander II. The extent of Fairfield's work is depicted in 'The Fairfield Fleet', an oil on canvas completed by Arthur Burgess in 1907, and now on display at the Museum of Transport in Glasgow.

The craftsmen at Fairfield excelled at working with wood in their state-of-the-art, 20 000-square-foot mill. There was no overhead belting or shafts to clutter the shop. All machines were run by motors under the floor. Pneumatic, high-powered collectors gathered dust and shavings which were propelled by fans to incinerators. Over twenty different types of wood were received at Fairfield Shipbuilding in the rawest possible form — as giant timbers. Circular ripping saws and horizontal cutting machines were used to metamorphosize timber into board lumber, panelling, and veneers. The mill could reduce trees up to 42 inches in diameter.

The interiors of CPR's new liners were a treasure in decorative wood and woodworking. Over 46,700 square feet of mahogany was installed in each hull. Solid wood was the rule wherever possible. Veneers, used where solid wood wasn't practical, were applied in layers held together by adhesive. The passenger spaces of Hulls 442 and 443 were panelled in mahogany, satinwood, alderwood, and bird's-eye maple. Large-scale, hand-carved mouldings of mahogany, oak, and yellow pine framed the panels creating a sense of strength as well as opulence. It was the look of a grand railway hotel translated for the sea. Many woods were incorporated into cabinetry including oak, walnut, and birch most prevalently. Other cabinet woods installed included California redwood, canary, teak, tulipwood, pitch pine, ash, satinwood, white pine, and yellow pine. Fairfield, unlike many shipyards, even manufactured its own tables and chairs.

Twenty acres of boiler, furnace, and engine shops forged the monster-sized components which would eventually harmonize in propulsion of each *Empress*. CPR was not as adventurous as the Allan Line in selecting a power plant. It choose quadruple-expansion reciprocating steam engines instead of steam turbines. This decision further confirms Shaughnessy's somewhat conservative approach to CPR's Atlantic ferry.

An enormous loft, with skylight roof, was constructed for cutting templates. Almost all of the deck plating for Hulls 442 and 443 was marked, cut and pre-punched well before beams and frames formed the distinct outline of a ship. A little over half of the steel hull plates could also be prepared in advance.

From bottom to top, eight decks were installed in each *Empress*. The first steel deck was the Orlop Deck which by name alone defines the lowest deck in a ship. It was a partial deck which ran forward of the boiler rooms and aft from the engine room. The next steel deck was the Lower Deck which ran from bow to stern 8 feet above Orlop Deck. At the forward end of Lower Deck was accommodation for third-class and steerage passengers. The Lower Deck ran just above the waterline.

Ascending another 8 feet, one found the Main Deck which was covered by various lengths of 5-inch wide, 3-inch thick, pitch pine planking. The third-class dining saloon which seated 300 was located here between the funnel uptakes. Second and third-class cabins were located throughout this deck with lesser cabins located forward. Third-class cabins were small yet enjoyed comfortable features including wire mattresses, wash basins, and ventilation.

The Upper Deck was 8 feet higher than the Main Deck and ran the length of the ship like the two decks below it. It was also covered in pitch pine but not throughout. Successively higher decks had richer appointments. Teak began to appear in the alleyways and open passages of Upper Deck. This deck accommodated second-class passengers on the starboard side and a variety of crew members including stewards, engineers, firemen, and greasers on the port side. The third-class social halls were forward of the second-class cabin area. They consisted of a piano equipped room finished in Kauri for the women and a separate smoking room for the men. The ship's office and first-class barber shop were on this level. Also on the Upper Deck, just forward of the second funnel, was the mail room. To the starboard side of the mail room was the bullion room for shipments of gold and silver. The second-class children's nursery was at the aft end of Upper Deck.

The Shelter Deck was the fourth and highest deck to run from stem to stern 8 feet above the Upper Deck. This deck housed the completely separate first and second-class dining saloons. The first-class dining area, with space for 224, was in the centre of the ship to soften the effects of high seas. Also known as the saloon it spanned the breadth of the ship and extended 58 feet in length. The second-class passengers dined close to the stern in roughly the same amount of space but with seating for 296. First-class children were relegated to separate, but eminently acceptable, dining facilities at the forward end of Shelter Deck. Standards of the day dictated that children be neither seen nor heard in the first-class adult dining saloon. First-class children enjoyed a few extras in their facility. Engraved panels depicted youthful themes. Seats were adjustable so that each child could be raised or tilted forward to meet the dining surface. There was also special ventilation for the first-class children's saloon. The first, second, and third-class galleys were located between the first and second-class saloons. The ship's hospital was at the aft end of Shelter Deck with separate wards for men and women of four beds each.

The superstructure of the ship, that portion which rose above the Shelter Deck, consisted of a Lower Promenade Deck, Upper Promenade Deck, and Boat Deck. The vertical distances between these decks starting from Shelter Deck varied at 8 feet 8 inches; 8 feet; and 7 feet 9 inches. The Lower Promenade Deck, from the front of the superstructure aft, ran 410 feet all the way to the stern. This was considered a modern feature because it afforded second-class passengers additional open space with several built-in deck seats. Stretching the Lower Promenade was a precursor to the sun bathing decks prevalent on today's cruise ships.

The Lower Promenade Deck was covered in 5-inch x 2.75-inch planks of various lengths. Pitch pine was used inside and teak was used on the spacious open promenades. Six strolls around the Lower Promenade equalled one mile. The Upper Promenade Deck was covered in the same way but with planking one-half-inch thinner. The centre of the Boat Deck, inboard of lifeboats, was covered in teak planks 2.25 inches thick. A total of 18,027 cubic feet of pitch pine and 12,283 cubic feet of teak was installed on decks throughout the ship.

The Lower Promenade Deck housed the first-class library, café , and smoking room. The library was well forward, directly above the first-class children's saloon. All bookcases were covered by wood-framed glass doors. A total of 650 volumes were accommodated. Each volume contained a catalogue of the library's holdings for easy reference. The Library took in natural light from six, vertically rectangular, brass-framed windows overlooking Shelter Deck. Mottled Amboina panelling framed in oiled mahogany and overstuffed chairs with matching ottomans gave the library the feel of a private club. Velvet green upholstery was complimented by thick carpeting underfoot. Fringed Tiffany-style lamps accented walnut writing tables. For the wealthy, it was an enclave where one could find quiet solace, an escape from the tedium of an Atlantic crossing.

The first-class smoking room was aft at the end of the enclosed cabin. It was topped by a large, leaded glass, rectangular skylight installed athwartships. An exhaust fan was mounted in the skylight. The first-class bar was located on the port side, at the forward end of the smoking lounge. The dominant motif was oak with inlaid seascapes. A masculine tone was achieved with brown leather furnishings. A wrought-iron fireplace added a touch of intimacy to this exclusively male kingdom. Aft of the lounge was a veranda which served as a retreat for smokers desiring open air. Panels and windows from the *Empress of Britain* smoking lounge, upon her retirement under the name *Montroyal*, were reconstructed in the Sola Strand Hotel at Stavanger, Norway. The ex-*Empress of Britain* was purchased for £37,000 by Stavanger Skipsopphugging (Stavanger Ship Breakers) in 1930. Hotel Director Axel Lund purchased the entire lounge and fireplace which now form the hotel's Montroyal Hall.

The Lower and Upper Promenade Decks were the exclusive domain of first-class passengers. Suites and special cabins were decorated in different woods. They were often identified by type of wood (maple, oak, mahogany, etc.) before cabin number. A staircase of grand proportions and vestibule as wide as the ship provided access from the Promenade Decks to the first-class dining saloon on Shelter Deck. Refined liners at the turn of the century were also designed with a skylight-covered central well. More than just a glorious domed atrium in the ship's centre, it was the *epergne* of first-class social life.

On the *Empresses*, the central well rose from the first-class dining saloon on Shelter Deck through Lower and Upper Promenade Decks to a skylight on the Boat Deck. Below the skylight, on Upper Promenade Deck was the first-class music room. Old rose taffeta upholstery, Steinway grand piano, coal-burning fireplace, tufted banquettes, and plush sofas recessed in alcoves were featured in this elite recreation room. Polished satinwood was inlaid with tulipwood which mirrored diamond shapes woven into thick broadloom carpeting. Below the music room, visible through a baroque stained glass dome, was the café. The café was a relatively new feature at sea which permitted first-class patrons to indulge in light fare and beverages throughout the day. Padded chairs with arms, protected by linen slip covers and accented with fringe, provided seats for 44 passengers. There were matching sofas around the perimeter.

The room became known as the 'Italian café' because it was finished entirely in Italian walnut. The café was the venue for afternoon tea served in proper British fashion. It was where women could go while their husbands retired to the smoking lounge. The central well ran right through the forward end of the café. A balustrade supported by ornamental fretwork prevented tipsy passengers from falling into the first-class dining area below.

One of the outstanding features of the *Empresses* was the versatile layout of staterooms. Families were accommodated by selected cabins built in pairs with an adjoining door. Many cabins were easily convertible for use as a single, double, or triple owing to their large size. This also permitted interchangeability between standard first-class cabins and second-class cabins below Shelter Deck. One of the other valued features for third-class families was the children's playground which included an enormously popular sand pit. It was located on Upper Deck forward.

Canadian Pacific was rightfully proud of the many features incorporated in its new Atlantic liners. Company brochures promoted them as 'something beyond the highest point hitherto touched in travel to Canada. State rooms of all kinds are provided, some *en suite* with baths. To form a true conception of the cabins and magnificently appointed assembly halls, one must dismiss all previous notions of such accommodation.' Among some of the 'selling points' advertised were:

LARGE TWIN-SCREW STEAMERS
BILGE KEELS TO PREVENT ROLLING
LARGE CABINS
CAFÉ
CUISINE UNSURPASSED
CHILDREN'S NURSERIES
CRICKET PITCH
CPR TICKET OFFICE ON BOARD

There was also a description of the thermo-tank moderated fresh air system manufactured by the Thermo-Tank Ventilating Company of Glasgow:

VENTILATION AND HEATING BY THE THERMO SYSTEM, ENSURING COMPLETE CHANGE OF AIR (HEATED OR COOLED AS DESIRED) IN EVERY COMPARTMENT ONCE IN TEN MINUTES. OWING TO ABSENCE OF STEAM PIPES NO BAD ODOR, THUS REDUCING LIABILITY TO SEA-SICKNESS.

In cold weather, ship's steam at reduced pressure is supplied to heater tubes within each tank. Electric fans move outside air through the tanks and then distribute the warmed air to louvers near the ceiling in each cabin. The air is humidified by a needle which emits a fine spray of steam. Exhaust louvers at deck level remove the air from passageways to complete the ventilating cycle. In warm weather, cooling is accomplished by reversing the system and turning off the heater tubes. Stale hot air is then sucked out through the ceiling level louvers.

Each *Empress* was equipped with a refrigeration plant. It was supplied by J. & E. Hall Ltd, of Dartford, England. Three of their patented CO_2 machines were employed to keep 29,700 cubic feet of cargo space at a temperature suitable for carriage of dairy products. A fourth machine was used to keep provisions cold and make ice.

There were no passenger elevators installed on either *Empress*. There were, however, two lifts for provisions. One lift connected fresh and refrigerated stores with the galleys on Shelter Deck. The other lift connected the Shelter Deck with the Promenade Decks.

The *Empress of Ireland* was baptized in the Clyde on Saturday afternoon, 27 January 1906. This month also marked the award of the two-year Royal Mail contract. The Atlantic subsidy was split between the Allan Line and CPR. Royal Mail Steamer (RMS) *Empress of Ireland* was christened by Mrs Alexander Gracie, the wife of Fairfield's managing director. An immense throng of well-wishers must have had a touch of déjà vu from three months earlier when they watched the *Empress of Britain* slide down the ways. The launch platform, festooned with bunting, was crowded with over 90 dignitaries representing the shipyard and Canadian Pacific. Notably absent were the titular heads of builder and buyer. Sir William G. Pearce, Chairman of Fairfield, and Sir Thomas Shaughnessy were duly recognized *in absentia* by subordinates who extended cursory apologies.

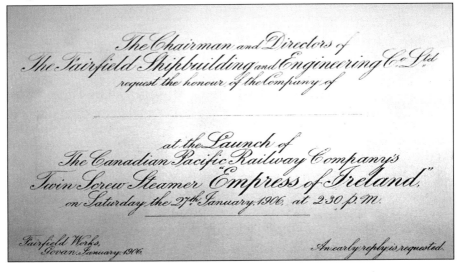

Blank invitation to the launch of the Empress of Ireland. (Keeper of the Records of Scotland).

Warning signals were sounded to clear the River Clyde. The *Empress of Ireland* travelled 928.5 feet at launch. Drag chains were used to arrest her powerful momentum. One by one they rumbled into life as each helped moderate the hull's rush to water. The *Empress's* propellers spun a bit as she hit the water. Five tugboats were on hand to escort her to the fitting-out basin. The crowd cheered. The tugs and a flotilla of small craft sounded their whistles in salute.

A gala luncheon was held after the christening ceremony. The usual launch-day fare of Medallions de Foie Gras in Aspic, Lobster Salad, and Truffled Quail was served. Champagne toasts were tendered back and forth between Fairfield and Canadian Pacific. Admiral Sir Digby Morant, one of the shipyard directors, presided over protocol. He kicked off the copious consumption of champagne by proposing 'Success to the *Empress of Ireland* and prosperity to the Canadian Pacific Railway Company'. The CPR, he went on, had spanned the Pacific to the Far East and made its Pacific fleet a great success. He predicted the new venture of express steamers from Liverpool to Canada would be even more successful. The forward thinking Sir Digby added that two new *Empresses* would not do. So far as Fairfield was concerned, more ships should be ordered with each one more advanced and luxurious than the one before.

Mr Archer Baker, CPR's senior representative at the luncheon, replied to Sir Digby's gracious pleasantry with a few words about the growth of Canadian Pacific. CPR's fleet, he began, had grown to a total of 54 Atlantic, Pacific, coastal and inland waterway steamers which consumed 3,000 tons of coal a day. Stacked end to end the fleet would extend for 3.5 miles. The company's payroll, afloat and ashore, including pensioners, covered 35,000 employees. He noted that the company's ambition for an 'All-red' route to the Orient was finally realized; 'All-red' being synonymous with 'All-British' as it was common practice to depict countries belonging to the Empire in red on maps. The advent of the Atlantic *Empresses* meant that a passenger could travel entirely under the British-owned CPR House flag from England to Hong Kong a distance of 11,841 miles. Passengers had the convenience of having to board only one train to travel from coast to coast. It was a marvellous enterprise which Baker extolled until concluding with thanks to Mrs Gracie for having named the *Empress of Ireland*. Mrs Gracie was presented with a silver casket as a souvenir of the occasion. Captain Mowatt, CPR's marine superintendent from Liverpool, proposed a toast to the Fairfield Company which was greeted with a hearty round of cheers.

The *Empress of Ireland*'s sea trials were conducted on 5 and 7 June in the Firth of Clyde. Although second to be launched, she was the faster of the twins. She broke 20 knots in progressive trials on 5 June and demonstrated a sustained speed of 19.6 knots during an endurance run on 7 June. The *Empress of Britain* was one-third knot slower on her trials.

On 12 June 1906, CPR ordered £4,611 in extras to be installed as the ship prepared for its maiden voyage from Liverpool. A partial list of these last minute changes includes: repair and testing of four Berthon collapsible boats provided by CPR; remote helm control above the wheelhouse; additional electric lights, switches, curling iron cabin heaters, and key holders for first-class staterooms; additional tip-up white wash basins; stained glass inserts for the top pane of rectangular windows; alterations to the design of plaster work in the music room; a ticket case for the ship's office; and gold silk curtains for the first-class dining room.

Fairfield realized a profit of slightly less than three per cent on the *Empress of Ireland*. The Board of Directors considered this small margin a 'loss' which they fully anticipated when fixing the contract price. At the time, Fairfield wanted the work and a continuing relationship with a good customer. An internal memo signed by Managing Director Alexander Gracie said that Fairfield mustn't make the same mistake again. In a new construction commercial contract issued shortly after completion of the *Empresses*, a fee of five per cent was specified.

The *Empress of Ireland* left Liverpool at 6:30pm on Friday, 29 June 1906, to begin her maiden voyage under the command of Captain Frank Carey. She sailed through the Irish Sea to Moville, Ireland, where she remained until the following day. Departing Moville at 1:30pm on 30 June, the *Ireland* completed 2,623 nautical miles en route to Quebec. Two days of very rough weather on 4 and 5 July prevented her maiden voyage from being a record breaker.

The maiden voyage was taken on the 'summer/intermediate' schedule when the St Lawrence was navigable through to Quebec. The sailing season ran from May through November after which ice began to lock-out passenger traffic. During the off-season Canadian Pacific liners disembarked passengers at Saint John, New Brunswick.

Upon reaching Father Point, Customs and Immigration officials boarded to begin their inspections. The inbound transit to Quebec would give them a six-hour jump on their duties after subtracting a couple of hours for gratuitous meals. During the winter season, Customs inspectors boarded at Halifax, Nova Scotia, and made the transit to St John. Customs officials were so enamoured of the *Empress of Ireland* that they did not complete their baggage inspection until well after she docked. Customs blamed the delay on the commingling of first and second-class bags.

Arrival time in Quebec on Saturday, 7 July 1906, was just after 5:00am, but this did not deter hundreds of well-wishers from coming out to greet the magnificent new vessel. The *Empress of Ireland* was fully dressed from stem to stern with colourful flags. From her bow, as a salute to her country namesake, she sported a British ensign on green background with the Golden Harp of Erin on the fly.

A full breakfast was served to saloon passengers while stevedores positioned cargo and luggage on the quayside. A new baggage handling area, covered walkway, and immigration shed had been constructed for the Atlantic *Empresses* at the breakwater extension. Many first and second-class travellers, assisted by porters, were able to make the first Canadian Pacific train at 9:00am. Some saloon passengers and third-class passengers had to wait for the 11:00am or later trains.

The return leg of the maiden voyage began on 12 July 1906. As part of ceremonies to commemorate the first eastbound crossing, Irish citizens from Montreal presented Sir Thomas Shaughnessy with an assortment of silk flags. Shaughnessy gave them to Captain Carey to be carried aboard the *Empress*.

The third crossing, which left Liverpool on 26 July 1906, was the *Empress of Ireland*'s fastest. She completed the 'open sea' journey in less than four days. Unlike the New York run, there was no formal Blue Riband pennant to designate the fastest ship on the Canadian run. However, speed to Canada was important because each new record meant faster delivery of mail. On her record run, the

Empress of Ireland travelled from Moville to Father Point in 5 days, 10 hours, and 30 minutes. Moville to Father Point was the focus of speed runs because that was the distance between ports of dispatch for mail.

On 8 October 1909, the *Empress of Ireland* left Liverpool on a westbound crossing carrying passengers and cargo under the command of Captain John V. Forster. The ocean crossing was uneventful and weather was clear for transit up the St Lawrence. On Thursday 14 October, Quartermaster John Murphy was steering the ship. The *Empress* passed Cape Chat (approximately 290 miles east of Quebec on the south shore) doing 16 knots at 9:40am. Two hours later, approaching the mouth of the Matane River, the forward momentum of the ship was abruptly halted. Passengers toppled over like dominoes as the ship shuddered from bow to stern and back again. Grinding and scraping noises were heard along the port side. The *Empress of Ireland* was about 2.5 miles from the south shore between Matane and the village of Ste-Félicité.

The new Empress of Ireland: *14,141 Gross Registered Tons and 570 feet in length overall upon delivery. She exceeded 20 knots on trials during June 1906. Funnels and masts were designed with a distinctive rake of about 2 inches per vertical foot. Deck and hull plating contained a total of 1,100,000 hydraulically installed rivets. Interior deck space amounted to over four acres. Canadian Pacific directed that ample cargo capacity be part of her design in case passenger traffic fell off. This gave the* Empress of Ireland *full lines and resulted in steady performance on the high seas. These images were reproduced from glass negatives. (University of Glasgow, Business Records Centre).*

Captain Forster and watchstanders on the Bridge lurched forward. They groped for the nearest handhold. Forster ordered Murphy to turn the ship hard to starboard. The ship first keeled over to starboard, then dipped to port and rumbled forward. The shock was over in a few seconds. Chief Engineer William Sampson inspected the holds and reported 20 feet of water contained in the forward stokehold. Lifeboats were not swung out. The *Empress* continued to Quebec riding two feet lower than her normal draft.

Passengers disembarked in Quebec early on Friday 15 October 1909. The tugboat *Cruizer* was hired to pump out the waterlogged holds. Late on Saturday, the *Empress* was moved to a berth near the Canadian Northern Railway grain elevator so that a diver could survey her punctured hull. At about 8:00pm, a fire started in a conveyor leading from the grain elevator to the wharf. Within 15 minutes, the elevator building was completely ablaze. Flames shot over a hundred feet in the air. The entire city was illuminated by the blaze which could be seen by small towns twenty miles down river.

Two service tugs rushed to the side of the *Empress of Ireland*. Hawsers were flying in the air before the tugs reached the ship. Boathooks recovered the hastily thrown lines and soon they were secured to each tug. The tugs started to pull the *Empress* away from the wharf into open water.

Quebec's waterfront was destroyed. Property damage amounted to $1,250,000. Canadian Northern's elevator, several freight cars, the Custom House, the Harbour Commissioner's building, freight sheds, and warehouses were all reduced to smouldering heaps of rubble. It was described as Quebec's greatest conflagration in three-quarters of a century. The *Empress of Ireland* was scorched but spared.

Although the *Empress* wasn't seriously damaged, fire destroyed the diver's equipment stored in a quayside shed. The examination of the hull was delayed for two days. Diver Joseph Begin worked for six days after new equipment arrived. He found several hull strakes (plates) damaged on the port side of the keel. A crescent-shaped opening 15-inches-wide was punched into the bottom. Several rivet heads had been shaved off. Temporary repairs using cement were completed by the G. T. Davie & Sons shipyard in Quebec's Louise Basin.

The Commissioner of Wrecks, Captain L. A. Demers, convened an inquiry on 26 October 1909, in Quebec. At this session, the cause of the accident was not determined. The most favoured possibility was that the *Empress of Ireland* struck a submerged 'derelict'. Close behind the sunken wreck theory was the possibility of an uncharted outcrop of rock. Poor navigation on the part of Captain Forster and his officers was dismissed as a potential cause. Of interest, however, was a discussion of the steering qualities of the *Empress of Ireland*. Witnesses for CPR said there was no truth to reports that she was a 'wild steerer'. One story, discounted by the inquiry, held that the first Master of the *Empress*, Captain Carey, gave up his command because her helm was unreliable. Perhaps there was some truth here. CPR ordered the *Empress of Ireland*'s rudder enlarged during her first year of service. The company said the alteration would 'improve her steering qualities' over the original rudder which CPR considered fully satisfactory. Engineering drawings for the enlarged rudder were started on 18 September 1906, less than three months after her maiden voyage.

On 27 October 1909, less than a day following commencement of formal inquiry, the *Empress* sailed for home with a skeleton crew and no passengers. Upon arrival in Liverpool, she was placed in dry dock for permanent repair. Thomas Miller, from the Board of Trade Surveyor's Office, found evidence of 'violent' damage to bottom strakes, frames, and floors intermittently along the port side. The keel was scored along the latter half of its length. The tips of two port-side propeller blades were chipped.

Captain Demers reconvened his inquiry in Quebec on 18 December 1909. The nature of the physical damage fully revealed in dry dock weighed against a finding that the *Empress* struck an uncharted rock. Witnesses recalled seeing splinters of wood surface along the port-side after the 14 October impact. This was corroborated by the discovery of a small piece of wood in one of the port-side butt straps. The surveyors concluded that the *Empress* struck a waterlogged hull with rigid features possibly an iron hull.

Accordingly, the inquiry ruled that the accident must have been caused by the 'submerged hull of a derelict probably held in suspension'.

This photo is often mistaken for the Empress of Ireland. *It is actually her sister ship, the* Empress of Britain.

2 The Crippen Curse

The dramatic events of 1910 set spinning into motion by Doctor Hawley Harvey Crippen are tangentially but inseparably linked to the *Empress of Ireland* story. Some observers find this true crime saga a fascinating morsel of digression in the history of maritime disaster. Others, with a penchant for providential cause and effect, insist that the *Empress of Ireland* was doomed by Crippen's curse. Here then is the extraordinary tale which captivated audiences on both sides of the Atlantic.

Hawley Harvey was born to Mrs Myron Augustus Crippen in Coldwater, Michigan, on 13 March 1862. His upbringing was unremarkable except for proper, hard working and religious parents. This home environment must have influenced the development of Crippen's quiet, above the fray, demeanour. He earned a degree in Homeopathic Medicine at Hospital College, Cleveland, Ohio, in 1883. Further practical study at several locations including London and New York completed his medical education. He had an interest in dentistry and presented himself as an eye, ear, nose, and throat physician. 'Doctor' was always used in his title even though he was not certified.

Standing erect, Crippen was a diminutive five feet three inches, crowned by fine, sandy blond hair. His forehead sloped flat back to eventually meet a receding hairline except for bulging outward just above and to either side of his eyes. The bridge of his nose was also flat creating a nuisance as his gold-rimmed spectacles repeatedly tried to crawl off his face. He sported the long, handlebar-style moustache popular at the time. The whole man, as a physical package, was hardly threatening. Holding his head forward and slightly downward added to a meek appearance and mild countenance.

As for the workings of his mind, Crippen was far from milquetoast. The Doctor was intelligent and extremely well spoken. He could speak French as well as some German. Disarming to meet, he almost always appeared calm, cool and collected. His attire befitted his white-collar position with suit jacket or frock coat and silk hat being the usual wear.

Dr. Hawley Harvey "Peter" Crippen.
(Original courtesy New Scotland Yard-Adapted by Prometheus Graphics).

In 1887, Crippen married Charlotte Bell, an Irish plumber's daughter. They had one child together, a son named Otto. Charlotte succumbed to cerebral haemorrhage four years after the marriage. Otto was sent to live with Crippen relatives in Michigan. Little is known about Crippen's first legally sanctioned relationship but one may reasonably surmise he was looking for something more in life — something bigger.

Bigger he got, two years after his loss, when he fell in love with a Rubenesque tart named Cora Turner. Through thick lenses, Crippen's watery grey eyes saw everything he lacked. She was gregarious, flamboyant, and exuded an exotic sex appeal through her garish, take-note, appearance. Cora's brown eyes first caught hold of Crippen's at a medical practice in Brooklyn, New York, where she was patient and he was staff physician. She was 17 and he was almost twice her age at 31. At the time, Cora was being kept by a wealthy, but married, businessman from Brooklyn. She enjoyed the finery but not her station. She got into trouble and later miscarried. She viewed Crippen as her ticket out, a direct line to respectability. He was a doctor, after all!

Cora relentlessly pursued the Doctor until he consented to marry her in New Jersey on 1 September 1892. She got what she wanted — financial security and a monumental boost in her social status. As Doctor Crippen's wife, she was now a long way from her origin as Kunigunde Mackamotzki — offspring of a German-Jewish mother and Russian-Polish father. Cora concealed her background of poverty by telling people she was the daughter of Baron Mackamotzki. Fantastic tales of Polish royalty aside, by marrying Crippen she had finally arrived or so she thought.

She soon learned that her new husband was not as well off as she had presumed. He earned a below average salary for his profession as a consultant and marketeer for Munyon's Remedies. Munyon was in the business of selling medicinals for common ailments. Cora also learned that his degree limited his ability to practice as an independent physician so it was unlikely she would be sharing the fortune of a wealthy provider. She had hitched her wagon to a mediocre star. Crippen, however, demonstrated management potential and was transferred from New York City to Munyon's London main office. His salary was £12 monthly plus commissions. Cora had her own money which made up the lion's share of their savings account. A streetwise woman, Cora set up this account to require her signature for withdrawal. The source of her funds was questionable, most likely a combination of prostitution and related gifts.

The Crippen story is rife with *noms de plume*. No one can begrudge Cora for making the unfathomable 'Kunigunde Mackamotzki' history. However, Cora Turner was not the end of it. She changed her name to Macka Motski hoping the alliterative play on her birthright would add some zest to her desperate attempts to achieve stardom in operetta. Lacking a newspaper magnate husband who could order the publication of mellifluous reviews, she was panned and gave up opera to try her hand at music hall. Reinventing herself once more, she dropped the ethnic name for a flashy, all new, sultry 'Belle Elmore'. Belle achieved limited success with infrequent performances first as a singer and later as a comedienne. Her nightclub act was performed in seedy venues before smoked-filled rooms of men. It was woefully bad Mae West before there even was a Mae West. Her shrill voice and risqué repertoire failed to entertain anyone in the audience, even the inebriated patrons. Her notoriety was at an all-time low when she crossed a picket line to work on stage in London only to be booed in infamy. Another performer, Weldon Atherstone, also deserted rank and file brethren to follow Belle on the stage. He too was booed, but to a lesser extent as Belle's singing had already cleared much of the auditorium.

While Belle's career nose dived, so did the Crippen marriage. At first, there were no rocks in the bed even though Cora was disappointed with her 'Doctor'. The first few years rolled along pleasantly enough from the inertia of fresh, marital bliss. Then, Crippen was sent to the United States for several months on business, opening the door for another American, Bruce Miller, to be the object of Belle's affection. Miller was a music hall singer on semi-permanent tour in England. He was also an ex-prize-fighter whose physique was more attuned to Belle's. She was free to receive Bruce with abandon. Her pre-Crippen ovariectomy would short circuit any extramarital pregnancy. Crippen had always known about Belle's inability to produce children. An indication of his lack of interest in raising children is the permanent relegation of his only child to Crippen's parents in Michigan. Otto was whisked away immediately following his mother's death. Flesh and blood never appeared to be important.

What was important? Keeping up appearances, displaying the trappings of a doctor, creating a quiet but unmistakable hint of high station mattered a great deal. To this end, Crippen would festoon Belle with jewellery and furs which could not be missed by friends and neighbours. They also leased a spacious Victorian duplex north of central London at 39 Hilldrop Crescent Road. Belle loved to use this setting for intimate encounters with Bruce while Crippen was away on business or during office hours. Belle did not attempt to hide her affair, revealing it upon Crippen's return from America. The once happy marriage had been reduced to farce complete with separate bedrooms.

The isolation of separate chambers further thickened the tense atmosphere at 39 Hilldrop Crescent. Doctor and Mrs Crippen each sought their own refuge from domestic misfortune. Belle, never willing to completely divorce show business, used her contacts in the theatre to win election as Treasurer of the Music Hall Ladies Guild. Crippen, not to be outdone by philandering Belle, started an affair of his own with a secretary he met at Drouet's Remedies. Drouet was a rival patent medicine outfit. The secretary's experience made it easy to steal her over to Munyon's where they both worked in offices on New Oxford Street. She was employed as typist, stenographer and assistant to Doctor Crippen. Her birth name was Ethel Clara Neave; however, habitual name changes being the rule in this story, Le Neve was substituted for Neave. Ethel thought it a bewitching enhancement. Crippen continued to use the initials 'H. H.' in his title but dropped Hawley Harvey for the more prosaic, Peter.

Attraction to young women could be counted among Crippen's weaknesses. It was self-prescribed for acute loneliness and marital pain, a case of the physician healing thyself.

Ethel, a London native, was a spry 19-year-old when they first met at Drouet's. Months passed but eventually, at Crippen's urging, they secretly consummated their affair in a hotel room near King's Cross under assumed names. This would become the routine for several years even after Belle learned of their once secret liaison.

Le Neve embodied the quintessential antithesis of Belle. She was unassuming, ladylike, always in control, and deferentially soft spoken. She quickly became an attractive oasis for Crippen who desperately needed comfort from the daily tortures of his grease-painted, increasingly steatopygic wife. The Doctor's new young lover was almost identical to him in height and build. He admired her fluffy light brown hair, styled to ensconce head and neck in the Gibson Girl fashion. This gave one the impression she was permanently shrugging her shoulders like an innocent child. Overall, she was well dressed, eloquent and an eminently acceptable escort for the two-timing Crippen. In the early days of their courtship, Belle captured her husband with unbridled exoticism. Now, demure Ethel, entranced him with large blue-grey eyes. They had a most engaging, hypnotic quality which she knew how to use. She mesmerized Peter Crippen but it was unnecessary for he was deeply in love from the start. He resolved to keep seeing Ethel for as long as he lived despite threats from Belle.

And threaten she did. Belle demanded Peter stop seeing his prim and proper mistress or Belle would resume her relationship with the American ex-pugilist, Bruce Miller. Such a threat to Crippen was laughable. He could not care less and the same was true of Bruce who had returned to Chicago to raise a family of his own. Miller had no idea his name was being used in an ill-conceived attempt to spawn jealousy. Frustrated, a conceited Belle started to randomly see other men to bolster her falling ego. She was in despair over unsightly cellulite and her expanding girth. Many years of unhappiness at home and a career which never got off the ground took its toll. Her face looked rough and spent beyond a woman of 36 years. Vanity shattered, she found true solace at the bottom of a bottle of brandy or cognac.

Crippen's billfold was usually as empty as one of so many liquor bottles accumulating randomly about the house, usually at the exact point of depletion. Household finances reached critical mass when Munyon's fired Crippen as their London agent. Unofficially, Munyon's told Crippen he was removed because his wife's scandalous, show-girl behaviour might tarnish the firm's image. At the time of Crippen's dismissal, Munyon's was unaware of the real scandal — Crippen's affair with an employee. Crippen was incredulous. He couldn't believe he was victim of life's unfairness especially from an employer hawking bogus cures. To lessen the financial squeeze, at Belle's insistence, they advertised the availability of accommodation at 39 Hilldrop Crescent. The *Daily Telegraph* advertisement offered prospective takers pleasant surroundings convenient to central London. To make room, the Crippens resided on the bottom floor with Belle's pampered, indoor-only, pedigreed felines. As many as four paying borders stayed with the Crippens but the scheme was short-lived. It seemed Mrs Crippen didn't do sheets. In fact, she had an aversion to housework of any kind, most notably her own, and she refused to do the laundry of guests. The malleable Doctor had to cook, clean, and haul in coal for their customers. These duties compounded his existing daily chores: most notably care, feeding, and sanitation of Belle's two cats. The guest house, absent elbow grease from its hostess, was much too great a strain on its staff of one.

Belle saw her role in the enterprise as an innkeeper/majorette-domo with overall responsibility for the entertainment and comfort of boarders. Some of the guests were treated to piano recitals in the parlour consisting of two numbers (the extent of her repertoire) accompanied by Belle's infamous singing. Others, such as Richard Ehrlich, a student from Heidelberg, were favoured with the hospitality of Belle's boudoir. One day at noon, Crippen returned home unexpectedly to retrieve health questionnaires which he forgot to stuff into his medical bag. He stepped into Belle's room and discovered Ehrlich and his wife passionately devouring each other. Crippen said nothing and quietly retreated. Caught in the act, Belle had no defence and had to abandon the guest house scheme. Crippen continued to generate income from his interest in a small dental office and from sales of various remedies. Even so, the expenses of a home, business, needy wife, and mistress must have been overwhelming.

Belle was not immune from the double burden of dwindling resources and spousal unfaithfulness. She coped with adversity through associations in the Ladies Guild, but just barely. Then, at the dawn of 1909, an unexpected event forever changed the tenor of Crippendom. Ethel became pregnant. She immediately shared the news with her landlady, Mrs Emily Jackson, and Peter, of course. Mrs Jackson was the first to know as Ethel's confidant. There were no other men in Ethel's world so the child was unquestionably Peter Crippen's. Belle was evil with jealousy, her own barrenness adding salt to the festering wound. Ever mindful of propriety, she castigated Peter for the embarrassment which would personally befall her. Ethel, however, was jubilant. She believed her pregnancy would force Belle to give Peter his freedom. Several months later Mrs Jackson would find herself consoling a maudlin Ethel. Ethel had miscarried. The pathetic triangle had turned again to expose its most jagged edge.

Belle was perversely relieved that everyone was back on the same playing field but would not let the matter rest. She saw this as her best and perhaps last opportunity to dethrone mistress Le Neve. Belle told acquaintances that Ethel was unperturbed by the miscarriage since she had no idea who the father was among her many suitors. She also carefully planted a rumour that the miscarriage was a hoax to cover up Ethel's wilful abortion.

One can imagine how difficult it must have been for Crippen to return home after a hard day of hustling to make ends meet: Belle, dishevelled, roots bleeding through bleached hair, nighttime make-up streaming and screaming, stumbling to greet her husband. She had had all day to store discontent and now, pumped up on liquor, unloaded in mocking histrionics. Crippen did not indulge her by joining the fray. He internalised his misery in quiet ignominy.

When it came to outward appearances, we do know that Belle as well as Peter maintained the image of a couple quite respectful of each other. The only clue to marital disintegration would be infidelity which was discreetly hidden on both sides for a number of years. Acquaintances from the stage or Ladies Guild regularly called on the Crippens, unaware of any problem. The couple never used these occasions to complain about their deeply troubled marriage. Even Belle's campaign to annihilate home wrecker Le Neve was executed with surgical precision perhaps in the misguided belief that reconciliation was possible.

The Crippens, who entertained frequently, invited two friends of the Guild over for dinner, drinks, and contract bridge. Their guests were the Flying Martinettis, retired acrobats, now somewhat frail from the punishment of countless performances. The Martinettis agreed to come over early in February 1910. Crippen insisted they join company on 31 January, even though Paul Martinetti was weak. As with prior occasions, the evening went well. Clara Martinetti would later recall what a pleasant evening the couples enjoyed. The Martinettis were having such a good time — they stayed well past midnight. Finally, during the early hours of 1 February 1910, they bid their hosts *arrivederci* after Crippen spent a lonely hour hailing a carriage outside in the freezing cold.

Throughout the long evening, Belle filled herself with cocktails, to the point of over-subscription. Not surprisingly, a few moments following the departure of their guests, she turned on Peter like a rabid lioness. She was angry because Crippen did not jump to the aid of Paul Martinetti when he experienced some difficulty on the stairs to the water closet. Belle had hit a heretofore insulated raw nerve with her pettiness. A hateful argument consumed them both.

Several weeks prior to this confrontation, Belle had furnished advance notice to Charing Cross Bank for withdrawal of over £600 but a lengthy withdrawal notice period (required on accounts earning premium interest) tied up the funds for months.

Crippen had also been busy several weeks before, only he was calling on the neighbourhood Chemist instead of a bank teller. The Doctor ordered a powerful sedative sometimes used as truth serum or in conjunction with morphine as a pain killer.

Hyoscine, made from roots of the naturally occurring Nightshade weed, Henbane, was so rare it took the Pharmacist a couple of days to procure. Crippen had observed clinical use of the drug while an intern at London's Royal Bethlehem 'Bedlam' Hospital where Hyoscine was used to subdue dangerous psychopaths and fiends. The dosage in these applications was hundredths-of-a-grain. Crippen picked up five whole grains of Hyoscine as soon as his order arrived at the pharmacy. There was no attempt to deceive the Chemist who must have thought Doctor Crippen was concocting another patent remedy. Crippen took the drug home and may have commingled it with an extensive assortment of household remedies to prevent the appearance of a suspicious bottle.

Fighting continued at fashionable 39 Hilldrop Crescent. The maelstrom which was the Crippen marriage, one that deprived Belle of her dreams, and denied Peter an attractive and loving wife, now spun hopelessly out of control. Belle's jeers about Ethel tore at Crippen's heart. Her alcoholically bloated form disgusted him. Although we will never know if Belle actually planned to leave Crippen, her invective rambled into new territory. She probably unwittingly revealed her plans to empty their bank account. She may have also decided that the best way to foil Crippen's permanent future with Ethel would be to deny him a divorce. Insinuating that Ethel had an abortion because she wasn't sure if Peter was the father must have been the proverbial nail in Belle's coffin. Pausing to catch her breath before launching into subsequent rounds of diatribe, Belle characteristically demanded another drink from her husband. He was only too willing to oblige. Crippen mixed Belle an extremely smart Hyoscine cocktail in the kitchen and promptly handed it to her. The combination of her drinking and the depressant was fatal. Unlike the American Groundhog of 1910, she would never live to see 2 February or her shadow again.

Crippen now faced an imbroglio of emotion from a single but unalterable act. First, a rush of relief from the horror of Belle's torment followed by soothing thoughts of Ethel which rationalized an otherwise unspeakable crime. Then, the realization that he escaped one maelstrom only to be staring down the throat of another. It was now the murderer who was short of breath as he considered the bothersome complications associated with killing one's spouse in the parlour. The consequences of murder swirled in his mind like headlines from a newsreel, obscuring reality to the point where his mind was no longer at the scene of the crime.

Crippen imagined Belle's corpse on a white enamel, shallow rimmed slab at a hospital mortuary, awaiting dissection. What was written on the tag dangling from her big toe? Was it Belle Elmore? The Baroness Kunigunde Mackamotski? The abbreviated Macka Motski? The original Cora Turner? Bruce Miller's tender assignation 'Brown Eyes', or just plain 'Mack'? If Belle had lived to a ripe old age, which Crippen thought unlikely even absent his hand, she would have proliferated more *noms de plume* than toes on her feet. Crippen continued to slide into a surrealistic morgue where lifeless Belle lay before him on her back with eyes shut. Crippen was dressed in surgical garb, mask, and brandished a formidable, razor-sharp blade. Reeking formaldehyde and corpse stench made him dizzy, bleary-eyed and queasy. Before proceeding with the imaginary autopsy he checked the body tag wired to Belle's toe. Turning it over to read the name, he choked upon finding 'CRIPPEN DID IT' written in blood. He violently tore the tag from its anchor slightly cutting his hand in the process. At the other end of the slab, Crippen aligned the blade across Belle's puffy throat. Unexpectedly, a twitch in her neck and Belle's eyelids snapped open like sprung window shades. Gasping for air while emitting a ghoulish howl, the murderer raised his blade high in the air when suddenly a familiar sound, the regulator clock in the parlour, resoundingly announced the hour. Crippen's momentary hallucination was over. His respiration gradually returned to normal. In Jekyll-and-Hyde fashion, the old Doctor H. H. Crippen resumed control. Imperturbable, he would now have to deal with the gruesome disposal of an immobile, reliably silent, Belle Elmore.

There is no evidence in the historical record to show exactly what happened after Belle gulped down her adulterated cocktail (Crippen's mortuary hallucination is an invention of your author). One theory is that Belle went to her bedroom and died peacefully in her sleep. This would have been convenient since her bedroom adjoined the bathroom. Crippen would only have to drag the dead weight a short distance to the tub where the grisly chore of dismemberment could be neatly contained and washed away without a trace. Once the body was landed in the bathtub, a medical background did not make the task any easier as Crippen had no post-mortem experience. Another theory is that Belle had a reaction to Hyoscine, not unprecedented in high doses, where she became uncontrollably violent. Crippen, who kept a revolver in the house allegedly to protect Belle's expensive jewellery and furs, may have used the weapon to force a dangerously agitated Belle into the bathroom. He might have shot her in the head to quell her loud aggression before it became too outrageous for neighbours to ignore. One neighbour, Mrs Louisa May Glackner, would later tell newspaper reporters that she heard Belle pleading for her life followed by a gunshot.

Crippen stayed at home for three days immediately following the murder, but he was not without work. He dislodged, removed and set aside a section of bricks from the coal cellar floor. In this section, a shallow pit was shovelled out. The thoroughly filleted Belle, consisting of flesh and parts of internal organs, was deposited in the excavation together with a pyjama top from Jones Brothers of Holloway. The balance of Belle's remains including torso skeleton, hands, feet, and limbs were incinerated in the kitchen stove. The pyjama shirt might have been wrapped around body parts to transport them from tub to stove. It may have initially become splattered with blood and body fluids during or after the murder while being worn by Crippen. In any event, it should have been incinerated in the kitchen stove with the rest of Belle. The head was rumoured to have been disposed of in the English Channel. Speculation was that Crippen tossed Belle's head over the side of a cross-channel ferry in a weighted hatbox or Gladstone bag. To complete the home burial, Crippen added calcium oxide, found in quicklime, to dissolve the flesh and control resultant odours. His mixture was apparently too wet or inadequately applied, making its net effect more preservative than corrosive. The floor of the cellar was restored. A strange and bungled cover-up had begun.

Crippen's cover-up failed because there really was no cover-up. There was no logical plan to perfect the crime. The weeks that followed were a tragic comedy of errors during which the murderer jumped from one loose, extemporaneous story to another. One of Crippen's first actions, on Belle's behalf, was to send a letter of resignation from the post of Treasurer to the Music Hall Ladies Guild. Miss Le Neve hand carried the letter to Melinda May of the Guild on the day after the murder. On the same day, Crippen went to Oxford Street and pawned much of Belle's jewellery for the sum of £195. He gave the balance of jewellery consisting of many valuable rings and a diamond brooch to his mistress. Ethel, daft from the joy of having Peter to herself and the jewels, unquestionably accepted Belle's disappearance. Crippen told her that Belle had left him and would never be coming back. He added a fabrication, saying that Belle left her jewellery behind because it wasn't good enough for her. Ethel, a bit too naive to be believed, was at 39 Hilldrop Crescent on the afternoon following the murder and didn't notice that Belle had left without taking anything with her. There was nothing missing from Belle's wardrobe; her personal items and toiletries were still in place. Ethel and Peter slept together in the house that night. For these events to hold true, all happening one day after Belle's demise, Crippen must have dispatched the body with demonic efficiency or hidden what was left from Ethel's view.

Crippen was far less effective when it came to explaining Belle's sudden departure from London. He told acquaintances that Belle had sailed to America immediately upon news that a close relative was about to die, possibly leaving behind a substantial legacy. Crippen never anticipated how meddlesome Belle's operatives would become. They forced encounters with him to extract more information about Belle. Crippen had to stumble through made-up details of Belle's family emergency in California when pressed by her loyal coterie. The ladies at the Guild were far from satisfied. Belle's tenacious Music Hall sisters wanted 'obtrusive' information like Belle's address, the name of the ship she sailed on, and an explanation for why she didn't draft correspondence during her crossing. Crippen eventually gave someone from the Guild the Hollywood, California, address of his son, Otto. He identified Belle's westbound ship for Mrs Martinetti as *La Touraine* of Compagnie Générale Transatlantique (French Line) without verifying the ship's sailing schedule. He also told Mrs Martinetti that Belle was completely overcome by events and very prone to seasickness so it should not be surprising that no correspondence was forthcoming.

Three weeks after the murder, the Music Hall Ladies Guild held their annual charity fund-raiser at the Criterion restaurant. Incredibly, Crippen attended the gala dinner ball with his mistress. He had purchased two tickets from Mrs Martinetti probably as a way to escape her relentless inquiries about Belle. Even more astounding, Ethel wore some of Belle's jewellery which Crippen had given her. One piece, a diamond brooch, stuck out like a sore thumb. Several women recognized it as Belle's 'rising sun' brooch and knew instinctively that something was quite wrong with the picture they were seeing.

Crippen decided that he had to stop the repeated entreaties from Belle's friends. In mid March, he began telling Clara Martinetti and others that Belle had become very ill with pneumonia. He added that Belle had travelled into the California mountains and could not be reached by mail. On 24 March, he sent a telegram to Mrs Martinetti advising her of Belle's passing. Crippen and Le Neve immediately departed for a week-long holiday to Dieppe, in northern France. Peter and Ethel may have quickly married during this flight from reminders of the old Mrs Crippen.

The lovebirds' escape to France was an extremely short reprieve from Belle's dedicated associates who would not let her die. Crippen had more explaining to do than ever. Once again he made a serious error by telling Mrs Smythson, of the Guild, that Belle was cremated. Mrs Smythson had demanded a gravesite address in order to send flowers. Crippen must have thought himself clever in coming up with cremation to foil any graveside memorial activity. Belle's friends, however, knew that cremation would have been quite unthinkable since Belle's family was devoutly Catholic.

The Music Hall Ladies Guild continued their detective work. Melinda May wrote to Otto Crippen in California to ask how his stepmother was getting on. Otto was married and had since moved from the address Crippen had furnished to the Guild. It took some time for Melinda's letter to get forwarded to the new address. Weeks later, a reply was received in which Otto writes:

> *The death of my stepmother was as great a surprise to me as to anyone... the first I heard of it was through my father, who wrote to me immediately afterwards.*

The women also investigated Belle's alleged 2 February sailing on *La Touraine*. It turned out that *La Touraine* was actually in the middle of an eastbound crossing to Le Havre. Belle's friends were convinced something dishonest and downright sinister had befallen her.

John and Lilly Hawthorne Nash, who had dined at the same table with Peter and Ethel at the Criterion Ball, were among those who suspected foul play. Mr and Mrs Nash had recently returned from performing on tour in the States, including shows in California. While in America, they found no evidence of Belle's death at various record offices. They appealed to a friend who was Superintendent of criminal cases at New Scotland Yard to investigate the matter. Chief Inspector Walter Dew was assigned to the missing person case. This was the same Inspector who a decade earlier worked on the Jack the Ripper case — a mystery which was never solved. Dew was assisted by a detective named Mitchell.

Dew and Mitchell went to interview Crippen on Friday, 8 July. They found the impassive little man at his office. The trio went to lunch at an Italian eatery during which Crippen ingeniously unburdened himself. He explained away all the concerns of the Ladies Guild using guileful male bonding. First, he admitted to his lunch companions that he had lied. The 'truth' was that following a bitter argument Belle left Crippen to join her lover in America. There never was a dying relative, substantial inheritance, or attack of pneumonia. Belle was alive and well somewhere in the States. Crippen told the two policemen that he simply couldn't bear the humiliation he would suffer at the hands of Belle's Bohemian friends so he made up stories to defuse their treatment of him as an inadequate man. Dew fell for it. The trio proceeded to 39 Hilldrop Crescent where a brief search was conducted, revealing nothing noteworthy. Crippen had not only dodged the bullet but should have received an academy award for a flawless performance devoid of even a nuance of guilt.

Crippen failed to realize that his handling of Inspector Dew was the finest hour in an otherwise haphazard and twisted cover-up. Without a corpse, New Scotland Yard had no crime to prosecute. The Chief Inspector was prepared to let the case become one of so many dormant in his missing persons file. Crippen, however cool on the outside, was actually rattled to the bone on the inside. He quickly closed up affairs at his office, gathered money and jewellery, and with Ethel fled to the Netherlands and later to Belgium. Crippen planned to start a new life for them both in Canada. They would escape initially to Montreal on a steamer out of Antwerp. Two days after Crippen ran, Monday, 11 July, Chief Inspector Dew was completing his report on the disappearance of Belle Elmore. He wanted to double-check the exact date of Belle's departure so he returned to Crippen's office. Lunch with Crippen on the previous Friday was so cordial — perhaps they would do it again. It was immediately obvious that Crippen had abandoned his office. Dew found notes from Crippen to co-workers announcing an indefinite absence from the dental practice. Dew knew then that his missing person case might be a homicide.

Dew and Mitchell spent the next three days searching 39 Hilldrop Crescent. On day three, Dew was beginning to wonder if Belle would ever turn up when he happened to bang his stick on the basement floor while gazing at the ceiling. The sound returned was hollow. An adrenalin pumping, second-strike against the floor drew his attention to a loose brick. The floor was taken up and a ghastly mound of flesh was discovered together with a Jones Brothers cotton pyjama top and a lock of peroxide-white hair. The wafting stench forced police to evacuate the basement repeatedly for air. A more intensive search of the grounds including manual excavation of the garden was undertaken in the hope of finding the rest of Belle. No other trace, not even an errant blood stain, was ever found. The police surgeon, Dr Thomas Marshall, was called but had little to do except perhaps verify the paltry remains as human. The tissue was removed and sent to a mortuary pending forensic investigation. Three years later, Ingleby Oddie, the coroner in the case, would note what he considered a bizarre coincidence. Weldon Atherstone was shot dead at almost the same time as Belle's remains were found. Weldon was the performer who followed Belle on stage only to be booed off during the artists' strike. Accordingly, your author posthumously adds 'Bad Luck Belle' to her many titles.

The discovery of a mutilated human being in the cellar combined with Belle's disappearance was all the newspapers needed to launch a sensational crime story. Belle had finally achieved the fame which eluded her in life. Internationally, headlines announced the murder of a 'famous' actress in London. On 15 July, Crippen first learned of his fugitive status from just such a headline in a Belgian paper. On 16 July, New Scotland Yard was widely circulating Police Bulletins which began with 'MURDER AND MUTILATION', in large bold-type followed by, 'Hawley Harvey Crippen, alias Peter Crippen... and Ethel Clara Le Neve, alias Mrs Crippen, and Neave. Wanted for the Murder of Cora Crippen, otherwise Belle Elmore.'

Crippen police bulletin. (New Scotland Yard)

The bulletins included photographs of Crippen and Le Neve, detailed descriptions, and handwriting samples. It advised steamship offices to be watchful. Belle's 'rising sun' brooch figured prominently in the police description of Ethel:

May have in her possession and endeavour to dispose of same — a round gold brooch, with points radiating zig-zag from centre, each point about an inch long, diamond in centre, each point set brilliant, the brooch in all being slightly larger than a half-crown.

The fact that Belle's brooch received so much play in the Police Bulletin is a credit to persistent women at the Guild who saw Ethel wearing it and so informed New Scotland Yard.

Crippen no longer had the luxury of a leisurely escape. Peter and Ethel needed to conceal their identities and get out of the country as soon as possible. They ended up travelling as Mr John Philo Robinson and his teenage son. Some newspaper accounts reported that Crippen was travelling as Reverend Robinson complete with clerical collar. It may be that Crippen told a variety of stories to travellers as he fled. Making it up as he went along would certainly be vintage Crippen. Ethel's 'Master Robinson' disguise was not very convincing. Her hair was trimmed like a boy and she was wearing men's trousers but a tight fit gave away her feminine build. Crippen shaved his moustache and removed his tell-tale spectacles. He also allowed his beard to grow. Fraudulent father and son booked passage on the next available steamer to Canada. That vessel was *Montrose*, scheduled to sail several days later on 20 July from Antwerp to Quebec.

The ship Crippen and 'son' boarded was built in 1897 for the carriage of dairy products and immigrants to Canada. *Montrose* belonged to the Elder Dempster Line until 1903 when Canadian Pacific bought her as part of its entry into Atlantic service. She had a single-funnel, four masts, and no first-class accommodation. Passenger capacity was 57 cabin-class and over 300 steerage. *Montrose* was under the command of Captain Henry George Kendall.

The *Montrose* had barely gotten out to sea when ship's company started to notice something askew with two of their cabin-class passengers. The Chief Steward noticed that Master Robinson had remarkably small hands and walked like a woman. He notified Third Officer R. S. Mowatt who shared this curiosity with Captain Kendall. Cabin-class passengers were quite noticeable aboard *Montrose* since there were a maximum of 57 berths and no higher level of accommodation. On this crossing only 20 passengers occupied cabin-class which made Crippen and Le Neve even more visible. The 36-year-old Kendall had just finished telling the stewards to keep a close watch on the Robinsons in Cabin 5 when he noticed some unusual behaviour. Two of his small group of cabin-class passengers, two men more specifically, appeared to be holding hands in a most affectionate manner. It was the Robinsons! Peter and Ethel thought they were out of public view behind a lifeboat but Kendall was able to see them through a porthole. He noted that 'The younger one squeezed the other's hand immoderately. It seemed to me unnatural for two males, so I suspected them at once.'

Did he suspect them of being homosexual? Kendall never admitted to this. It was possible for a father and daughter to be travelling as father and 'son' to avoid relegation to separate compartments. Ocean liners, reflecting the standards of the day, segregated unmarried adults by gender and excluded women entirely from some areas such as smoking lounges and game rooms. Kendall invited Mr Robinson and son to dine at his table. This would be an opportunity to learn more about the mysterious couple.

Meanwhile, newspapers worldwide were immortalizing the butchered Belle Elmore. Crippen was dubbed 'the North London Cellar Murderer'. Like the O.J. Simpson case in Los Angeles many years later, the Crippen story totally dominated the news. It also dominated public discourse on the street, at work, in hotels, restaurants, and at home. People were shocked by a doctor killing his wife, horrified by evisceral details, and lynch-mob angry at the alleged perpetrator. If Crippen murdered his wife and cut her up in the world of today, it would be short-lived, third-page news.

Canadian Pacific's S.S. Montrose *originally owned by Elder Dempster and Company. Full view.* (Peabody Essex Museum, Salem, Massachusetts).

Crippen had been at-large since 9 July. New Scotland Yard, as indicated in their wanted for murder and mutilation bulletin, was keen on watching steamship agents and ocean liners. Crippen had plenty of time to book passage westbound between abandoning his home and the discovery in the cellar. If he had sailed on or about 9 July, he was near arrival at a major eastern harbour. Belle's fate was front-page news in New York City on 14 July and city piers were under observation the very next day. Cunard Steamship Line's new landing, Pier 56, at 14th Street, was the site of one such pierside watch. Pier 56 was newly built, uptown, in 1907 to accommodate the arrival of Cunard's four-stack, speedy behemoths *Lusitania* and *Mauretania*. Cunard's previous dock, Pier 51 at 12th Street, wasn't high enough to embark passengers through hull portals which were now two decks or more above street level.

Of Cunard's two large sister ships, neither requires introduction. *Mauretania*, under construction in 1906, was made famous when her funnels were laid end to end along side the hull for a publicity gimmick. Automobiles, two abreast, drove through sections of three stacks as a demonstration of *Mauretania's* enormous scale. She went on to enjoy a long life including 22 years as transatlantic speed record holder. The *Lusitania*, like Belle, was destroyed before her time. *Lusitania* was cut down by German torpedoes but the fatal poison may have been ammunition and coal dust in her belly. *Lusitania* first tied up at Cunard's new pier in September of 1907. Less than three years later, when she arrived in New York on 15 July 1910, she was closely scrutinized by none other than Mrs Isabel Ginnett, the President of the Music Hall Ladies Guild.

Mrs Ginnett, a close friend of Belle's, was in the United States while her husband toured with an equestrian show. Isabel was famous in her own right as ex-bareback rider and circus performer 'Madame Ginnett'. Now, as President of the Guild, she had the good fortune to be in New York in perfect position to avenge Belle's death. She went down to Pier 56 to meet the *Lusitania* returning from Liverpool. She fully expected to capture the demon Crippen and that 'hussy' accomplice Le Neve. She studied all disembarking passengers ready to finger Crippen for two policemen who accompanied her to the pier. After intensely scanning all disembarkees, Madame Ginnett, in the relentless tradition of Guild women, continued her self-appointed work. Convinced that *Lusitania* was not Crippenless, she boarded the vessel using the authority of her police escorts and interrogated stewards and a few remaining passengers. She repeated this practice during the next few days with several other inbound liners including White Star's *Cedric*; French Line's *La Lorraine*; and American Line's *St Paul*.

The Marconi installation on board *Montrose* had a transmission range of 150 miles and a receiving range of up to 600 miles. *The Montrose* also had a fresh supply of major newspapers taken on board just before leaving Belgium. Captain Kendall pored over the newspapers and studied the many feature stories about Crippen and Le Neve. He was also aware that a £250 reward was offered by New Scotland Yard for information leading to their arrest. During the first day at sea Crippen failed an important test of his disguise. Captain Kendall called to 'Mr Robinson' several times while on deck but his greeting fell on deaf ears. It suddenly dawned on Ethel that they were the Robinsons. She awkwardly reminded her 'father' that the Captain was attempting to engage him. It was too late; Kendall knew he was dealing with people on the run.

Dinner the first night out at Kendall's table must have been more uncomfortable than the night Crippen and Ethel spent at the Ladies Guild charity ball. What intrigue and drama with Kendall determined to resolve whether the Robinsons were homosexuals or axe murderers and Ethel trying pathetically to pass herself off as a young man. Among Master Robinson's transparent characteristics were: ill-fitting clothes, feminine build, ladylike handling of food using two dainty fingers, and a voice which started deep and then flew into outer space. Crippen sat to the Captain's right at the end of the table. Crippen was making small talk about the weather and started to steer the conversation to Shakespeare. He would be a harder nut to crack than the thinly veiled Miss Le Neve. Kendall knew from newspaper descriptions that Crippen had gold fillings. Kendall entertained his table with a tireless set of amusing sea stories until Crippen finally opened up wide to let out a hearty laugh. The gleam of gold shot out like a star. Kendall knew then that he was dining with the murderous fiend, Doctor Hawley Harvey Crippen.

To further confirm his conclusion, Kendall was said to have tossed a coin into Ethel's lap to see if she would spread her legs to catch it as a girl would wearing a skirt. A boy would be expected to have closed his legs to catch the object. We can only guess at Ethel's reaction because this event is a piece of Crippen fiction. Another version of this story had Master Robinson closing 'his' legs to catch a ball on deck. Kendall did confirm his identification of Crippen by comparing newspaper photographs of Doctor Crippen to passenger John P. Robinson. To match the newspaper photo to Crippen's pseudo-identity, the Captain took a piece of chalk from the ship's chart-stand and began to colour over Crippen's spectacles and moustache. Thinking back to dinner, Kendall remembered that the bridge of Robinson's nose was irritated and dented. Most curious for a man who didn't wear glasses. Kendall completed alterations to Crippen's photo and studied it for a time. There was more than a chance resemblance. Kendall's artistry unmistakably translated into the fictitious Robinson. Kendall had to act fast as *Montrose* would soon be out of radio range.

With a £250 reward, better than a third of his annual salary, potentially burning a hole in his wallet, Kendall became very secretive. He ordered Stewards to discreetly gather up all English language newspapers on board. This was apparently done to avoid alarming Crippen and Le Neve but it also kept the story out of the hands of those who might feel entitled to share the reward. Captain Kendall went to the Marconi cabin on 22 July and handed the wireless man, Llewellyn Jones, the following historic message:

3 PM GMT Friday 130 miles West Lizard — Have strong suspicions that Crippen London Cellar murderer and accomplice are amongst Saloon passengers. Moustache taken off — growing beard. Accomplice dressed as boy. Voice manner and build undoubtedly a girl. Both travelling as Mr and Master Robinson... Kendall.

The message was sent to the attention of Arthur Piers, Canadian Pacific's Steamship Manager in Liverpool. Piers passed it on to the Liverpool police who forwarded it to New Scotland Yard in London. Kendall gave Jones a letter absolving Jones from any responsibility for the message in the event Kendall was wrong.

New Scotland Yard had no idea if Kendall and his information could be relied upon. They also had no reason to doubt it. On 23 July, Dew boarded White Star's 17 knot *Laurentic*, in Liverpool, to chase Crippen across the North Atlantic.

'Operation Handcuffs' with Dew travelling under the unimaginative cover 'Dewhurst' had begun. *Montrose* was a far slower 13 knot ship so Dew expected to make up *Montrose*'s three day head start and possibly pass her.

Laurentic, built in 1909, equipped with a single-funnel, was the first ship to use the propulsion configuration later used on *Olympic* and *Titanic*. It consisted of port and starboard screws powered by expansion engines plus a low-pressure steam turbine to power the third screw in the centre. *Laurentic*'s reputation for speed, as reinforced by the Crippen chase, would later be partially responsible for

Captain Kendall's marconigram to Canadian Pacific's Liverpool office
advising Arthur Piers that Crippen and Le Neve were on board the Montrose.
(New Scotland Yard).

her selection to run a secret World War I mission: Great Britain needed to bolster
the weakening pound sterling and finance procurement of war hardware. This
required the transfer of gold bullion to North America. On 25 January 1917, four
miles from the North Irish coast, *Laurentic* hit two mines laid by German
submarine U-80. She sank rapidly taking the gold and 354 of her crew to the
bottom.

The *Montezuma*, also owned by Canadian Pacific, passed *Montrose* in the
opposite direction eastbound on 25 July. Kendall saw this as an excellent
opportunity to update New Scotland Yard so he asked the Captain of the
Montezuma to forward a wireless report to London. The text of Kendall's
messages about Crippen had a discursive tendency, as though Kendall was
convincing himself that the killer was actually on board his ship. The 25 July
Marconigram to *Montezuma* is typical:

> With reference to wireless I sent regarding Crippen I feel more fully
> convinced that it is him. All descriptions corresponding fully with information
> from papers and police report received in London. Is very reticent. Also
> accomplice. They have no baggage except a small cheap grip bought on
> continent. Is still letting beard grow but shaves upper lip. Managed to examine
> his soft grey felt hat while at lunch. Name inside Jackson's, Boulevard de Nord.
> Grey felt hat of accomplice no lining, packed inside of band to make fit. Both
> wearing brown suits and white canvas shoes. Noticed accomplice using safety
> pins in pants. According to conversations with him he has travelled all over the
> States. Up to present he has no suspicion of being watched on board... Kendall.

On 27 July, the gendarme's Atlantic greyhound *Laurentic* closed on the villain's older Canadian Pacific immigrant steamer. Ship-to-ship wireless was used to contact the *Montrose*. Inspector Dew sent the following Marconigram:

Will board you Father Point. Please keep any information till I arrive there strictly confidential... Dew Scotland Yard on board Laurentic.

Newspaper audiences were thrilled. They were enthralled not only with the story but with the ocean liner chase. Newspapers published charts showing each vessel's North Atlantic track, their progress west, and the points from which Marconigrams were sent. Readers were also treated to photographs of the ships, the Captains, and even the wireless operators. People could visualize *Laurentic* at full steam, digging into the sea, her funnel leaving a long flat trail of smoke over a ferocious, horizon-long wake. They imagined the drone of her engines and the hum of her shafts beating like the heart of a giant predator racing for the kill. On her Boat Deck, the induction coil of her Marconi device feverishly sparked out the letters of messages which would be Crippen's undoing. In her belly, dutiful stokers gave *Laurentic* her lifeblood, frantically shovelling coal into her roaring boilers. Would Scotland Yard overtake the *Montrose* and get their man? Would the suspicious couple really turn out to be Crippen and Le Neve? Was it shipboard life as usual on the *Montrose* or a game of Captain Kendall and mouse? Where and how would the arrest be made or would the clever little man evade capture? The press and the public were in rapture. It was one of the most suspenseful criminal dramas of the century fuelled by the marvel of Marconi's new invention. Today's true crime stories pale in comparison.

As *Montrose* approached the easterly reaches of Newfoundland on 29 July, wireless activity from Belle Isle filled the airways. Many of the messages were directed to Crippen like the following one from a major news organization:

You are accused of murdering your wife in London. Please deny it. Write a complete statement at once.

These messages were, of course, kept from Crippen. Inspector Dew was exchanging numerous wireless messages with Captain Kendall to prepare for *Montrose*'s arrival at Father Point. One of the concerns both men shared was a possible suicide attempt by Crippen before the arrest could be made.

To keep Crippen busy, Kendall shared books from his personal library located in the Captain's cabin. On several occasions, Crippen visited Kendall in the Captain's stateroom to discuss their respective reading. On one such occasion, Crippen handed Kendall *The Four Just Men* by Edgar Wallace which Crippen had brought with him from the ship's library. Kendall was aghast. Crippen had just handed him a murder mystery! This reminded the Captain of something in his private collection. Kendall opened his bookcase, handed Crippen a volume and said 'Have you read that? It's about a man who murdered his wife.' The book was *The Murder of Delicia* by Marie Corelli. If Crippen intended this encounter to be a minor power play in support of his innocence, he lost to the Captain's quick and bold intellect. Crippen twisted his lower lip between his fingers and stared out the

Captain's porthole. The strain of remaining composed must have been intense. After thanking Kendall for the murder story, Crippen dismissed himself and retreated to his cabin.

Crippen had a habit of pacing about the open decks apprehensively, especially at odd hours. He couldn't help but notice that activity in the Marconi shack was at a fever pitch. He stopped to chat with lead Marconiman Llewellyn Jones to see what all the fuss was about. Jones cleverly made up a story about ice being sighted off the tip of Belle Isle. He told Crippen he was sending out ice warnings to the Commanding Officers of nearby ships including the *Royal George*. Crippen never suspected that he was actually the subject of all those messages. On the Boat Deck, in conversation with Kendall, he described Marconi's wireless as 'a wonderful invention'.

On 31 July, the climactic chase was over. *Laurentic* had won the handicapped transatlantic race arriving comfortably ahead of *Montrose* at Father Point on the afternoon of 29 July. Inspector Dew dropped the 'Mr Dewhurst' cover and co-ordinated with Canadian authorities in preparation for the arrest. Chief Constable McCarthy from Quebec would be the arresting official with assistance from Detective Dennis. Inspector Dew didn't want to give the fugitives time to react if he was seen coming aboard. Crippen might be armed and Captain Kendall indeed thought he had seen the shape of a revolver on Crippen during the crossing. Jean Baptiste Belanger, Captain of *Eureka*, loaned Inspector Dew his Navy pea-coat and white combination-cap with visor to ensure a successful ruse. The *Eureka* was a Dominion Government Steamer based at Father Point.

The *Montrose*'s whistle was heard at Father Point as early as 4:30am on Sunday, 31 July 1910. Local residents and reporters dressed hastily and gathered in a drizzling rain to feast on the arrival of *Montrose*'s infamous passengers. The *Montrose* slowed to a stop off Father Point at 7:30am unaware that she would soon enjoy a reception worthy of a fabulous new ocean liner. As a further precaution against tipping off Crippen, Inspector Dew and the arresting officers decided to use one of *Eureka*'s tenders for the transit out to *Montrose*. While *Eureka*'s lifeboat tendered out the incognito Inspector, the ship's surgeon, Doctor C. H. Stewart, kept an eye on Crippen. Crippen and Stewart, almost shoulder-to-shoulder, were looking out over the ship's starboard rail on the forward Promenade Deck near the main saloon stairway. They watched *Eureka*'s lifeboat approach with the welcoming committee of three plus several seamen.

'What a lot of men in that small boat... are they all pilots?' inquired Crippen.

Doctor Stewart pointed out that there is only one pilot for the ship but the others were perhaps friends embarking for an excursion to Quebec. Crippen grew suspicious. He postulated that the men must be coming on board for a medical inspection but Stewart said such an inspection was not expected at Father Point.

Inspector Dew climbed up the rope ladder thrown down for his arrival with the Chief Constable ascending just one rung behind in perfect unison. Inspector Dew went right up to Crippen, tapped him on the shoulder, and greeted him with a self-satisfying 'Good Morning, Doctor Crippen'.

The murderer recognized his nemesis immediately. The blood drained from Crippen's face as he belatedly swallowed the words 'I am Doctor Crippen'.

Dew, Crippen, and McCarthy adjourned to Captain Kendall's cabin. The arrest was uneventful except for Crippen's reaction. He was angry not surprised. Perhaps angry at himself for throughout this story he is his own worst enemy. Definitely angry at Captain Kendall for his interference and mockery. Crippen later confided that he was relieved the suspenseful chase was over. Crippen was handcuffed after listening to Chief Constable McCarthy read an arrest warrant signed by the Attorney General for the Province of Quebec. A search of the man in custody revealed no weapon. Le Neve was arrested moments later on the same warrant in Crippen's cabin and also handcuffed. Just before her arrest, the stewardess saw Le Neve toss a package out through the cabin porthole. Le Neve was taken to Cabin 8 where she sobbed hysterically for much of the twelve-hour continuation voyage west to Quebec. Crippen was kept completely separate from Ethel in what was the 'Robinson's' stateroom.

The sleepy town of Rimouski had been deluged with reporters, photographers, and throngs of people who wanted to catch a glimpse of the London Cellar Murderer and his accomplice. Captain Kendall signalled the *Eureka* which came alongside with a human cargo of about 40 reporters. They were allowed on board for the transit to Quebec but were not permitted to interview Crippen or Le Neve. In Canada, where the good Doctor had hoped to begin a new life and cheerfully bid Captain Kendall adieu, he now stood in shackles awaiting extradition. He thought he was about to be paraded in front of taunting reporters like a circus freak. He was mortified. Unable to contain himself, he fell to the deck and declared a horrible curse on Captain Kendall's head. His eyes bulged right out of their sockets as Crippen proclaimed 'You will suffer for this treachery, sir.' This evil vexation received coverage in the Montreal *Daily Star*.

Crippen was arraigned in a crowded Quebec courtroom on 1 August. Le Neve did not appear as she was still in shock from her arrest. The crowd outside the courthouse numbered in the thousands. When Crippen was taken out of the courtroom, extra police had to be called in to push the crowd back. The carriage Crippen was riding in almost overturned when someone startled the horse. A woman spectator was almost crushed under one of the carriage wheels.

Someone who would not miss the chance to see justice done was Mrs Isabel Ginnett, President of the Ladies Guild. She travelled to Quebec from New York and was interviewed by local authorities in the presence of Inspector Dew. Mrs Ginnett, who always boasted that she could spot Crippen anywhere, was able to identify three diamond rings, a diamond brooch, and a cluster ring with large diamond as unmistakably the property of Belle Elmore. These five items were found stitched to Crippen's underclothes.

If not jewellery, what was in the package which Ethel tossed overboard? Was it the revolver Crippen was alleged to be carrying? This remains one of the mysteries of the Crippen case.

Crippen was extradited in quick order, less than three weeks. There were complications associated with processing an American fugitive arrested on Canadian waters for a crime committed in England. The Fugitive Offenders Act provided a waiting period of 15 days prior to extradition to allow the accused time to dispute the proceedings. Crippen and Le Neve were both willing to go back and did not seek legal counsel to try and block their return. New Scotland Yard booked passage for their return to London on White Star's *Megantic*, the sister ship to *Laurentic*. So as not to alarm passengers, Inspector Dew changed names again. He travelled as 'Mr Doyle'; and prisoner Crippen became 'Mr Nield'. Ethel was on board as well under guard in a separate cabin. *Megantic* began her eastbound crossing on 20 August. Angry crowds jeered *Megantic*'s arrival in Liverpool. The prisoners were also ridiculed at stops on the train trip from Liverpool to London.

On 5 October, Captain Kendall received a reward cheque drawn on the Bank of England for £250 payable to him and no others. It was signed by then British Home Secretary Winston Churchill. The reward was not shared with the Chief Steward or Third Officer Mowatt. Earlier, when Kendall was besieged by reporters immediately following Crippen's arrest, he was asked if he would share the reward. Kendall replied tersely that he was unaware of any reward and added that those under his command were always willing to do their duty. Kendall probably felt entitled to the whole reward by virtue of his position and decision to send the first message which threw New Scotland Yard into the chase. Ironically, he never cashed the cheque. It was framed and hung on the bulkhead in his cabin.

The arrest warrant used by Canadian authorities remanded Crippen for the murder of 'an unknown woman'. Upon arrival in London, Crippen was formally charged with the murder and mutilation of his wife. Le Neve was charged with being an accessory to murder after the fact. The trial began on 18 October and lasted five days.

Crippen insisted he was innocent. He claimed that the remains found at 39 Hilldrop Crescent were not Belle and that they must have been there when he moved into the house. This meant that the remains had to be at least 5 years old. Unfortunately for Crippen, the Jones Brothers pyjama shirt found with the remains had only been on the market for two years. His defence strategy unravelled.

The prosecution had to prove that the remains found were indeed Mrs Crippen. Doctor Bernard Spilsbury, a young pathologist, stole the show. He confirmed traces of Hyoscine in the tissue; found evidence of Belle's ovariectomy; and showed that the hair found matched Belle's natural colour. The jury convicted Crippen after deliberating for twenty-seven minutes. Crippen was hanged on 23 November 1910, at Pentonville Prison and buried there with Ethel's letters and a photograph of his love. Crippen's effigy may be seen today in the Chamber of Horrors at Madame Tussaud's Wax Museum in London.

Le Neve was acquitted and had to flee the country to avoid reporters. She left England in November 1910. Veiled in a grieving widow's black outfit she boarded White Star's *Majestic* in Southampton and sailed to New York hoping to find a new life as Crippen had once promised. Never finding herself and always afraid of being recognized, she returned to Great Britain six years later travelling as Ethel Nelson. She later married and took her new husband's name which was Smith. They had a son and daughter together. Ethel became a grandmother and died in Dulwich of heart failure at the age of 84. She had been through enough.

The Crippen case dramatized the power of wireless communication. At the time of Crippen's arrest, there were sixty ships fitted with a Marconi set. Within a matter of months, many times that number were installed on ships all over the world.

The *Empress of Ireland* had a Marconi set installed when she was built. It was just one element of numerous features which made her a safe ship.

Dr. Crippen disembarks White Star's S.S. Megantic *in handcuffs at Liverpool landing stage escorted by Inspector Dew.* (British Library)

3 A Safe Ship

The *Empress of Ireland*'s wireless shack was equipped with a 1.5-kilowatt Marconi transmitter, a receiver, and an emergency set. The expression 'shack' had its origins from the makeshift cabins added to ships before radio rooms became part of ship design. The wireless shack on the *Empress of Ireland* originally appeared at the stern of Lower Promenade Deck. It was later relocated to the Boat Deck, just forward of the engine room skylight. A wireless operator was on duty at all times. In an emergency, help was as close as the nearest ship.

If help was not nearby, the *Empress* was designed to contain flooding with a system of watertight bulkheads and doors. She had ten transverse bulkheads which formed eleven watertight compartments. The bulkheads were arranged starting with number 1, in the bow, and extending aft so that any two adjacent compartments could be flooded without loss of the ship. The Upper Deck was the vertical limit of compartmentalized watertight integrity. This meant that the ship should float with two compartments filled through Main Deck. The distances between bulkheads ranged from 22 feet to 87 feet with the longest distance residing in the middle of the ship. Bulkheads 4 through 6 defined the middle — an expanse 175 feet long. These large areas in the engine and boiler rooms were also divided by a centreline longitudinal bulkhead not intended to be watertight.

To permit access fore-and-aft on Main Deck and below, openings were cut in various locations through watertight bulkheads. Watertight doors with sill plates were installed in each opening. The *Empress of Ireland* had twenty-two horizontal-sliding and two vertical-sliding watertight doors. Every one of these doors had to be closed manually. The operator had to align and fit a metal crank-key over a square-headed pinion on the deck one level up from the door. The crank turned gears which ran along a rack fixed to the door. An average steward was able to crank a watertight door shut in one full minute. Daily drills were held at 10:00am to ensure that the crew knew their emergency stations and to practice closing all watertight doors. These exercises repeatedly demonstrated that the crew could seal all compartments in a matter of minutes. Of course that was under ideal conditions when the crew was waiting around for the drill to begin. To be effective, this system required action on the part of twenty-two separate stewards. In an emergency, would every one of them reach their watertight door assignment to carry out their duty? Technology was available to install remotely operated watertight doors such as the hydraulically operated doors on *Lusitania*. It is not known if this was a consideration in the design of the *Empress of Ireland*. *Titanic* had vertical sliding watertight doors fitted with an electro-magnetic clutch which could be controlled from the Bridge or manually using a lever mounted on the bulkhead next to the door. A back-up system consisting of a float switch closed *Titanic*'s watertight doors automatically if water began to fill a compartment.

The *Empress of Ireland* was constructed with a cellular double-bottom which ran the length of the ship. The double-bottom was almost 5 feet-deep at the keel, tapering to 3.5 feet at each side of the ship where it stopped without extending

upward. The double-bottom could ballast over ,500 tons of water. A 200-foot-
long bilge keel, which functioned like a longitudinal fin, was attached amidships
on each side, below the waterline. This V-shaped appendage lessened the
tendency of the ship to roll without adding costly resistance.

*One of the quadruple-expansion engines in a Fairfield Shipyard promotional
photograph.* (Keeper of the Records of Scotland).

There were two quadruple-expansion engines, one on each side to rotate each propeller, and to power a bank of electric dynamos. Each engine had four cylinders. The high-pressure cylinder at 36 inches diameter and first intermediate cylinder at 52 inches diameter were fitted with piston valves. The second-intermediate cylinder at 75 inches diameter and low-pressure cylinder at 108 inches diameter had flat, sliding valves. The piston stroke was a whopping 5 feet 9 inches. The engines themselves were incredibly fiendish-looking with all their reciprocating arms and articulating valve mechanisms. They were also very tall, towering from their base in the hold through three full decks. Each engine weighed over 545 tons. The engine room itself occupied a space 71 feet long, 65 feet wide and 30 feet high. The engines were designed to produce 18,500 horsepower.

To satisfy the appetite of these goliath machines, a 220 pound per square inch steam plant was installed forward of the engine room between Bulkheads 4 and 6. Watertight Bulkhead 5 split this space into two separate boiler rooms all residing below the waterline. The forward boiler room contained three double-ended boilers forward and one single-ended boiler aft. The after boiler room was structured in reverse but with two single-ended boilers forward, followed by the mirror image, three double-ended boilers aft. Each single-ended boiler had four furnaces and each double-ended boiler had eight furnaces for a grand total of 60 furnaces. A midships passage through Bulkhead 5 connected the two boiler rooms. The aft end of this passage was fitted with a 5.5 foot   2 foot vertical-sliding watertight door. This passage was at the bottom level of the boiler room in the ship's hold. A similar arrangement connected the after boiler room to the engine room through Bulkhead 6 which also had a vertical-sliding watertight door.

The *Empress of Ireland* was really a four-class ship in terms of accommodation, whereas dining was separated into the traditional three classes. The specifications for passenger berthing called for 310 first-class; 468 second-class; 488 third-class; and 270 steerage for a grand total of 1,536. Many sources lump steerage accommodation into third-class when quantifying capacity but this fails to take into account the monumental difference in sleeping arrangements. Third-class passengers had cabins, some of which were removable for conversion to cargo space. There were no cabins in steerage. Steerage passengers slept in bunks arranged vertically two per tier.

Lifesaving equipment was installed in accordance with Board of Trade requirements in effect at the time. As with *Titanic*, this meant that there were not enough lifeboats to save everyone on board. The original fitting-out consisted of 16 steel lifeboats manufactured by the Seamless Steel Boat Co., Ltd, plus four collapsible Berthon boats. Of the sixteen lifeboats, seven were installed on each side of the Boat Deck. They were identified by odd numbers on the starboard side and even numbers on the port side. The remaining two steel lifeboats were installed at the extreme stern end of the Lower Promenade Deck. Each 2.5 ton steel lifeboat was fitted under davits. The 28 foot Berthon boats were installed on the Boat Deck to either side of the engine room skylight. The maximum number of passengers which could be carried, assuming all lifeboats were successfully launched, was 940. Twice as many seats were needed to successfully rescue a fully-booked ship plus crew. As for personal flotation devices, the original equipment approached the quantity required. A total of 1,770 adult life belts, 150 youth life belts, and 24 life buoys were delivered with the ship. Nine of the life buoys had miniature lamps. The Bridge was equipped with a 30-inch Firebrand megaphone for hailing purposes.

The *Empress of Ireland* had her lifesaving capabilities updated shortly in advance of revised Board of Trade standards which became effective in January 1913, after loss of *Titanic*. The davits were extended to nest sixteen Englehardt collapsible wooden lifeboats under the original steel lifeboats. An additional four Englehardts were added to the Lower Promenade Deck. The lifeboat capacity doubled to handle 1,860 people in a total of forty boats. The quantity of life belts on board was increased by 180 bringing the total for adults and children to 2,100; more than enough to handle a catastrophic event with a few to spare.

The ship was fitted with special telephones that served as a navigational aid rather than communication device. They were manufactured by the Submarine Signal Company but had nothing to do with ships that travel under the sea. Submarine Signal phones were used to listen for underwater warning bells placed along selected harbour approaches and coastal routes. The sound was received by tanks containing microphones which were attached inside the hull below water level. A telephone line connected the 'listening' tanks to receivers on the Bridge. An officer on watch could listen separately to port or starboard microphones and determine from which direction the warning bells originated. Many modern liners were fitted with this system including *Titanic*. One of the formerly Bridge-mounted submarine phones is on display in the *Empress of Ireland* exhibit at the Maritime Museum, L'Islet-sur-Mer, Quebec.

There were a number of human 'fixtures' on the *Empress of Ireland*. Chief Engineer William Sampson, born and raised in Ireland, had been with the *Empress* since her fitting out at Fairfield's. He made the maiden voyage and never missed one thereafter. The 'Chief' had thirty-four-years experience, almost all of it at sea. He lived in Liverpool.

Another Irishman, a deck officer, joined the wardroom shortly after the maiden voyage. He was a tall man of slim build and extremely well-liked by everyone. His name was Mansfield Richard Steede. He was born in Whitegate, County Cork, on 22 September, 1872. Steede was raised on Main Street in Whitegate where his father was a local trader. At the age of fourteen, possibly after a row with his father, Steede left home to answer the call of the sea out of Liverpool. His early nautical experience was honed on the four-masted barque *Silverhorn*.

Steede made the shift to steam by joining the Elder Dempster Line where he advanced rapidly. He was rewarded with command of an African coastal steamer.

Steede was later assigned as one of Elder Dempster's Marine Superintendents on the west coast of Africa. His favourite pastime was to paint in watercolour. Returning to Liverpool, Steede married the former Miss Stuart and had three children one of whom was his namesake. Although he possessed an Extra Master's Certificate, Steede signed on with Canadian Pacific as a second officer aboard the *Empress of Ireland*. This would allow him to be with his family in Liverpool every fortnight.

The Duke and Duchess of Connaught sailed on the *Empress of Ireland* from Liverpool to Quebec on Friday, 6 October 1911. Captain Forster was in command. The Duke had been appointed Governor General of Canada. Naturally, CPR gave the Royal party the best accommodation — the Duke and Duchess Suites. These suites were upgrades installed in anticipation of this special crossing. The Duke's was located aft of the first-class café on the port side. It consisted of a full bath, two beds with sofa, and a sitting room which included a writing desk and sofa bed. Detailed orders could be communicated to the steward from the comfort of bed as a deluxe telephone handset was situated above each headboard. The walls were papered in Lincrusta, an embossed, richly textured paper. The furniture was large scale and lavishly upholstered to match complementary carpeting, drapes, and comforters. The Duchess Suite was similarly configured on the starboard side.

The first-class saloon passenger list devoted almost one page to the Royal party. They were identified as follows:

Field Marshal His Royal Highness
The Duke of Connaught
and Strathearn, K.G., etc.

Her Royal Highness
The Duchess of Connaught

Miss Pelly (Lady-in-Waiting to
H.R.H. The Duchess of Connaught)

Lieut. Col. H. C. Lowther,
C.M.G., M.VO., D.S.O.
(Military Secretary and Secretary)

Capt. W. Long, D.S.O. (Aide-de-Camp)
Lieut. Hon. A. Ramsay, R.N. (Aide-de-Camp)

The *Empress of Ireland* was six-years-old at the time of the Duke's official voyage. He described her internal arrangements as 'superb'. The *Empress of Ireland* had that magical quality known to a small circle of ships which made the traveller feel both safe and at home. She also had a loyal following among the Irish who fancied crossing on a vessel named after their homeland. A smart layout plus a reputation for steady performance in rough seas made the *Empress of Ireland* a top choice among rich and poor.

The Duke of Connaught greatly enjoyed Mansfield Steede's company. Steede was an engaging conversationalist who could entertain in any social circle. At the conclusion of the sailing, the Duke presented Steede with a special gift. It was a diamond-adorned gold tie pin.

The Duchess sitting room. (National Maritime Museum, London).

On 11 July 1913, the *Empress of Ireland* was among some 35 liners and cruisers which participated in the Royal Review of Merchant and Naval Vessels at Liverpool. Queen Mary and King George V presided over this salute to British sea power and opening celebration for Gladstone Dock. The *Empress of Ireland* was lined up in the Mersey river at position 13 in the good company of Cunard's *Mauretania* and *Carmania*.

By this time Mansfield Steede had risen to the position of Chief Officer. His wife, with three children in tow, was attempting to get out to the *Empress* to visit on the day of the Royal Review. A red carpet had been laid up to the Mersey Harbour Board's yacht *Galatea* for embarking the Royal party. Mrs Steede and children started to walk down the red carpet to catch a tender to the *Empress*. A policeman tried to stop Mrs Steede advising her that the landing was reserved for the Royal party. She replied 'If it's good enough for the King, it's good enough for me'. The policeman wisely allowed her to pass.

The Passengers' Certificate issued to the *Empress of Ireland* by the Board of Trade was renewed for one year in February 1914. The Board of Trade surveyor restricted the ship to carriage of 714 third-class and steerage passengers. This restriction was continued from the prior Passengers' Certificate based on a total lifeboat capacity of 1860. At some point, one additional Berthon boat was installed on each side of the Marconi shack. This raised the lifeboat capacity to 1960.

On 15 May 1914, the *Empress of Ireland* was preparing to cross from Liverpool to Quebec. Emigration officials thoroughly inspected the ship for compliance with Board of Trade safety requirements. A bugle was sounded and the order 'OUT ALL BOATS!' was given. All sixteen steel lifeboats were swung out. Emigration officer Thomas E. Thompson summarized this inspection in a report to the Board of Trade dated 4 June 1914. He found that at least two men climbed into each lifeboat to ship the rudder and pins. These sailors were identified by badges attached to their coats showing their boat number. Other men on deck cleared the fall lines. The lifeboats were readied in every way up to the point of lowering. Four minutes elapsed from the order until all boats were ready.

Thompson also reported a satisfactory result from inspection of all watertight doors which were operated for the drill. After the lifeboats were secure, a fire drill was ordered. Designated watchmen placed emergency lighting (oil lamps) in critical passageways. Hoses were pressurized and extinguishers, chosen at random, were inspected. The crew was found to know their duties and carry them out without confusion. All equipment worked properly. Thompson's report noted that 2,212 life belts plus 150 youth life belts were carried. That was 120 more adult belts than declared in the survey made for the Passengers' Certificate three months earlier.

On 22 May 1914, the *Empress of Ireland* docked in Quebec after an uneventful but pleasant crossing. Canadian Pacific's Superintendent of Life Saving Appliances, Captain Hugh G. Staunton, ordered a lifeboat drill on the following day. Three boats were actually lowered and tested in the water. Two Englehardt collapsible boats were opened and readied for use. The ship was taking on coal alongside which prevented the exercise of more lifeboats during the drill.

The *Empress of Ireland* passed all her safety inspections during the month of May 1914. The report made by Emigration Officer Thompson did not find any deficiencies, an extraordinary result for a government inspection. The *Ireland's* crew certainly seemed well trained and ready for any emergency. This was not surprising because safety was a matter of corporate policy at Canadian Pacific.

CPR's letter of instruction to its steamship Captains said that safe navigation was paramount. Safety of lives and property came first and no savings of time on a voyage was 'to be purchased at the risk of accident'. CPR's policy was generic compared to a letter sent to Cunard's Captains following the loss of White Star's *Titanic*. Alfred Booth, Chairman of Cunard, instructed his Captains to be on guard against the 'folly' and 'stupidity' of those commanding other ships at sea. He wrote, 'if your ship is lost or damaged it will be poor compensation to us, and to you, to know that you are technically free from blame'.

Ship's company looked forward to the 96th voyage on the *Empress of Ireland* because they were on the return leg to Liverpool where most of them resided. One aspect of shipboard life would be different for officers and crew. A new Captain had been assigned to the ship. He relieved Captain James A. Murray on 1 May 1914, in Halifax. The crew would be a touch uneasy until they adjusted to the whims of their new Master as every ship had 'its own long splice'. The new 'old man' had a reputation which preceded him. He was the man who caught Crippen… Captain Henry George Kendall.

Advertising the
'Empresses'
of the Atlantic.

4 Bon Voyage

Captain Kendall gazed across the harbour and began to recall the events which brought him to the pinnacle of his career — command of the *Empress of Ireland*. He always believed you made your own luck up to a point. Pride blurred his focus as he reflected whimsically on the incredible journey which delivered him to the Bridge of the *Empress*.

Kendall was born in the Borough of Chelsea on 30 January 1874. He lost his father at an early age leaving Kendall the only male presence to guide the household. He possessed an independent streak emboldened by the loss of his father. This did not serve him well in school as he often received corporal punishment for his mischievous behaviour.

Kendall's immediate family were not seafarers. There was a Captain John Kendall who went down with his ship generations earlier but the sea was not a Kendall legacy. Many of Kendall's juvenile contemporaries were mesmerized by the coming and going of ships on the Thames. Kendall was not so moved.

Kendall had a sharp mind capable of thinking things through concisely and pragmatically. At age 15, he weighed his options in life. He wanted adventure, the freedom to get a taste of the world. With no legacy, and no particular talent or business leanings, Kendall chose the sea. It was a logical decision which permitted a clean break from home. His mother, sisters, and other relatives gave him a farewell party prior to his joining the crew of *City of Berlin*. His mother died shortly thereafter.

The *City of Berlin* was an Inman Line steamship on the Liverpool-to-New York run. She was a three-masted, single-funnel barque built in 1875 by Caird and Company, Greenock, Scotland. Kendall joined her in December 1889, two years after the ship had been fitted with new triple-expansion engines. She could do 16 knots and had a record crossing of 7 days, 14 hours. She was also the first Atlantic steamer to be fitted with electric lights. The *City of Berlin* was an excellent vessel for a young sailor's first steamship.

A couple of rough North Atlantic crossings convinced Kendall that he needed a more southerly itinerary. He also wanted to get the feel of a ship powered exclusively by sail before they became extinct. He signed on to the *Iolanthe* as an apprentice. She was bound for Normanton, Australia, with a load of steel rails for construction of northern Australia's first railroad.

Kendall had been at sea aboard *Iolanthe* for five months when she completed a transit of the Timor Sea and entered the Gulf of Carpentaria. Crew members had grown tired of looking at each other. Fights were commonplace. One altercation between an African-American and West Indian went too far. The American stabbed the West Indian several times. Blood gushed out of the victim in three different directions before he collapsed on the deck.

Kendall and a shipmate named Louie were the only witnesses to the crime. This fact was not lost on the perpetrator who claimed self-defence. The witnesses' account supported a charge of attempted murder. The Captain planned to turn the case over to the proper authorities upon arrival in Normanton. In the interim, Louie became ill while at the top of the mizzen mast and almost fell to his death. He was successfully lowered to the deck and died before sunrise. He had been poisoned. The Captain choose to bury Louie at sea instead of keeping his body on ice for an autopsy ashore. The American had conveniently eliminated one of the two witnesses.

Kendall testified against the American as sole witness. The Court saw the matter as a fight between sailors which got out of hand but not worthy of a charge of murder. The case was dismissed based on self-defence. Exonerated, the American slasher was sent back to the *Iolanthe*.

Kendall was literally in the predicament of his life. A return to the *Iolanthe* would be suicide. The American would eventually try to settle the score for testifying against him. Kendall's pragmatism made desertion the only choice.

He decided to run to Croydon which was 100 miles inland from Normanton. Croydon was a small town which was born out of a gold rush. To reach Croydon, Kendall subsisted on wild dates. He found work and hospitality but no gold.

Kendall wanted to return to the sea so he made his way back to Normanton. To his surprise, the *Iolanthe* was still in port. As a deserter, he would be subject to extremely harsh treatment if he survived his nemesis — the slasher. After a few tense moments, Kendall slipped away hidden on the coastal mail steamer *Yaralla*.

The Captain of the *Yaralla* was not very pleased to find a stowaway on board his vessel. Worst still, the Chief Officer recognized the stowaway as a deserter from the *Iolanthe*. Rather than delay the mail, Captain Ussher of *Yaralla* continued on to his next stop. Ussher was not about to be accused of harbouring a deserter so he deposited Kendall on Thursday Island with the mail.

Thursday Island is one of a group of islands which make up Torres Strait between Cape York, Australia, and New Guinea. It was frequently visited by steamers transiting the South Pacific. Cape York is the arrow-shaped peninsula in the northeast quadrant of Australia which appears to point at New Guinea. The owner of the largest of three hotels, Mrs McNulty, looked after Kendall during his stay on Thursday Island. To support himself, Kendall worked on boats which served as dive platforms for the pearl harvesting industry. One evening he was bitten by a scorpion while on board a pearl boat. The bite was between his thumb and forefinger. It caused his arm to swell to twice its normal size. Natives on the Island saved Kendall's life by sucking out the wound and keeping him awake to avoid his lapsing into unconsciousness. After spending over a year on Thursday Island Kendall was homesick. He used his hard earned pearl fishing money to help a Norwegian Captain finance a commercial voyage back to England via Cape Horn. The cargo was most unpleasant, consisting entirely of fertilizer made from seagull droppings. This foul but much sought-after mixture was called guano. Kendall held his nose and joined the Norwegian's crew of eleven as an able-bodied seaman.

Kendall and his shipmates had a brush with death when the Norwegian

Captain's forty-year-old vessel almost foundered in a gale off the coast of New Zealand. The mizzen mast was torn from its roots. During the continuing 12,000 mile journey, bad weather stripped off the top of the main mast. The 350 ton barque leaked like a sieve.

Food ran short to the point where the crew considered butchering the ship's mascot — a pig named Dennis. Crew members used to drape their clothing over Dennis to warm garments before going on watch. Kendall later described Dennis as 'a good shipmate with excellent habits'. Fortunately, provisions were obtained at a South American port of call before it was necessary to consume the beloved mascot.

Kendall and his shipmates finally arrived in London, having been towed up the Thames, 197 days after leaving the South Pacific. Kendall's sisters thought he was dead. It had been over two years since his farewell. Kendall never sent a card or letter. His sisters told him of his mother's passing.

Kendall's first regular leadership position on the North Atlantic came as Fourth Officer aboard the Beaver Line's *Lake Superior*. She was a 5,000 ton, single-screw 13-knot steamer on the Liverpool to Quebec run. Just one crossing reminded Kendall of his earlier decision to sail a warmer route. Kendall had initial doubts about a career on the North Atlantic but quickly succumbed to the call of the sea. He wrote in *Adventures on the High Seas*:

> ...the formidable fogs of Newfoundland made me seriously consider whether I had chosen rightly. Despite the longing to thaw out in pleasanter seas, I began to like this northern route, presently it gripped me, and eventually I was reluctant to be released. All the conditions and perplexities had become part of myself.

Newspapers, during the first three months of 1903, were peppered with stories about the imminent acquisition of an Atlantic fleet for Canadian Pacific. Kendall was then employed by the Beaver Line which was previously absorbed by Elder Dempster. Kendall, who religiously read newspapers to keep on top of current events, lost no time in protecting his career. He visited Arthur Piers, CPR's Steamship Manager.

Piers relieved Kendall of his anxiety when he put forth the resume required for retention by CPR. Officers with an Extra Masters Certificate and a commission in the Naval Reserve would be kept on. Kendall possessed both qualifications.

In 1907, Kendall was assigned to *Empress of Ireland* as Chief Officer under Captain John V. Forster. During his twelve months as Chief Officer he observed the enormous popularity of the *Empress of Ireland*. She was always near capacity and carried her share of very important persons such as Earl Grey, Governor General of Canada; Rudyard Kipling; and the man whose invention made Kendall famous, Guglielmo Marconi.

Kendall was more than just a skilled mariner. He was a gregarious Captain who loved to entertain passengers with an amusing anecdote or occasional oratory of his own making. The following is an edited extract from an invocation recited by Kendall at sea on 31 May 1908, from the original at Canadian Pacific Archives:

Through everlasting fog our way we plod
along the banks where dwell the luscious cod...

The Captain sleepless in his aerie stands,
a thousand souls committed to his hands.
Attentive, lest the lifting veil disclose
some ghostly bark, or errant, jagged floes.
Ceaseless, we charge the atmosphere forlorn
with the grave pliant of our relentless horn;
the dismal windows drip with sickly tears,
and ocean's self in moisture disappears...

Then may our 'Empress', with her Godly crew,
a prosperous and easy course pursue,
and may the changeful, fickle-minded sea
respect her chequered red and white Burgee!

In 1908, Kendall with some eighteen years of experience and all his tickets punched, was given command of the steamship *Milwaukee*. In the next six years, he became a seasoned and well-known Captain in command of *Monmouth*, the infamous *Montrose*, and *Lake Champlain* (renamed *Ruthenia*). In 1912, Kendall, while Master of *Lake Champlain*, went to the assistance of Allan Line's *Corsican* after she struck an iceberg near Belle Isle.

Kendall had temporary command of the steamer *Lake Erie*, filling in for her Skipper who was recovering from illness. Upon docking in Boston, the local theatre guild gave Kendall and his senior officers free tickets to see 'Caught by Wireless'. The tickets were to a luxurious private box. Just before the curtain went up on the second half of the performance, the theatre manager called the audience's attention to the real life hero of the Crippen affair seated up in the box. Kendall received a standing ovation from theatre goers.

The *Empress of Ireland* was Kendall's fifth full-time command which he assumed at age forty. He completed one round-trip from Halifax to Liverpool with return up the St Lawrence to Quebec. The upcoming voyage would be Kendall's first in charge of the *Empress of Ireland* outbound from Quebec.

Captain Kendall surveyed last minute preparations for sailing from the port wing of the Bridge. It was afternoon on Thursday, 28 May 1914. Preparing for a transatlantic crossing was slightly less hectic than it is today. The *Empress of Ireland* had seven days to load 2,600 tons of coal and 1,100 tons of cargo. Today, the QE2 is lucky to have 8 hours turnaround time between crossings. Of course, in 1914, cargo handling was primitive with coal being loaded hand over hand in buckets from lighters alongside.

The *Empress* was fully booked in third-class and steerage with 714 passengers. However, first and second-class berths did not sell well for this particular crossing.

Captain Henry George Kendall
(Courtesy David St - Pierre.)

Two-thirds of the first-class berths were empty and second-class was only half full. This was unusual for an Atlantic *Empress*. The stewards looked forward to a less demanding crossing.

Gunn's Limited had the contract to provision CPR ships. Their representative, Mr Paulhus, was having tea with Chief Steward Augustus Gaade following the loading of provisions. They sat in the alcove of the first-class dining saloon nearest the Chief Steward's quarters. On the table was the receipt for provisions which included 7,000 pounds of fresh beef and pork, 1,200 ready-to-roast chickens and several tons of produce.

Paulhus and Gaade had a good working relationship. Paulhus was thankful for that. Gaade could not afford to visit for long what with all the demands of sailing day. He was a veteran of the CPR Line, professional in service to passengers and loyal to his employer. He had served on the *Empress* since her maiden voyage. Gaade concluded the amicable meeting by swallowing the tea in his saucer, standing, and brushing down the cuffs of his blue steward's jacket. He promised to have a look around Montreal for a couple of days on the return from Liverpool. Gaade then disappeared out the forward door of the dining room and into the main stairway vestibule. Paulhus disembarked just before 4:15pm, the planned departure time.

Precious cargo was on the manifest. The Nipissing Mine of Cobalt, Ontario, was shipping 212 silver bars valued at $1,099,000 to London. The shipment arrived in Quebec by train the day before. The bullion was in two groups: 49 bars valued at $275,000 and 163 bars containing the balance of $824,000. It had been judiciously guarded by hired police who watched the bullion as it was loaded into a hatchway over the ship's side. Captain Kendall kept a keen eye on the proceedings from his perch way up on the Bridge. One of the guards who paused momentarily to lean against the bullion caught sight of Kendall's stare and quickly jumped to attention. Such was the power of command and respect for the Master of the *Empress of Ireland*.

Passenger luggage had been brought on board throughout sailing day. This was a labour-intensive process often performed piecemeal by wheeling the bags in barrows to the correct gangway and then loading by hand. Substantial trunks and supplies were loaded by the ship's steam winches. Baggage was staged on deck for sorting. CPR furnished passengers with 'WANTED' and 'UNWANTED' tags at time of booking. Bags labelled 'UNWANTED' were sent to luggage holds segregated by class. Saloon passengers were allowed 20 cubic feet of space after which excess baggage charges could be assessed. 'WANTED' bags were promptly delivered to the appropriate stateroom.

One of those loading baggage was an 18-year-old Assistant Steward from Liverpool. He completed 49 voyages on the *Empress* having first signed-on at age 14. Trim and slim, the happy-go-lucky lad never had a bad word to say about anyone. He had curly brown hair, an ear-to-ear smile with a slight gap between his upper front teeth, and big ears. His disarming manner in handling passengers and wisecracking popularity among crew members begged adoption of an identity less formal than William Lawrence Hughes. Shipmates called him 'Billy Boy'.

Saloon passengers were personally escorted up the gangway to their staterooms by a cabin or bedroom steward. Once there, a number of other preliminaries had to be attended to. One was to advise your cabin steward of the proper time for your call preparatory to dinner. Another was to be introduced to the bathroom steward who would be drawing your daily tub at such time and temperature as you instructed. The final detail on the first day was to negotiate with Chief Steward Gaade for the best seats in the first-class dining saloon.

The passengers who would later be occupying saloon seats on 28 May were distinguished by the expected qualities of wealth, position, and fame. Among the wealthy was Ethel Sabina Grundy Paton. She was a socialite from Sherbrooke, Quebec, whose only burden was the weight of her indispensable jewellery.

Mrs Paton was born in Wales. She came to Sherbrooke as a child when her father, Frank Grundy, became Vice-President of the Quebec Central Railway. She married William E. Paton, the owner of a wool manufacturing concern of the same name. Paton Manufacturing Company, Ltd, was started by William's father. The Patons had a son who stood in line to run the family founded business.

Master Paton did not accompany his mother on the *Empress of Ireland.* She was crossing alone to rendezvous with her brothers Fred and Robert who were journalists working in Egypt. Mrs Paton boarded using the highest gangway which was reserved for first-class passengers. It provided admission to Shelter Deck and the exclusive environs above. Mrs Paton was escorted to her stateroom on the Upper Promenade Deck by 34-year-old Stewardess Helena Hollies. Paton occupied Cabin 32 near the second funnel. Her fare was £40.

Also travelling first-class was millionaire Major Henry Herbert Lyman of Montreal. The bald and bearded 59-year-old married for the first time at age 57 to the daughter of New York's Rev. William Kirkby. Henry Lyman had been so totally devoted to his ailing mother, work, and other interests that he never had time to fall in love. Following his mother's death, he became smitten with Miss Kirkby. Mr Lyman had promised his young bride a romantic tour of Europe. Their sailing on the *Empress* marked the start of it. Mrs Lyman not only provided love and companionship, she did his listening for him as Henry had become very hard of hearing. He used an ear trumpet to reduce the deficit.

Mr Lyman was educated at McGill University where he completed graduate studies in 1880. He immediately went to work for his father in Canada's largest wholesale drug company. The firm became known as Lyman Sons & Company when Henry was elevated to partner in 1885. The firm was reorganized as Lymans Ltd upon the death of Lyman senior. Lymans Ltd grew into a large and profitable enterprise.

Henry Lyman was very well known throughout Great Britain, Canada, and the United States due to his many affiliations. He joined the Royal Scots of Canada as an Ensign and retired at the rank of Major. The Royal Scots were the precursor to the Royal Highlanders. He was an amateur entomologist whose passion was butterfly collecting. Lyman received a great deal of recognition through lectures and writings about his avocation. He was member and fellow at entomological societies in Ontario, New York, Cambridge, and London. The American Association for the Advancement of Science also honoured him with a Fellowship. The evening before the sailing he spoke before the Montreal Entomological Society.

An energetic man, Mr Lyman was involved in so many things that his biographical introductions seemed to go on for days. His other affiliations included Fellow of the Royal Geographical Society, Vice-president of the Graduate Society of McGill University, Governor of Montreal General Hospital, Director of the British and Colonial Press Service, and founder of the Imperial Federation League. In this last capacity, he was an outspoken proponent of British Imperialism and of Canada's duty to help in the military defence of the Empire. Lyman's participation in all these varied interests was performed on top of his financial and business obligations. For the Lymans, a voyage on the *Empress of Ireland* must have been a welcome chance to spend some time together.

A robust composite of wealth, position, and fame was realized in first-class passenger Sir Henry Seton-Karr. Of Scottish heritage, he was famous as a big-game hunter, explorer, mountain climber, salmon fisherman, author, and golfer. His rugged spirit was akin to Teddy Roosevelt's but he also possessed the refinement of a titled gentleman. These manly qualities and uncommon good looks served him well in winning the affections of Ms Edith Pilkington. Edith belonged to the William Pilkington glass family of Liverpool — a lucrative and well-established concern. Sir Henry completed law school with honours and gained admittance to the bar in 1879. A year later, the 27-year-old married Edith. It was not long before Henry reaped the benefits of marrying into a good family. He was elected to Parliament, on the conservative ticket — a position he held for 20 years, and was eventually knighted.

Sir Henry enjoyed mountain climbing in the North American Rockies and in Norway. In East Africa, Sir Henry the hunter claimed to have stumbled upon the birthplace of the human race while tracking a wild lion. He discovered several

Palaeolithic objects underfoot which he sincerely believed had their origins in the Garden of Eden. Seton-Karr said that he may have handled the 'very spade with which Adam digged'.

When Sir Henry sailed on the *Empress* he was 61 years old. He had married Jane Jarvie Thorburn of Edinburgh following the unexpected loss of his Pilkington bride. The dashing adventurer had physically matured into a slightly wider, balding, walrus-moustached but no less dashing adventurer. He was a dead ringer for the trademark banker icon made famous by the Parkers Brothers' board game. One can picture him attired in tweed sports jacket, silk cravat, flannel vest, and sporty knickerbockers — never too busy to share an adventure or two.

Prior to joining the *Empress*, Sir Henry had been hunting in British Columbia. He rated British Columbia as the last word in outdoor recreation for sportsmen. One of his kills on this trip was a modest-sized moose. He had the antlers packed away with his 'UNWANTED' baggage.

Travelling without his wife and two children was Clayton R. Burt. Clayton was manager of the Russell Motor Car Company factory in West Toronto. The company was sending him over to Europe in first-class to investigate overseas automotive manufacturers and suppliers. Russell imported some parts for their cars such as the magneto for electric starters.

Mr Burt was a hearty man with rough, handsome features. He enjoyed his work and waxed poetic about the Russell-Knight motorcar. The Knight was a long vehicle noted for power and comfort. Mr Burt boasted of upholstery over twelve-inches thick. Russell Motor Car Company advertising informed prospective buyers that the Knight was 'made up to a standard, not down to a price'. The car's price was true to this slogan. The discriminating customer could acquire a Russell-Knight for the upscale price of $2,975.

Another first-class passenger with a connection to the automobile industry was Mr Charles R. Clark. He was returning to London after attending business meetings in Detroit at the Hupp Motor Car Company. Clark was sales manager for Whiting Ltd, a distributor of Hupmobiles in the United Kingdom. Hupmobiles were distinctive automobiles easily recognized by their squat, aerodynamic noses, fine-mesh grills and flared fenders.

One way to identify passengers who were at the upscale end of the social register was to observe those travelling with their own attendants. Personal servants did not have their names spelled out on the passenger list. They would receive mention based on their function immediately following the names of those they served such as the so-and-so family 'and maid'. A fare of £15 was charged for each servant. On 28 May, the *Empress of Ireland* first-class saloon list identified three families travelling with 'maid'. They were Mrs Cullen, daughter Maudie, and Master Cullen of Toronto; Mr and Mrs O'Hara and Miss Helen O'Hara also of Toronto; and Mr and Mrs Laurence Irving of London. The Cullen's 'maid' was actually the children's nanny, Miss Jennie Blythe.

The Irvings were, perhaps, the most famous passengers travelling on the

Empress. Laurence Irving was a well-known stage performer who had a difficult legacy to fulfil. His father was the world-renowned Shakespearean actor, Sir Henry Irving. Sir Henry's work was the inspiration for later thespians such as John Gielgud and Laurence Olivier. There was, however, one role which Sir Henry did not excel at: husband and father. He walked out on his family when Laurence was just a boy. Mrs Irving raised her two sons alone.

Laurence Irving wanted to follow in his father's footsteps but his mother and estranged father discouraged him. Sir Henry refused to allow his son to act in Sir Henry's theatrical company. He wanted Laurence to join the Army. The struggling Laurence was so distraught, he shot himself. Fortunately, the apparent suicide was unsuccessful. Laurence fully recovered and the family began to support his desire to become an actor like his father. He was even allowed to join his father's theatre company. It was here that he met his wife, Mabel Hackney.

The senior Irving died following a performance of 'Becket' at the Grand Theatre of Bradford, England, in 1905. Laurence continued to work hard at acting and was beginning to be recognized in his own right. In 1910, he wrote and performed the lead in 'The Unwritten Law' which was adapted from Dostoievsky's *Crime and Punishment*. In 1914, Laurence Irving's company toured Canada with 'The Unwritten Law' and a play called 'Typhoon'. The tour was partially underwritten by the British-Canadian Theatrical Organization. The Irvings and Martin Harvey & Company were the first to produce theatre exclusively for tour in Canada. The Irving's productions were considered a triumph even though 'Typhoon' had received mixed reviews.

In 'Typhoon', Irving played a Japanese patriot, Doctor Takeramon, who uses diplomatic credentials in an attempt to undermine French control of Northeast Indochina. Irving's wife plays his nemesis, Helene, an attractive temptress working for the French. Takeramon eventually succumbs to Helene's control and falls hopelessly in love with her. Caught between a traitorous love and failure to carry out his patriotic duty, Irving as Takeramon commits suicide. His last lines in 'Typhoon' were 'What is death? Death is nothing but the passing to another life'.

'Typhoon' had been staged at His Majesty's Theatre in Montreal but the last performance of the Irvings prior to sailing on the *Empress of Ireland* was of 'The Unwritten Law' at the Walker Theatre in Winnipeg on 23 May. The closing sequence of this drama finds Mrs Irving (Sonia) imploring Laurence Irving (Rodion) to make the sign of the cross before an icon-rich altar. Laurence refused saying he will not worship bits of pasteboard but rather the spirit which is Sonia. He then turned his back on the altar and made the sign of the cross before Sonia as the curtain fell. Ironically, Laurence's father made the sign of the cross as the curtain fell on his last performance in 'Becket'.

Laurence and his father were both extremely intense professionals who drove themselves relentlessly to achieve success. Laurence could also be demanding of his audience. No one seated before a Laurence Irving play would dare cough or clear their throats. This is because Mr Irving had been known to stop performances when a theatre-goer interrupted the actors with a troublesome hack. Performances resumed after Irving sarcastically offered offenders a cough suppressant.

Irving's entire company scheduled their return on the *Empress of Ireland* but there was insufficient time to break down scenery and pack costumes for the 1600-mile journey from Winnipeg to Quebec. The company, including the Irvings, Mabel's maid, and Laurence's valet rebooked on White Star's *Teutonic* which sailed on Sunday, 31 May. There was no compelling reason why Irving and his wife had to delay their departure until the entire company was ready to sail. Accordingly, he and Mabel changed their tickets back to the *Empress of Ireland.* Their maid, Hilda Haggerston, and valet wanted to sail with the rest of the company on *Teutonic*. Laurence acquiesced in the case of his valet but Mabel refused to make an ocean voyage without private staff. Hilda reluctantly sailed with the Irvings.

Laurence Irving's off-stage presence was equal to his power before the footlights. He was perfectly cast in the role of ocean liner notable. Lesser personages aboard the *Empress of Ireland* easily recognized Irving even though he covered his gangly build with a flamboyancy of outerwear. Silk scarf, opera cape, fur-collared overcoat, drooping felt hat, and his penetrating marble-black eyes made Irving one of the most intriguing images to ever grace the Upper Promenade.

As Irving strolled the decks of the *Empress*, he was in deep thought about his next production. He had completed a manuscript based on the character of Napoleon. The only copy of his work was in the Irvings' stateroom. He was anxious to get home and see to the details of production. Mabel was also excited about the new play having boasted about it in general terms during an interview at the King Edward Hotel in Toronto. Upon arrival in London, the childless couple looked forward to a reunion with their dogs which had been patiently waiting out the Canadian tour.

Dogs, cats, birds and other pets were permitted on board the *Empress of Ireland.* CPR charged a very reasonable tariff for their passage. The particulars of passengers' pets embarking on 28 May are not known.

There was a story about a pet which appeared in the New York *Times*. It was not about a passenger's pet. The Times reported that an honorary crew member skipped the sailing after two years of loyal service. The four-legged deserter was an orange tabby cat named Emmy. Captain Kendall looked upon Emmy's service favourably. He probably found her to be a good shipmate. Some even considered her the Captain's cat.

Emmy made a cautious but deliberate exit from the ship as the departure hour neared. Her brazen attempt for unauthorized shore leave was observed by jealous souls in the ship's company. A steward was dispatched to retrieve the wayward mouser. Emmy was returned to the ship after she was found hiding in a quayside shed. Undeterred by this forced conscription, Emmy soon made another run for it. She dashed in, out, and around human obstructions on the gangway until safely ashore. As removal of the gangway was imminent, ship's company abandoned further attempts to return Emmy to duty.

Officers and crew went about their duties which now involved getting to underway stations. The newest officer on board actually had nothing to do with getting the ship underway. He was the ship's surgeon, Doctor James Frederick Grant. The 26-year-old doctor had a boyish, actor Tom Hanks look. Grant, who had no prior experience at sea, was making his second voyage on the *Empress of Ireland*. A native of Victoria, British Columbia, he received his medical degree from McGill University in 1913. His internship was at Montreal General Hospital. The medical chief at Montreal General, Dr William Alexander Molson, believed that Grant needed a change of air to improve his vitality. Sea air was the specific prescription which Dr Molson had in mind. He recommended Grant's appointment to surgeon aboard the *Empress of Ireland*.

Doctor Grant's on-board residence was Cabin 300 on the starboard side of Upper Deck just ahead of the forward funnel. This cabin was especially designed for the ship's physician with extra built-ins for storage. As part of getting underway, Doctor Grant made a last minute check of the ship's medical facilities. Everything was in place, including his diploma from McGill which hung authoritatively from a bulkhead in the dispensary. Passengers were expected to settle their on-board medical expenses directly with the ship's physician. This was because ocean liners' doctors performed their professional duties as an independent contractor. Canadian Pacific did not expect passengers to pay for injuries or illnesses which were caused by the ocean voyage. CPR picked up the tab for the most common malady in this category — sea sickness.

Mal de mer rarely affected passengers during the outbound transit on the St Lawrence. The two days prior to entering the North Atlantic were a great time to get to know the ship and observe other passengers. Wealth, position, and fame were not the only curiosity factors. Some saloon passengers were interesting because of their profession or connection to other passengers; others because they were an enigmatic party of one.

Mr Lionel Kent was Director of the Energite Explosives Company of Widdifield, Ontario. Kent, who was born in Ireland and raised in Detroit, had chosen Montreal for his home ten years earlier.

Another prominent Montrealer sailing on the *Empress* was Mr Louis A. Gosselin. Gosselin was an attorney in the law firm which represented Kent's company. No explosives concern could function without adequate legal counsel. Gosselin had a reputation as one of the best in his profession. He was a fastidious dresser. Lionel Kent, not to be outdone by his attorney, also dressed to the nines. Both men wore tapered jackets with tails and collars starched hard without points. They were booked in adjoining suites, Cabins 40 and 41, on the Upper Promenade Deck.

One deck below were the first-class staterooms of Frederick J. Rutherford of

Montreal, and acquaintances. Like the Irvings, Mr Rutherford changed his booking from another ship to the *Empress*. Frederick Rutherford was scheduled to sail on the *Baltic* but changed to the *Empress* to accompany Mr J. J. Cayley. Both men had staterooms near the smoking lounge. Mr Rutherford was a purchasing man for J. C. Watkins (The Right House) of Hamilton, Ontario, and subsequently for Ogilvy & Sons of Montreal. Mr Cayley was Rutherford's successor at the Watkins firm. This was the 33rd crossing for Fred Rutherford. Also connected to Mr Rutherford was a third acquaintance in the first-class section, Mr Walter Hirxheimer of Montreal. Mr Hirxheimer raised the ire of ship's company prior to sailing. He attended a bon voyage party in Quebec where some of the ship's officers were present. When a toast to the *Empress of Ireland* and men who sail her was proposed, Hirxheimer, a drinking man, refused to partake.

Occupying a berth on the Upper Promenade, but travelling *tout seul* without connection to other passengers, was Mr F. P. Godson of Kingston, Ontario. He was in Cabin 21 on the port side next to the music room. Godson, a graduate of Cambridge, was born in Wiltshire, England. He had just completed two years of study in mining and geology at Queen's University in Kingston, Ontario. He was returning to summer at his parents home in Fenbury, Worcestershire, England. When he said goodbye to friends in Kingston, he jokingly closed with 'If I don't drown on the way over, I will be back to college in the fall'.

Some passengers were fascinated by their fellow travellers who came from distant shores. One such traveller who could not be overlooked was a stylish young woman of seventeen from Blenheim, New Zealand. Her name was Tiria Townshend. She was a stout, athletic person who embarked fashionably dressed in flared, ankle-length jumper dress, ruffled blouse, and cutaway jacket joined by mother-of-pearl buttons. Ms Townshend, as did 'Lady' Paton, and many other passengers wore exquisite hats. Tiria's hat was typical, with brim flared to one side, silk rosettes, and genuine Ostrich quills. Her Aunt, Wynnie Price, was escorting Tiria on a trip around the world. It was not unusual to encounter people from South Pacific origins aboard an Atlantic *Empress*. Canadian Pacific arranged their entire passage from Australia or New Zealand to Vancouver by steamer and overland by rail to embarkation quayside in Quebec.

Second-class accommodation on the 28 May sailing of the *Empress* became the afloat headquarters for the Canadian Salvation Army. Salvationists from all over the world were travelling to London, the city where the Army was founded. The occasion was the Army's third worldwide conference which they called an International Congress. The *Empress of Ireland* was selected by Canadian Salvationists to transport their contingent of 171 members to the international celebration of fellowship, prayer, and music.

Marching bands were a favourite source of music at these international gatherings. The Salvation Army Territorial Staff Band, from Toronto, was one of the bands scheduled to parade down Regent Street in London. The band's conductor was a talented 35-year-old who was clean-shaven except for an unruly, bushy moustache. His name was Adjutant Edward James Hanagan. He had his wife, Edith, and seven-year-old daughter, Gracie, with him.

The Commander of the Canadian Salvation Army, which included the Canadian territories and Bermuda, was David Matthias Rees. Rees was a biscuit baker at Huntley & Palmer's before he joined the Salvation Army. The distinguished, silver haired Rees travelled second-class with his wife Ruth, the former Miss Babington. One of their sons, Harding, and a daughter, Madge, occupied cabins with other members of their contingent based on gender. The 60-year-old patriarch of Canada's Salvation Army was not new to journey by steamship. In the course of doing the Lord's work for many years, Rees had travelled around the world. He was looking forward to his upcoming retirement.

The Commander of Salvation Army personnel in the United States was Evangeline 'Eva' Booth, a daughter of the Army's founder, William. Eva had considered booking her United States contingent on the *Empress of Ireland*. It seems that Canadian Pacific was offering attractive rates round trip for £10 per person. These competitive fares might have been the work of William Measures, an official in CPR's Toronto passenger office who happened to be a member of the Territorial Staff Band. Eva decided to book her troops on White Star's *Olympic*. The *Empress* was not big enough to hold all the American and Canadian Salvationists in second-class.

As it was, the Canadian Salvationists occupied many second-class cabins to capacity. Four Toronto officers shared a cabin at the aft end of Upper Deck. These bunkmates included Captain Guido Whatmore, Captain Rufus T. Spooner, Lieutenant Stanley Bigland, and Lieutenant Alfred Keith. Lieutenant Keith was the son of another Salvation Army officer, Ensign Keith, of the Toronto Children's Home. Young Lieutenant Keith had smooth skin devoid of facial hair. He wore perfectly round, tightly-fitted, wire-rimmed spectacles. This gave him an intelligent but otherwise generic look.

Sharing a second-class cabin with CPR official Will Measures were Staff Bandsmen Ernie Aldridge, Kenneth McIntyre (son of a Salvation Army Colonel from New York) and Edwin P. Gray. Mr Gray was an artist on the staff of the Toronto *Daily Star*. He went by the nickname Teddy. Teddy was a popular and devoted member of the Salvation Army. He was a regular contributor of drawings to the War Cry, the journal of the Salvation Army. Teddy excelled at drawing caricatures but possessed the talent to render anything the *Daily Star* needed. His work sometimes captured life's darker side such as devastation from fire or the cold remains of a motorcar accident.

Teddy's persona was far from dark. He was a handsome, vivacious young man who loved his work and his fiancée, Miss Sadie Bilham. The happy couple planned to be married within a fortnight of Teddy's return. Since Sadie would not be accompanying Teddy on the *Empress of Ireland*, he called on her at the Bilham residence during the evening of 26 May. It was an opportunity to spend some time together before Teddy sailed to the International Congress.

Herbert Wood in *Till We Meet Again* relates an awkward but amusing exchange which took place between Teddy Gray and Sadie's father. Teddy asked Mr Bilham for some time alone with Sadie. Mr Bilham innocently told Teddy to make the most of his last night. He suggested the couple enjoy the seclusion of the Bilham's parlour. Both parties were embarrassed when the *double-entendre* registered.

The normally high-spirited Gray was not made uncomfortable by a moment of impropriety. He was in a gloomy mood to begin with. Teddy was uneasy about making the ocean crossing. Gray was in such a state of trepidation that he took dramatic steps to soothe his anxiety. He made out his last will and testament leaving everything to Sadie. He also took out a $2,000 life insurance policy naming Sadie as beneficiary. In the privacy of the Bilham's parlour, Teddy told Sadie about the extraordinary precautions he had undertaken earlier that day. She was not pleased. Refusing at first, she reluctantly accepted a copy of Ted's will. The couple shared an unusually long and silent embrace before joining Sadie's parents. The Bilhams sensed Sadie's upset as the young lovers emerged from the parlour. At the conclusion of Teddy's visit, Mr and Mrs Bilham and Sadie stood before the open front door. Joy in their hearts dismissed an unexplained visceral emptiness as they wished Teddy 'bon voyage'.

Gray wasn't the only passenger to take out last-minute life insurance. Staff bandsman Ernie Evans took out separate policies for himself and his wife. Mr and Mrs Evans were travelling with their baby. Ernie told E. C. Wickham, a family friend from Toronto, that he took out life insurance because he was apprehensive about the crossing. Evans said that the insurance proceeds would care for his aging mother. Evans also shared his premonition of undefined trouble with Captain Weeks from the Earlscourt Salvation Army.

Alice Bales of Southbank, Middlesborough, England, had a bad dream about the *Empress* but she never told anyone about it prior to sailing nor did she do anything as dramatic as purchasing life insurance. Miss Bales was a petite 21-year-old who looked much younger. She was often described as girlish. Her long hair flowed unfashionably down around her shoulders. She had been in Canada for eighteen months and was excited about returning to her mother's in England. Alice stayed in Toronto with a successful uncle who made the arrangements for her trip home. Her uncle described the *Empress of Ireland* as 'a peach of a liner'. Alice was unmarried but she looked forward to a friend's wedding where she might be lucky enough to catch the bride's bouquet. Miss Bales was travelling with £200, a fair bit of jewellery, and wedding presents.

One of Miss Bale's cabinmates was also going to a wedding. Rose Butler was headed to Surrey, England, where she would attend her sister's wedding. Rose was a maid at the R. W. Prittie residence on High Park Boulevard in Toronto. Rose's employer, Mrs Prittie, crossed from Liverpool to Quebec on the voyage of the *Empress* just prior to Rose's sailing. Mrs Prittie said 'Now Rose, I've brought your ship over so you can take her back'.

Rose planned to marry her sweetheart, an Englishman named John Dwyer, upon return from Surrey. Rose withdrew the entirety of her modest life savings from the bank just prior to boarding the train for Quebec. Mrs Prittie admonished Rose for financial recklessness. Rose knew she should save some money but emptied the account anyway. She was afraid she would run short of funds during the visit. Sharing the cabin with Rose and Alice was Miss E. Willmot of Campbellford, Ontario.

The *Empress of Ireland* had several couples on the manifest who were new to matrimony. Thomas H. Greenaway and Mary Greenaway, formerly Miss Dalzell, shared their vows only three days prior to embarkation. The Greenaways planned to visit relatives in England after the close of the International Congress. Tom's brother, Bert, was also on board. Another newlywed couple sailing on the *Empress* was Mr Reginald Frank Simmonds and wife Mary, the former Miss Mahony. They were bound for their home in London following a two-week honeymoon in Canada. Married for one whole week were Captain and Mrs John Edward 'Eddy' Dodd from Toronto. Captain Dodd was the sub-editor of the *War Cry*. His wife's name was Violet.

Some passengers had honeymoons to look forward to in their immediate future. After all, the *Empress* was scheduled to arrive in June which is a favourite time of year for weddings. First-class passenger Doctor Murdoch Alexander (Alec) Lindsay, a native of Halifax, was to be married to Kathleen Webb of Warwickshire, England, at a mid June ceremony. The 32-year-old rugby and tennis star left Halifax in 1908 to complete his medical degree in Edinburgh, Scotland. He returned to Halifax in 1912 to become pathologist at Victoria General Hospital. Second-class passenger James J. Lennon, a Winnipeg insurance salesman, was crossing to Ireland for his ceremony. Third-class passengers Christian and Theophile Bartschi were farmers who homesteaded in Stettler, Alberta, eleven years earlier. The brothers had carved out a satisfactory life for themselves and were returning to their native Switzerland to 'claim their brides'.

Third-class accommodation on the *Empress of Ireland* was a melting pot of working class, often first generation, immigrants. Many still retained their native tongue. Their reasons for sailing on the *Empress* were as varied as their ethnic backgrounds. Mr and Mrs Magnus Luren were returning to Stavanger, Norway, after settling in Minneapolis, Minnesota. It had been 15 years since they said goodbye to their homeland. They planned to join native brethren who had been celebrating the centenary of Norway's constitution. Harry Yudin of Toronto had a more compelling reason to reach his homeland. He had left his wife behind when he sought a new life in Canada. Now his wife was dying. His friends and co-workers took up a collection to pay for his trip back to Libau, Russia.

Some people booked in third-class because they simply couldn't afford better accommodation. The Mawbys of Toronto wanted to show off new daughter Kathline to overseas relatives. They planned their trip to coincide with Kathline's second birthday which was the day after sailing. Mr Mawby had to remain behind for an hourly wage while he sent his wife and daughter on the *Empress* alone.

Mr and Mrs E. N. Gattrell of Johannesburg were travelling third-class for the first time in their lives but could afford more. When they were shown to their cabin, Mrs Gattrell had quite a negative reaction to the sparse accommodation. She said she wouldn't stand it. She dispatched her husband to find Chief Steward Gaade in hopes of securing more suitable quarters in second-class.

Mrs Gattrell had second thoughts about waiting around for her husband so she joined him in his quest. The Gattrells went up one deck and found the Chief Steward in conference with a couple of assistants. Mr Gattrell asked for a word with Gaade. The Chief Steward pleasantly obliged him. Gattrell offered $40 for an upgrade to second-class. Chief Steward Gaade shook his head in negative reply while looking at the denomination of the bills. He explained that the Salvation Army party was larger than expected and 'overcrowded' second-class. Apparently Gaade was unsure of second-cabin availability prior to sailing. The Gattrells went below.

Over 200 third-class passengers were factory workers from motorcar production facilities in and around Detroit, Michigan, and Windsor, Ontario. The majority were foreign nationals living in Detroit. Some of these assembly line labourers were migrating to their native homes because of summer layoffs. Others had their fill of North America and never planned to return. Most were young families returning to native homelands to visit parents, talk of prosperity, and show off never before seen grandchildren.

Mr James Allgrove of Windsor, Ontario, saved for years to send his 29-year-old wife Florence and daughters Vera and Evelyn, ages six and three respectively, to London. Mrs Rose Reeves and 5-year-old daughter Dora, of Ford City, planned to visit relatives in Wellingboro, Huntingdonshire. Mr Allan Reeves would sail over in early December to escort them home for the holidays. Mrs Reeves was no stranger to the *Empress of Ireland*. She first came to Canada on the *Empress* four years earlier.

There was a scattering of Salvation Army personnel in third-class accommodation. George Philip Felstead's family was in third-class while he shared a cabin with other bandsmen in second-class. George, a carpenter by trade, was the lead bass horn on the band. The instrument he played was donated by Mr J. C. Eaton shortly following music performed in front of the Eaton residence at Christmas time. George's 15-year-old son Willie was a talented musician who could hold his own as first horn. Mrs Felstead, Willie, and daughter Gladys paid for their third-class passage to follow Mr Felstead and the band. Mrs Felstead also wanted to see her elderly parents. A premonition befell Mrs Felstead which made her remark to friends that she would never see her aged father again. On two separate occasions a small bird flew into her room to perch on the foot of her bed. Each time the bird remained for an alarming period of time. Mrs Felstead took this as an ominous warning. Her presentiment infected Willie who said 'I don't want to go to England'.

Mr Felstead told a neighbour, Mrs Ruttan, that his wife was superstitious. 'She wants me to make out my will', he said. George Felstead refused to do so.

As the Gattrells would soon discover, travelling in third-class meant sharing a cabin with strangers. This was the case for an English woman named Sarah Woods. Mrs Woods, a widow, was in poor health and ambivalent about making the trip. She had been living in Toronto for months but was told to sail home to Birkenhead, England, where her sister could care for her. Sarah's physician insisted she make the trip. Reluctantly, Mrs Woods went to the steamship brokerage of Plenty & Wilson in Toronto, and booked a berth in Cabin 629. Mr Plenty advised her that it was the last berth available in third-class for the 28 May sailing. Sarah considered switching to an Allan Liner but let the *Empress* booking stand. She looked forward to travelling on a ship with the Salvation Army Staff Band. They would comfort an old woman's loneliness.

Most parties travelling in third-class were sailing *en masse*. The Delamont family was typical. Five members of the family were booked on the *Empress of Ireland*. They included Mr and Mrs John Delamont of Toronto; Bandsman Leonard Delamont of Moose Jaw, Saskatchewan; Lieutenant Elizabeth Delamont of Prince Albert, Saskatchewan; and Bandsman Arthur Delamont also of Moose Jaw.

It was not unusual for one or two crew members to miss a scheduled sailing. Sailors have a thousand and one reasons to explain missing ship's movement. The return to homeport should have been reason enough to be on board. Thoughts of home were not on the mind of five firemen and two trimmers who apparently jumped ship intentionally. Perhaps they witnessed Emmy's desertion earlier and decided to join her.

Some passengers genuinely missed their intended departure on the *Empress of Ireland*. Mrs Charles Atkins was booked on a CPR rail/steamship ticket from Vancouver. She left Vancouver three weeks ahead of time to ensure her arrival in Quebec on sailing day. She made stops in Winnipeg and Toronto to visit friends and make social calls. By the time she reached Montreal, an attack of heat prostration prevented her from continuing on to Quebec. Robert Dunn, another Vancouver passenger, was booked in Cabin 263. On his way to Quebec, he received a cablegram from his office which diverted him for a business matter. The *Empress* sailed without him.

Among other noteworthy passengers who did make the sailing were Mr Wallace Leonard Palmer and wife. Palmer was associate-editor for the London *Financial News*. He had organized a tour of North America for British manufacturers in search of business opportunities. The Palmers had tickets to sail on 14 May but delayed their departure to see the Honourable J. A. Murray, Minister of Agriculture. Murray was encouraging investment and colonization of land in New Brunswick.

The mother of Captain A. J. Hailey, Master of the *Empress of India* was on board. She had travelled from New Zealand to spend a month visiting with her son in Vancouver. The *Empress of India* sailed west out of Vancouver bound for Hong Kong on the same day the *Empress of Ireland* left Quebec. Mrs Elizabeth Hailey was travelling to England to visit relatives.

David Johnston, originally from Edinburgh, Scotland, owned a 12-acre farm and two lots along the St John River in the Parish of Kingsclear, New Brunswick. He purchased the property in April 1913. Johnston, 40 years old, was son of Sir Henry Johnston, Senator, College of Justice — one of the Law Lords of Scotland. He had served in the Boer War as a mounted yeoman. Johnston booked passage on the *Empress of Ireland* when he learned that he had inherited his brother's estate. He sold his farm two weeks before embarking on the *Empress*, never planning to return.

Another passenger originally from Edinburgh was Mr Robert A. Cunningham from Winnipeg. He had been a chemistry professor at the Manitoba Agricultural College.

The Government of Manitoba sent Cunningham to Scotland to serve an indefinite period of duty representing the provincial immigration office. He would also be able to spend time with his parents in Edinburgh. Cunningham occupied Cabin 206, an outside stateroom on the starboard side of Shelter Deck.

Returning home to Scotland was Mrs Jane Elinslie, a trained nurse, from Aberdeen. She finished a protracted visit with her daughter, Mrs Joseph Harrison, of Moosomin, Saskatchewan. Mrs Elinslie was looking forward to reunion with her family in Aberdeen. Alexander Bunthrone and George Johnston, ages 20 and 22 respectively, were returning to their homes at Faulkland, Fifeshire, Scotland. The two young men had been working on a ranch near Santa Barbara, California.

Mr and Mrs John W. Black of Ottawa, Ontario, were travelling to Paris for a meeting of the International Chambers of Commerce. Mr Black, 40 years old, was born in Glasgow, Scotland. He moved to Ottawa eleven years earlier and established himself as an accountant in a substantial lumber company. Black was representing the Ottawa Board of Trade.

Like Rose Butler, 19-year-old Grace Kohl was travelling to Surrey. This was her second North Atlantic crossing in as many weeks. She often spent time in Brooklyn, New York, where her cousin Herbert Henshaw was President of the Brooklyn Life Publishing Company. The young Montrealer was crossing to visit an aunt.

Mr George Bogue Smart of Brockville, Ontario, was Superintendent of Child Immigration for the Canadian Government. He lectured and wrote extensively about immigration issues and had been invited to join the Author's Club of London. As an immigration official Smart travelled frequently and was often provided excellent accommodation. This voyage was no exception. Smart was assigned Cabin 212, forward of the saloon on Shelter Deck.

Mr Smart, Ms Kohl, Mr and Mrs Palmer, Mrs Hailey, David Johnston, and Mr Cunningham were all travelling in first-class cabins. Mrs Elinslie, the two ranch hands from California, and the Blacks were in second-class.

One first-class passenger was married to the Colonial Secretary of the Bahamas. Her name was Ella Hart-Bennett, wife to the Honourable William Hart-Bennett. She moved to Nassau in 1905 when her husband assumed his post. She founded the Nassau branch of 'Our Dumb Friends League', an animal rescue and treatment office. She was known for her keen literary taste and for two books she authored: *An English Girl in Japan*, and *A Bahamas Souvenir Almanac*. She was also a member of the Imperial Order of Daughters of the Empire. Mrs Hart-Bennett was looking forward to a summer in Europe — an escape from the Bahamian weather. Miss Alise Lee of Nassau, daughter of close family friends, travelled with Mrs Hart-Bennett.

There was one American in first-class. She was a potential 'Molly Brown' known for her strong will, love of athletics, and prominence in social circles. She also had a reputation as an excellent swimmer. She was Mrs Frank. H. Dunlevy from Denver, Colorado. Mr Dunlevy was a real-estate financier and agent who maintained an office in Denver's Friederich building. The couple had been married for seven years. They were listed in Denver's annual social register for 1913, the cover of which reads 'a directory devoted to ultra society'. Weeks prior to sailing, Mr Dunlevy corresponded with one of the vice-chairmen at CPR to ensure his wife was properly looked after. On embarkation day, an official of the company introduced Mrs Dunlevy to Captain Kendall. The official instructed Kendall that Mrs Dunlevy was entrusted to his personal care during the voyage. Grace Dunlevy was given the suite formerly used by the Duchess of Connaught.

Twenty-four Americans were booked in second-class. Among them were Mr and Mrs George C. Richards of Terre Haute, Indiana, and Mr Gordon Charles Davidson of San Francisco, California. Mr Richards was born in England and educated at the Bristol School of Mines. He was travelling with Mary Gray and her 6-year-old daughter. Charles Gray (Mary's husband) was Mrs Richards' nephew. Richards was President of the Lower Vein Coal Company in Terre Haute. The Richards' party was crossing to Sheffield, England. Mr Davidson was a 30-year-old teaching assistant at the University of California, Berkeley, where he earned a Master's Degree in 1908. The University's Board of Regents had recently honoured Davidson with a travelling fellowship in Pacific Coast History. His fellowship required one year of study abroad which was to commence upon his crossing via the *Empress*. The travel was an opportunity for Davidson to research his doctoral thesis about the Northwest Trading Company.

Four of the twenty-four Americans were from Rochester, Minnesota. They boarded the *Empress* for travel to Hamburg, Germany. Reinholdt Bach, a seventh generation lineal descendant of composer Johann Sebastian Bach, and his daughter Edith left Rochester on 23 May. Joining them were family friends, Mr Herman Kruse and his daughter Freda. Mr Kruse was active in the Rochester Commercial Club. Freda was a trained nurse. Mr Bach was 78 years old. He had a fear of travel by train, especially at night, so stopovers were made in Chicago and Niagara Falls.

Bach said he had much more faith in the reliability of ocean liners.

Reinholdt Bach's history is a colourful one. He married Barbara Bauer of Portage, Wisconsin, in 1858 and settled in Marion, Minnesota. He prospered as an Olmsted County farmer and as the father of twelve children. He was a talented musician in his own right and hand-made violins as well as a home pipe organ. The Bachs retired to Rochester in 1912. Mrs Bach passed away one year later. Reinholdt looked forward to adding to his knowledge of the family's genealogy so he was crossing with valuable historical records about his lineage.

Several Chicagoans were on board. There was 55-yearold Fannie Mounsey, mother of nine children (6 girls, 3 boys). Her husband William had operated a moving and express company in Chicago on Milwaukee Avenue. She was travelling with Mrs John Fisher and her 23-year-old son Wilfred of Chicago Heights. The three were going overseas to spend time exploring their native Keswick, England. The Fishers talked an ambivalent Mrs Mounsey into making the journey. They lured her with CPR's promise of two day's scenery along the St Lawrence. Hugh Lenter Heath and his 4-year-old son Jack were visiting Hugh's father in London. The occasion was the retirement of Hugh's father, General Heath, from the British Army. Johannes Gard, 45 years old, and Arthur Evensen, 25 years old, were crossing to their homeland in Norway. Like the Lurens, and a number of other passengers, they planned to visit during the hundredth anniversary of Norway's constitution. Stephen Clark booked to Liverpool to visit his Aunt, Mrs Margaret Sharp. He told none of his friends in Chicago that he was going overseas.

Mr and Mrs Henry Freeman of West Allis, Wisconsin, planned two months abroad. Mr Freeman was on the Board of Directors for the First National Bank of West Allis. He had overseas business to transact in his capacity as a department head with the Allis-Chalmers Company. Mr and Mrs Freeman were 52 and 50 years old respectively.

Mr Alexander Matier from Indianapolis sent his family to Belfast for the summer on an earlier crossing. He waited until the St Lawrence opened for the season and booked his passage on the *Empress*.

Mrs F. E. Boynton from St Thomas, Ontario, booked second-class passage on the *Empress* to go to the aid of her dying mother in Herefordshire, England. Mrs Boynton had a large sum of cash with her for the journey and planned to sail with her son. Her husband refused to allow their son to go and further encouraged Mrs Boynton to travel on a steamer out of New York. Mrs Boynton did not share her husband's fears even though she was reported to have lost a sister on *Titanic* according to the Montreal *Daily Star*.

Two others who were apparently not superstitious were Mr A. J. Burrows and a man named Death. Mr Burrows of Nottingham, England, was beginning his thirteenth ocean crossing in first-class. Mr A. H. Death of Regina, Saskatchewan, was on a business trip travelling second-class.

Ordinary Seaman J. H. Price would be part of an event which was not routine immediately following his crossing on the *Empress*. Price was scheduled to receive the Albert Medal for heroism. As a crew member of *Devonian*, he saved two passengers from the burning hull of the immigrant ship *Volturno* on 9 October 1913. Gale-force winds made rescue almost impossible. Price's rescue boat capsized alongside *Devonian* just after off-loading rescued passengers. Seaman Price was from Liverpool.

Colonel Sidney Maidment and Commissioner David Matthias Rees at the ships rail awaiting departure on 28 May 1914. (War Cry).

Captain Kendall had hoped to get underway for Liverpool by 4:15pm but the final hour prior to underway had become hectic. The last boat train arrived an hour late at the quay. Most of the Salvation Army contingent had yet to embark. Their luggage and instruments were expeditiously transferred from the train to the ship.

The appearance of the Staff Band at the gangway stirred a few heads. For passengers who knew a large group of Salvationists were expected, there were probably comments made like, here comes the 'Sally Ann', this being friendly slang for the Salvation Army. Passengers unaware of the Salvation Army booking thought the *Empress of Ireland* was being raided by the Royal Canadian Mounted Police. This is because the Staff Band selected red tunics and Mountie-style Stetsons for their band uniforms in order to be both impressive and unmistakably Canadian at the International Congress.

Chief Officer Steede had given the order to single-up all lines at 4:00pm. A bugle call was followed by stewards who canvassed the decks repeating 'All ashore that's going ashore!' A group of Salvation Army bandsmen collected their instruments from the piles of baggage and began an impromptu bon voyage serenade. They started with 'O, Canada', followed by 'Auld Lang Syne'. The third-class gangway was broken down and secured. The first-class gangway was not stowed for sea because the pilot would use it to disembark. Captain Kendall gave the order to cast off all lines at 4:27pm. The band began playing 'God Be With You Till We Meet Again'. The melody was soft and slow to start. It then became powerful as all the brass rejoiced in crescendo. The distance between the ship's side and her mooring increased imperceptibly at first, like the music. Moments later, the pier rapidly trailed behind. The blare of the band was temporarily muffled by the *Empress*'s deep-throated whistle. The *Empress of Ireland* was underway!

The mighty ship's whistle cued the quayside throngs. Hundreds who had been waving and shouting farewells now erupted in one last cheer. A frenzy of hand-held Union jacks waved goodbye as toddlers and parents gave the *Empress* a patriotic send-off.

Mr Paulhus, the victualler who provisioned the ship, did something uncharacteristic on the afternoon of 28 May. After leaving Chief Steward Gaade, he would normally proceed directly back to the centre of Quebec City. This time he stood and watched as the *Empress* untied her umbilical cords and slowly steamed down river.

The officers on the Bridge felt that intoxicating rush known only to those who drive ships on the high seas. It was a feeling of independence from the landlubber world left behind. It was also a sense of confidence in technological advances which made it possible to cross the sea on demand. But it was really all about the timeless maritime tradition of captaincy. One person was held absolutely accountable for safe passage of life and property across a sometimes unforgiving sea. The authority and respect which came from that awesome responsibility was attractive to junior officers. Loyalty and hard work might someday make them Master of their own world afloat. At the moment, Captain Kendall was Master. The *Empress of Ireland* was big, black, beautiful, and belonged to him.

Emmy the cat was watching the send-off of her former nest from a perch atop freight shed number '27'. As the ship's departing whistle echoed off the quayside, her eyes grew wide and locked on streams of smoke merging behind the funnels. She uttered a protest but it went unheard.

The Bandmaster's little daughter, one of 138 children on board, insisted her protest be heeded. Gracie Hanagan, when presented with a berth nearest the cabin's porthole, flatly refused to sleep there. 'I don't want to sleep there,' she said. 'That's where the water will come in.'

Second-class life. An alcove in the second-class dining room. (Peabody Essex Museum, Salem, Massachusetts).

5 'For God's Sake - Get a Life belt'

Edith Hanagan had a solution to objectionable Upper Berth 'C'. She suggested that her daughter sleep in Lower Berth 'B' on the inside wall away from the porthole. The precocious Gracie accepted.

Joseph Wallet made a quick inspection of his first-class stateroom. He appreciated the ergonomical detail apparent throughout the cabin. Especially pleasing was the polished mahogany locker over the wash basin. There was ample space for storage of toiletries and pharmaceutical bottles. Wallet opened the right hand door of the *armoire*. He unconsciously noticed life preserver stowage inside the wardrobe on a shelf. Satisfied with the accommodation, Wallet proceeded to the nearest Promenade Deck. A steward entered the cabin to unpack and hang garments.

Wallet had spent most of his career employed by shipbuilding related businesses in Northern England. When the conundrum of middle-age struck, he found fulfilment in religion. He joined the United Methodist Church of Westcliff-on-Sea where he became pastor. Wallet was on holiday in Canada. The steamship ticket was a gift from his congregation.

Once up on deck, Reverend Wallet encountered Mr J. J. Cayley, already at the rail. They chatted like old friends even though this was their first introduction. The confraternity of the saloon made such instant bonding possible.

Some passengers initiated casual conversation using the age-old ice-breaker of weather. Toronto travellers had an unusual bit of weather news to relate. On Tuesday, two days before sailing, the sky over Toronto was a dichotomy of serenity in one direction and a brooding storm in the opposite direction. Heat lightning silently erupted to the east in a violent spectacle. The Toronto *Daily Star* found Mother Nature's gyrations so peculiar that an editorial was run on the morning of Thursday, 28 May which chronicled the strange 'writing in the sky'. The editorial described light which escaped from behind luminous clouds forming a 'golden chain' which looked 'ominous' like a written warning. Tuesday's sky and the subsequent editorial kept people talking on street cars, at work, in church, and on outbound steamers.

All ocean liners quickly develop their own reputation among the travelling public. A vessel's history or specifications were often reduced to a few well-turned phrases or nicknames. No singular nickname, like 'Old Reliable' for the *Olympic,* ever stuck to the *Empress of Ireland.* However, the ease with which she handled rough seas on her maiden voyage did establish her respectability. Leave it to passengers to perpetuate this image in colourful ways. Every departure found passengers at the rail singing the ship's praises with 'She's as steady as a rock'. The more technically minded would try to impress fellow travellers with 'It's her bilge keels which prevent her from rolling — she has the largest of any mail steamer'. Novices, who had no idea what a bilge keel was, saved face with overly enthusiastic nods of agreement. A frequent comment by distinguished gentlemen was 'You can stand a whisky-and-soda on the rail and not lose a drop'. One can imagine Sir Henry Seton-Karr engaged in just such an experiment to the delight of young Tiria Townshend while her Aunt looked on in feigned approval.

The rituals which passengers shared on departure day did not enthral David Johnston. He had mixed emotions over abandoning life in New Brunswick to return to Scotland. On the other hand, he had come into his own. The legal and financial matters of his brother's estate would keep him pressed for about a year. After that, the world would be his oyster. Mr Johnston proceeded to the ship's office two decks below. He was anxious to have money from the sale of his farm and other funds locked in the Purser's safe. He handed Assistant Purser Ernest Hayes an envelope containing over £1,800 in drafts drawn on the Bank of Montreal. These drafts were all payable upon demand to David Johnston,

Others who visited the ship's office that afternoon were Walter Herxheimer of Montreal, Doctor Alec Lindsay from Halifax, first-class passenger Charles Clark of London, and the American from Indiana — George Richards. Herxheimer placed a book containing fifteen International Mercantile Marine travellers' cheques of $50 each in the Purser's safe. Doctor Lindsay set aside $90 and £80 for safekeeping. Mr Clark placed $48 in the safe. Mr Richards deposited $100 in cash and $480 in travellers' cheques. All cash was sealed in safety envelopes which were signed by the depositing passenger.

Afternoon tea was served during the King's Hour according to custom. Reverend Wallet and Mr Cayley, like many passengers, remained at the ship's rail. Riparian splendour was preferable to afternoon tea. Besides, thought Wallet, there would be plenty of opportunity to enjoy tea during the voyage.

As the *Empress* gracefully steamed down river, wide-eyed passengers studied the unblemished farms and pine forests along the riverbank. Beautiful images of tin roofs, green fields, and rolled hay slipped into each person's line of sight. For some, the pace was too fast. New majesty was abeam while they were still absorbed in the vista rapidly fading astern. For others, nothing was missed. It seemed as though these astute observers were committing a lifetime of natural beauty to memory.

Late afternoon wind across the open decks brought on a slight chill. People began to vacate their coveted positions at the rail. Some waited for sunset in deck chairs facing the stern. There was no charge for the chair but reservations were required. Stewards affixed labels to each deck chair with the passenger's first initial and surname to identify reserved positions. Many proceeded below to have a peek at their dining room and note how to get there from their cabins. Attire was relaxed on embarkation night but a fair number of first-class passengers wore black tie anyway. At minimum, some time was needed to straighten one's appearance before dining. A bugle call was the formal announcement of dinner at 7:00pm.

Grand descents to first-class dinner were a trademark of the French Line beginning with the *France* of 1912. It was an opportunity for notables to pose and for women to show their deportment and finery. On the *France*, stairs cascaded into the first-class dining room from a balcony above. As one stepped down, a vast culinary exposition came into view but more importantly one was seen by those already seated. Canadian Pacific's Atlantic *Empresses* had doors at the bottom of the main stairway making a direct descent into the dining room impossible. Nonetheless, a descent was still required from staterooms on the Upper and Lower Promenades to the vestibule where people gathered forward of the dining room. The entrance was less dramatic but the scrutiny more intense.

The first-class dining room was elegant. The ceiling was finished in bright white enamel and walls were covered in cream enamel. Richly sculptured mouldings with gilded accents were abundant in a variety of patterns. Doors, chair rails, and alcove woodwork were highly polished Spanish mahogany. Eight semicircular tables lined each side of the dining room in alcoves of two tables each. They could accommodate up to five adults comfortably on plush tufted banquettes. This arrangement was also comfortable for table stewards because each diner could be served face-to-face. Two oversized portholes (16 inch) provided natural illumination for each semi-circular arrangement. Stained-glass round panels, co-ordinated with the decor, concealed the potentially *mal de mer*-inducing portholes. When looking at the ship from outside, the location of the first-class dining room was readily identifiable by these pairs of larger portholes. A variety of shimmering electric light fixtures was installed overhead. Directly above each alcove table was a three lamp electric fixture with cut glass, acorn-shaped globes. Inboard from the alcoves were four sets of long fore-and-aft tables on each side. Inboard once again were two sets of fore-and-aft tables. One of these tables was designated for the Captain and his invited guests. Stewards could rotate chairs at the fore-and-aft tables by means of a foot pedal. This eliminated the unpleasantness of pulling chairs back and scrambling into one's seat. All dining room chairs and banquettes were finished in crimson morocco leather. There was enough space to serve all first-class passengers at a single seating.

An ornate mahogany sideboard rose high above seated patrons at centreline against the rear wall. Opposite the sideboard at the other end of the saloon was the central well. It is here where the five piece orchestra entertained under the direction of ship's musician Mr Norman. This strategic location permitted Strauss waltzes and other mellifluous rapture to waft upward into the café. The selection of dinner music on 28 May included Gounod's 'Funeral March of a Marionette'. Alfred Hitchcock would use it fifty-years later as the theme for his television series *Alfred Hitchcock Presents*.

Very little is known about who dined with whom in the first-class saloon. Captain Kendall did not dine at his table on the first evening. He was either on the Bridge or only steps away in his cabin during the outbound transit. He planned to make his first appearance in the dining room at breakfast. He would be fresh and ready to entertain with an amusing sea story.

The rose of Sherbrooke, Ethel Paton, and big-game hunter Sir Henry Seton-Karr were sharing pleasantries and dined together at another table located closer to the central well. 'Billy Boy' Hughes, who had just finished with baggage detail, was now assisting waiters in the dining saloon. He wore the traditional steward's jacket with epaulets which reminded him of the outfits organ grinders used to dress their monkeys. Hughes placed an assortment of breads on each centreline table. Mrs Paton and Sir Henry, like passengers in that era, were not overly concerned about their weight. As the meal progressed, 'Billy Boy' Hughes noticed that Paton and Seton-Karr were consuming a lot of food and required another serving of bread. Hughes warned them not to eat too heavily or they would become sea sick in the wee hours of the morning. Mrs Paton laughed at the prospect. The fastidious Sir Henry raised his serviette for a dignified pat of his moustache and then wiped his lips.

Reverend Wallet ended up dining with the man he met at the Upper Promenade Deck rail — Mr J. J. Cayley. The two were one table over from the Captain's table. Cayley dominated dinner conversation with tales of his wife and children. The Irvings were naturally invited to dine at the Captain's table and began their meal in the presence of Clayton Burt and Grace Dunlevy. Realizing that Kendall would not be joining them on the first night, the Irvings requested temporary freedom from their perceived obligation to dine at the Captain's table. They moved to the privacy of a table in the rearmost alcove. Reverend Wallet later described where the Irvings sat as 'the most obscure corner of the dining room'.

The second-class dining room was configured something like the first-class saloon but with rectangular booths at the sides instead of alcoves containing semi-circular banquettes. The Salvation Army Staff Band, looking ever so smart in their new uniforms, occupied two sets of fore-and-aft tables in the centre of the room. Salvationists were overflowing with excitement about their journey and the sites to be seen in London. They talked about their meeting at the Albert Hall, the variety of brilliant uniforms to be seen from around the world, and the good natured rivalry among bands. Some members shared their childhood memories of growing up in Great Britain. Ensign Ernie Pugmire was so famished when he sat down to dine that he consumed all the olives on a pickle tray intended to serve six adults. Pugmire was not scheduled to attend the International Congress but filled in at the last minute for his brother Bert who decided not to go. Alice Bales was seated near the cheerful band members opposite a dreadful woman who made dinner a most unpleasant experience. The unidentified woman repeatedly called into question the ship's safety. 'I don't like this boat at all,' she said.

Alice needed to recover from her tablemate's ugliness. She left the dining room not expecting to do much before retiring for the night. To her surprise, a game of quoits was in full swing on deck (like a game of horseshoes using a ring instead of a shoe). Alice's spirits soared when she was invited to join the game. She made a few respectable tosses at the circular lines painted on deck sometimes hitting the higher valued inner circles. Alice was thrilled with her performance and looked forward to other activities offered on such a big vessel.

Someone who enjoyed his specialized work and was fond of large liners was Adelard Bernier. He was one of the pilots hired by CPR to help guide their Atlantic *Empresses* up and down the St Lawrence River between Quebec and Father Point. Pilots are experts at harbour and riverway navigation but their role aboard a vessel is entirely subject to the discretion of the Captain. Kendall allowed Bernier to give helm and engine (steering and speed) orders to watchstanders on the Bridge during the outbound transit. The Captain could instantly countermand any order which he felt ill-timed, unsafe, or otherwise incorrect.

Bernier had seven years' experience driving the *Empress of Ireland* as one of Canadian Pacific's preferred pilots. He had good reason to be fond of large liners. Their owners paid a higher fee based on draft plus, unlike tramp steamers, paid expenses for the pilot's trip home. In this case, after disembarking at Father Point, Bernier would be reimbursed for the trip back to Quebec.

The officers on the Bridge from eight to midnight were Second Officer Roger Williams and Fourth Officer Tunstall. There were two Quartermasters assigned to each watch. They would take turns at the helm for a total of two hours per watch. James Francis Galway of Kensington, Liverpool, was at the wheel from ten until midnight. He was beginning his fourth crossing on the *Empress*. He had three years' experience as Quartermaster but accumulated it by job hopping between competing lines.

The second-class dining room began to clear at about 8:30pm. There was a prompt exodus from the first-class saloon when the orchestra stopped playing at 9:00pm. The evening was young and warm enough for a relaxed stroll on deck. There was plenty of time to post a letter, play cards, indulge someone in a game of chess, or have a glass of port. Some gentlemen escaped to one of the male bastions to enjoy a smoke. Laurence Irving who enjoyed a good cigar visited the first-class smoking lounge at the rear of Lower Promenade Deck. Doctor Grant went to the café for a cup of coffee.

A few passengers planned their exit from dinner to minimize exposure and return to their cabins. Others selected a path which would maximize their presence on the vessel. In the latter category was Mrs Paton who exited through the front of the saloon and climbed the main staircase to the Upper Promenade Deck. This strategic move placed the music room along the way to her cabin. She could glide into the belle époque of the music room to assess the suitability of those assembled. If conditions were unfavourable, she could gracefully excuse herself and retire for the night. Perhaps she would encounter the American real estate queen from Denver, Grace Dunlevy, ensconced on one of the richly upholstered Victorian sofas. As it turned out, the first-class music room was unusually quiet. Mrs Paton retired for the night.

At 9:20pm, the pilot snacked on something he put aside from lunch earlier in the day. He watched the inbound collier *Alden* safely pass the *Empress* port-to-port or leftside-to-leftside. No manoeuvring was required as both ships passed at a straight reach in the river. To the *Alden*, the *Empress* with all her electric lights and wisp of smoke appeared aglow like a giant floating birthday cake.

Salvation Army musicians and vocalists worked off the excitement of dinner with impromptu performances. Ensign Oliver 'Ollie' Mardall and a couple of other vocalists climbed the port side aft stairway to explore the Lower Promenade Deck. They completed one lap around the deck and then paused to enjoy the beauty of a new moon. Inspired by the moon and stars, Ollie and companions started singing contemporary tunes. Before long, a few passengers gathered and started a protracted sing-along. This unscheduled concert concluded with several hymns including 'There's a Mansion up in Glory' and another song with the refrain 'Never to be remembered, our sins are washed away. Oh, what peace and joy we've had since we began to pray!'

The second-class social hall was the next space aft of the second-class dining room on Shelter Deck. Salvation Army Adjutant Harry Green transformed the room into a jubilant festival when he started to play a few melodies on the upright piano. Rufus Spooner, a Salvation Army Captain from Moose Jaw, Saskatchewan, coaxed a few lads into playing 'Dead Man' on the open deck to the rear of the social hall.

Around 10:00pm, Purser Alexander Betteley McDonald told his first assistant Ernie Hayes to close down the ship's office and lock the safe. One of the last items to go into the safe was a toy boat made of tin. It was used to collect donations for the Royal National Life Boat Association.

Doctor Grant grew tired of the café and moved on to the first-class smoking lounge. A couple of poker games were in full swing. There was also a foursome of bridge. Doctor Grant ordered a cocktail from the cheerful smoking room bar steward. His name was Tom Gerrard, although everybody knew him as 'Tom'. He was yet another fixture on the ship, one of those memorable characters who made repeat passengers feel welcome. Doctor Grant closely observed one of the poker games while he munched on one of Tom's sandwiches.

'Billy Boy' Hughes was finally finished with embarkation day drudgery. He entered the ship's 'glory hole'. This was his on-board residence: a tight, 16-berth sleeping area located between the Stewards' and Assistant Stewards' quarters on the port side. He tossed his 'monkey' suit at the bulkhead where a brass hook caught it reliably as always. Hughes stepped up on his berth and efficiently jumped down into his pyjamas. He tried to fluff up the company pillow but it was a futile nightly ritual. Hughes looked forward to a restful night and a sailor's joy of the first full day at sea.

Mr and Mrs Gattrell took a last stroll around the ship before subjecting themselves to night time in third-class. They encountered a woman and her children for whom berths had not yet been prepared. Mr Gattrell kissed his wife goodnight and the two retired to separate cabins. Mrs Gattrell shared with three other women, one of whom was Irish.

Chief Steward Gaade started his nightly walk-through at 10:00pm. It was an opportunity to check on his staff, be informed of any special requests made by passengers, and to inspect the public rooms. Gaade started his rounds in third-class and worked his way up the decks to first-class. Stewards were responsible for closing portholes in the alleyways between cabins no later than 10:00pm. They were also supposed to keep track of porthole closure in outside cabins. If a passenger in a Shelter Deck or lower cabin wanted his porthole open, it was an exception to be noted in orders to the night watchmen. These procedures were generally followed but compliance was not absolute. Gaade was more concerned with issues like cleanliness and stowage. The night watchmen would see to the ports. The Chief Steward finished his rounds at about 11:45pm. He selected a vacant first-class stateroom for his accommodation. It was Cabin 218, located on Shelter Deck, only two cabins forward of the main staircase on the starboard side. It was an inside stateroom with no porthole which was eminently acceptable after the strains of embarkation day. Gaade closed his door just as the clock struck midnight.

All entertainment had ceased and public rooms were deserted except for the first-class smoking lounge where a poker game continued. Though most people were in their cabins, not everyone could sleep. James Rankin, a supernumerary CPR engineer taking passage back to Liverpool, was unable to sleep due to an irritating rash. He was assigned Cabin 510 on the starboard side of Main Deck. To soothe his discomfort, he smeared his body with salve.

Ensign Pugmire was fully awake in Cabin 432 which he shared with the Commissioner's son and Captain James Patrick Myers. His insatiable appetite for olives caused a severe case of indigestion.

Watchstanders were relieved at midnight. Junior Marconi operator Edward Bamford relieved his boss, Ronald Ferguson, in the wireless shack. Ferguson joined the Marconi company at Liverpool in 1910 and served on *Megantic* and *Mauretania*. Bamford was making his first trip on the *Empress of Ireland* after three voyages on the *Michigan*. On the Bridge, First Officer Edward J. Jones and Third Officer Charles Alwyn Moore took over from Williams and Tunstall. Quartermaster John Murphy assumed his duty at the helm replacing Galway. This was the same Murphy who was steering on 14 October 1909, when the *Empress* struck an unknown submerged object. Quartermaster Sharples replaced Gulcher. Relieving reports between watchstanders noted no exceptions. The transit had gone smoothly. A Bellboy named Charles Spencer assumed duties as Bridge Messenger. Pilot Bernier's job was almost done. Eighty more minutes of transit time would place the ship off Father Point where the river opens substantially in width. Bernier would there disembark by tender.

Fog, more than any other factor, made the St Lawrence a hazardous river to navigate. There were other factors such as heavy traffic, little warning to shallow water, and tidal currents but all these were manageable in the absence of fog. At times, the river is totally obliterated by fog like the time *Montrose* delivered Doctor Crippen to his arrest. In those cases, the obscurity was omnipresent and appeared to be standing still. At other times, the fog acted like a self-propelled apparition driven in a particular direction following deliberation. Readers familiar with the original science fiction television series *Outer Limits* will recall the opening sequence where an oscilloscope displays an undulating electronic wave. The viewer is warned not to adjust the television while the wave takes shape. The wave is disorganized at first with erratic highs and lows. It then gathers itself into a regular rhythm, flattens, and takes off. This is precisely how phantom fogs on the St Lawrence behave. They are weak collections of mist at first. They build in intensity and height then seem to flatten a bit as they propel themselves across the river.

At 12:30am, the ship sailed into a fog bank. Slow speed, which equalled about 8 knots, had just been rung on the engine order telegraph for the approach to Rimouski. Jones ordered the Quartermaster to sound fog signals. The steam-powered whistle was mounted at the front of the forward funnel just below the top joint. Murphy pulled the whistle's cord for one long blast. The *Empress* emerged from the fog before another signal was needed. This was the second time fog signals had been sounded during the evening. The ship had sailed into a fog bank on the prior watch.

Ship's company were trained to close portholes upon hearing the ship's fog signals. Night Watchman William Morl was responsible for Cabins 201 through 229 on Shelter Deck. He closed all portholes in alleyways and in vacant cabins but did not disturb occupied cabins. A key was needed to close port holes so passengers couldn't reopen them.

The poker players in the smoking lounge ran out of steam. So did Doctor Grant who retired to his cabin. Steward Tom Gerrard sealed the liquor cabinets and cleared the few remaining empty glasses.

The outbound transit came to full stop near the south shore at 12:50am. The mail tender, *Lady Evelyn*, steamed out from Rimouski to meet the motionless *Empress*. Although totally unwarranted, the Royal Mail transfer had a sinister feel to it. It was late at night. The river was unusually tranquil with barely a ripple to catch the new moon's light. The familiar beat of the liner's machinery went ominously silent. A dwarfed vessel came alongside in commando fashion to the exact point where a door mysteriously opened. Sacks of routine and registered mail got tossed into the void. Deep voices exchanged indiscernible greetings, or were they instructions? Then suddenly, a couple of sacks of mail were tossed back at the little mail boat and she escaped into the night.

Royal Mail steamers began using Rimouski as a postal transfer point in 1876. This practice continued for decades making Rimouski an essential link between Canadian North America and Europe. Trains loaded with Royal Mail rushed between Ontario, Quebec City, and Rimouski actually shortening delivery time over transit by ship or ferry. The Royal Mail trains were not subject to unpredictable fog and congestion delays often experienced by ships on the St Lawrence.

One of the most interesting items posted on the *Empress* was a card sent by artist Teddy Gray to his fiancée Sadie. Teddy drew a caricature of himself in his band uniform complete with Mountie-style Stetson. He then took the card through the ship to get bandsmen and Salvation Army officers to sign it. The card was overflowing with signatures by the time Gray posted it for off-loading in Rimouski.

Newlywed Eddy Dodd wrote a dispatch to the *War Cry*, which he posted in time for the mail tender. He described the scene at Union Station in Toronto. Salvationists gathered to send off their brethren even though the train wasn't scheduled to leave until 11:30pm. A small chorus at the station platform sang 'Over the Sea' and many other tunes to wish the travellers farewell. Colonel Sydney Maidment read the 46th Psalm. The train left the station one hour late keeping well-wishers there past midnight. Dodd commented on this late departure in his dispatch. He wrote:

> *The train (from Toronto to Quebec) did not pull out until 12:25 AM. Unusual, yet unusual things are always happening in the Army! No one was surprised.*

Major George Attwell posted a colour postcard of the *Empress of Ireland* to his twelve-year-old son, Cecil, in Toronto. 'Dear Cecil,' he wrote, 'Lovely trip so far. I will post this at Rimouski. Love from Mama & me, Papa.'

Many other cards and letters were posted on board since there was plenty of time to do so. A postcard of the ship was a cute way to remind loved ones that they were in your thoughts. Captain George Wilson, a devout Salvation Army officer, violated the adage, 'neither a borrower nor a lender be'. He borrowed his wife's Bible for the voyage. Wilson posted a letter to his wife Annie thanking her for the Bible. He then borrowed the postage for his letter from William Wakefield of Vancouver.

At 1:20am the *Empress* slowed again to discharge the pilot. She came to almost a dead stop one mile north of the Father Point gas buoy. The pilot's boat *Eureka* met the ship on cue. A mild wind sporadically blew from the south shore so the *Eureka* planned to cross the stern and come up along the leeward side. At the last moment, *Eureka* elected to recover the pilot to starboard as the wind was negligible. Adélard Bernier shook hands with the Captain and parted saying, 'I don't think you'll run into much fog'. He then went down using the gangway still rigged to the ship's side expressly for his departure. From where a cargo door opens to Main Deck, he met the travelling CPR Agent who was also leaving. First the Agent, and then Bernier descended by rope ladder, not missing a rung, until safely on the deck of *Eureka*. The instant Bernier's foot hit the deck, the tug went to full throttle quickly parting company with the hull of the liner. *Eureka's* second-in-command logged the time as 1:30am. The pilot exchanged a casual salute with the officers on the starboard wing of the *Empress's* Bridge. He wished them 'smooth sailing', out of habit, not intending to be heard. For a moment, Bernier stared up at the green-coloured starboard side light where the officers were huddled. Then he went into the tug's cabin in search of warmth.

First Officer Jones ordered full speed ahead. The order, rung smartly on the engine order telegraph, was immediately answered by the engine room. The vessel shuddered a bit at the stern as the propellers dug into the water. She worked up to 15 knots on course north 50 east, roughly diagonally across the St Lawrence. The river is thirty miles wide at Father Point so there is plenty of room to manoeuvre. The St Lawrence continues to open wide along the Gaspe Peninsula until it eventually reaches the Strait of Belle Isle — gateway to the North Atlantic. This is why Father Point was considered the traditional start of ocean crossings from Canada. Chief Engineer Sampson retired for the night in his private quarters at the aft end of Upper Deck on the port side.

At 1:36am, high up in the crow's nest, one sharp clang was sounded on the lookout's 10-inch brass bell. John Carroll reported sighting the light from Cock Point buoy. Jones thought he had a visual fix on Cock Point but then it temporarily disappeared. Fog must have shut it out. Jones held a Master's certificate for twelve-years and had two trips on the *Empress* as Second Officer but was a little uncomfortable with the sudden changes in visibility. This was his first trip on the *Empress* as First Officer. Best to call the Captain who was warming up with a beaker of coffee in his cabin.

Kendall appeared, coffee in hand, at precisely that moment. Jones had not yet sent the messenger to request his presence on the Bridge. Captains had an uncanny way of doing that. At 1:38am, the lookout sounded his bell again. This time he reported an object off the starboard bow. Carroll shouted, 'Object on the right!'

Kendall grabbed a pair of binoculars from the stowage locker against the bulkhead. Visibility was good. He and Jones could see a ship's masthead lights on the horizon at 3-to-4-points off the starboard bow. A point equals 11.25 degrees which placed the bearing to the unknown vessel at about 40 degrees to the right of the *Empress*'s bow. Kendall estimated the distance to the stranger at about six miles more or less.

The next step for Kendall and his Bridge watch was to determine the intentions of the contact they observed. It was clearly another steamer. Was she inbound, outbound, or dead in the water? If she was an inbound ship, there wasn't much time to work out the navigational picture since the two vessels would be headed toward each other at a very fast rate. The *Empress* at full speed opposing a tramp steamer at 10 knots meant that the two could close each other at half a mile per minute. They might be on top of each other in as soon as twelve minutes. A scenario ending in collision would be indicated if the bearing to the other steamer held steady and the distance between the vessels kept decreasing. At this point, Kendall and Jones needed to carefully observe the bearing of the contact to see how it changed over the next minute or two.

Before taking a bearing and getting a firm understanding of what the other vessel was doing, Kendall decided to 'stand on' his planned track at Cock Point buoy. It was not unusual to alter course near Cock Point to run an outbound transit parallel to shore. Kendall elected to make the turn down river first and then obtain a bearing on the other steamer. Jones gave Murphy the order to port his helm and steady on new course north 76 east at 1:41am. This was a turn of slightly over two points to the right.

Helm orders in those days were the opposite of the direction one intended to steer. A port helm order meant a turn to the right. A starboard helm order turned the ship to the left. The helm direction identified which way the plane of the rudder was oriented. When the plane of the rudder pointed left, the force of water against it drove the ship to the right and vice versa. An easy way to visualize old helm orders is to think of tiller orders in a small boat. One pushes the tiller away from the intended direction of travel.

Kendall climbed up to the Navigational Bridge to take a bearing using the binnacle-mounted prismatic compass. Visibility was still good but fog was gathering along the shore. The lights on the masts of the other vessel clearly showed an inbound ship which appeared to be opening to the right of the *Empress*. Kendall observed the bearing at north 87 east or about one-point off the starboard bow. He estimated the distance between vessels to be about two miles or about 4 minutes away from passing. After dropping back down to the enclosed Bridge, he thought he saw the other ship's green starboard sidelight, further verification that the two ships should pass each other along their starboard sides on roughly opposite courses.

Alfred Severin Gensen Toftenes was the man on the opposite course. He was a tall, blond Norwegian who worked for Klaveness Line on board their cargo vessel *Storstad*. The Dominion Coal Company chartered the *Storstad* to haul coal from Sydney, Cape Breton Island, Nova Scotia, to Quebec and Montreal. The *Storstad* was 440 feet long, 58 feet-wide and weighed 6,028 tons. She was registered in Christiania, Norway, by Aktieselskabet Maritime, a joint stock steamship company. The *Storstad* was constructed with frames running parallel to the keel and horizontally up along the interior shell. Vertical support came from transverse cross-members. This framing system was patented by British naval architect Joseph Isherwood. Conventional ships, including ocean liners, were constructed with vertical frames supported horizontally by side-members called stringers. *Storstad's* longitudinally reinforced hull combined with her chisel shaped bow made it possible to bust through ice. Her non-conventional design also made the *Storstad* a potentially dangerous weapon.

Toftenes was considered an experienced sailor. He had held a Master's Certificate for seven years. He rose from *Storstad's* Third Officer to Chief Officer in three years from the date he reported aboard. At age 33, he had been Chief Officer for about six weeks. On the Bridge with Toftenes was Third Officer Jacob Saxe, Helmsman Peter Johannsen, and Seaman Knot. The officers were complemented by a crew of thirty-six. *Storstad* was headed for Father Point where they would embark a pilot for the transit upriver. Toftenes had been gradually altering course to close the south shore after passing Metis Point. Just after reaching a steady heading west southwest, two clangs of a bell rang out in rapid succession. The *Storstad's* lookout, Seaman Ludwig Fremmerlid, reported lights ahead to port. Toftenes could see the masthead lights of a large liner about one-and-a-half points off the port bow. He watched the liner for several minutes. He could see her change course, first seeing her starboard green sidelight then her masthead lights in line and finally her port red sidelight. Since the bearing to the liner was to his left and the liner was swinging to her right, Toftenes planned on passing port-to-port.

As if dispatched by Crippen's ghost, a phantom fog from the south shore propelled itself across the river in a north-westerly direction. The pocket of fog was oval shaped with its longest diameter oriented in a line from south-west to north-east. The north-eastern tip of the fog enveloped the *Storstad* first. A minute later, the *Empress* was surrounded.

The distance between vessels was still closing. Kendall could no longer see any lights from the *Storstad*. In the minute before fog reduced Kendall's visibility to zero, he saw that the *Storstad* was still at the same bearing. Kendall thought there was no risk of collision because he believed the *Empress* had already crossed the intended track of the *Storstad*. If true, the *Empress* was then on the north side of the *Storstad* ready for a starboard-to-starboard passing. But then Kendall gave an order *in extremis*, a command reserved for imminent collision. He ordered both engines full astern. Jones rang the order on the engine order telegraph and sounded the backing signal, three shorts blasts, on the ship's whistle. The backing signal woke up Tiria Townshend. The sound of engines going full astern rattled the Chief Engineer in his aft-end cabin. He immediately proceeded below to check on his engines and find out why such demands were made on them.

Chief Officer Toftenes answered with one long blast of the *Storstad's* whistle. This announced his intention to hold his course. He had standing orders to call his Captain to the Bridge in the event of fog. A request for Captain Andersen to come to the Bridge was not made at that time. Toftenes noticed that the liner was still one-and-a-half-points off his port bow just before fog made her disappear. Toftenes decided it would be prudent to slow his forward progress. He went to the engine order telegraph and pulled the lever toward him until it pointed at 'STOP'. The engine room acknowledged momentarily. The harmonic drone of *Storstad's* triple-expansion engine faded until silent. The decoupled shaft stopped revolving. The wide blades of her single propeller, denied power, stopped churning. Absent background noise, creaks in *Storstad's* hull were suddenly apparent. Each creak like successive turns on a ratchet raised the level of tension on the Bridge.

Kendall heard *Storstad's* whistle, coming from one-point off the starboard bow. The engine order telegraph still showed the *Empress* at full reverse. Three hurried blasts erupted from the whistle in a second warning to the inbound steamer. This wasn't the first time in Kendall's career that he reversed his engines. In 1908, as Captain of the steamship *Monmouth*, he was heading up the St Lawrence in the fog when he heard whistles ahead. He reversed his engines to come to a complete stop. The whistles belonged to outbound battleships *Indomitable* and *Indefatigable*. The *Indomitable* had the Prince of Wales, later King George V, on board. His Royal Highness was returning from a celebration in Quebec. Both battleships were headed toward the *Monmouth* at 24 knots. Kendall successfully got out of their way with a 'FULL AHEAD'. Unfortunately, he drove the *Monmouth* up on to an ice floe in the process.

Storstad answered again with an especially long blast. The screaming whistle rattled its mount on the funnel as well as the watchstanders in the wheel house. Current suddenly became the focus of concern. A two-knot current might be enough to drive the *Storstad*, which was rapidly losing steerage way, into the unknown liner. Toftenes did not want to be adrift in the fog especially with a large ship somewhere off his port side within a couple of minutes of passing. Toftenes ordered 'AHEAD SLOW' to work up to 4 knots. No whistle was sounded at that moment.

Kendall listened carefully to the *Storstad's* long retort. It sounded further to the right, maybe four-points off the starboard bow. This was good news. The two vessels would pass each other with some room to spare. The forward momentum of the *Empress* seemed arrested. Kendall ordered 'ALL STOP' on the engines. His heading was virtually unchanged at north 75 east. The Quartermaster sounded two long blasts. This was the signal for dead in the water.

Storstad sounded a third single long signal. She had started to steam ahead. Toftenes wanted to correct for drift so he ordered Johannsen to port his helm 'a little'. This would drive him to the right, opening the distance between vessels consistent with his assumption of a port-to-port passing. Toftenes called Captain Andersen on the voice tube and told him it was 'getting hazy'. The Captain asked his Chief Officer if Father Point light was visible. Toftenes said it had just been shut out by the fog. No mention was made of the whistle signals exchanged with the outbound liner or that another ship was in close proximity. While Toftenes listened carefully to his Captain's voice resonating in the brass tube, Third Officer Saxe noticed that the ship wasn't swinging to starboard fast enough. He grabbed Johannsen's wheel and spun it hard-a-port to hasten the Chief Officer's order.

For an instant which must have seemed like an eternity, the Bridge of the *Empress* was silent. Her engines were still. Kendall flashed back to his episode with the battleships. He felt their commanders quite lucky to have steamed through the fog at high speed without hitting anything. As for his current situation, was he exercising caution or had he lost control of the navigational picture? Kendall knew the St Lawrence was a very busy waterway. The Dominion Coal Company alone had 14 ships plying their way up and down the river. Less than two years earlier, the *Empress of Britain* collided with a Norwegian collier named *Helvetia*. The accident sank the *Helvetia* in the same area where Kendall now sat motionless. The Captain of the *Empress of Britain* was criticized for going too fast in the fog. Kendall's moment of reflection personally reaffirmed his actions. He stuck his head in the chart room behind the wheelhouse to check the time.

*Thomas Andersen,
Captain of the*
Storstad.
(Drawing by John
Andert).

Third Officer Moore was keeping a scratch log which would be used to complete the official log. Moore, seeing Kendall straining to catch the time, called out, '1:47am, Sir'.

Kendall broke the silence, 'Better remind them we've stopped, Mr Jones.' Jones sounded two long blasts.

Captain Andersen was already half-dressed in preparation for embarking the pilot at Father Point. He hastily tied his partly-laced boots. Andersen's wife who routinely joined him on voyages asked if he was nervous. 'I don't know why, but I am,' he said.

Captain Andersen proceeded from his cabin to the Bridge almost immediately. He barely got to the compass when he sighted the liner. He could see the entire hull of the *Empress*, her masthead lights, and most shocking of all her green starboard sidelight. The much larger *Empress* appeared as a giant wall of steel crossing rapidly in front of the *Storstad* from left to right. Andersen ordered full speed astern. Toftenes began sounding the backing signal — three short blasts. The *Storstad*, loaded with 10,400 tons of coal, began to shake as her engines reversed.

Captain Kendall may have been getting nervous sitting in fog with no way on. He poked his head into the chart room at 1:53am. Two minutes later, Kendall saw the *Storstad's* forward masthead light and both red and green sidelights at less than one ship length off his starboard bow. The *Empress* was a sitting duck. Kendall started to bark orders in a last gasp to save his ship. He had to shout to be heard over the blare of *Storstad's* backing signal. The watchstanders snapped into action after retrieving their jaws from the deck. Kendall looked carefully at *Storstad's* bow to see which way she pointed. Kendall saw that his starboard rear quarter was the target. He could also see that the *Storstad* was under power. She had a discernible bow wake. The collision angle made by the starboard bow of both ships appeared to be 75 degrees. The *Storstad* was headed at the *Empress* at almost a right angle. The *Storstad's* backing signal woke up a number of passengers including Reverend Wallet, and the Freemans' from Wisconsin.

Ludwig Fremmerlid saw the giant liner materialize out of the fog to his left. Instinctively, he jumped to safety farther back on deck. Captain Andersen's wife put on her deck shoes and an overcoat. She was headed for the Bridge to join her husband.

Mr John Fowler of Vancouver was booked in third-class forward on Lower Deck. The cacophony of fog signals woke him up. He stuck his head out of his porthole to see what was going on. He noticed a patchy state of fog hovering over the water. Portholes at Lower Deck level were only 5 feet above the waterline. To his amazement, the anchor, hawse pipe, and bow of another ship converged rapidly upon him. The fog seemed to dissipate as the ship got closer as though it was getting out of the way. Fowler yanked his head back in and started to close the porthole.

Boatswain's Mate Alexander Radley was on the Shelter Deck checking to see that hatches and booms were properly secured for a North Atlantic crossing. He also wanted to check on Seaman R. Crayton who was the forecastle lookout. A forward lookout on deck was considered redundant to the crow's nest lookout so the former performed tasks such as washing the deck. Crayton was so engaged.

Boatswain Radley, with 25 years at sea, recognized the perilous chorus of whistles raging in the dense night air. Before finding Seaman Crayton, Radley glanced to starboard and saw the *Storstad* bearing down. Radley raced into the forecastle where fifty crewmen were berthed. He banged on doors and shouted a warning to men who were fast asleep from the exhaustion of embarkation day.

Seaman Price, hero of the *Volturno* fire, was responsible for gathering up the sea ladder used by Pilot Bernier. He was walking forward on the starboard side of the Shelter Deck out in the open where cargo is handled. Price was preparing to stow the ladder for its next use in Liverpool when he saw the *Storstad* driving toward him. She seemed to be sheering away with her starboard sidelight clearly visible.

Kendall's only hope was to try and kick his starboard rear quarter out of the way so that the *Storstad* passed down his side maybe one hair-length away. He thought there was a slight chance that the two ships would simply bump along each other's side causing minor damage. Kendall ordered his engines ahead full and the helm hard-a-port. On the starboard wing of the Bridge, Kendall tried to hail the

Storstad using the 30-inch megaphone. It was too late. As the last blast of the *Storstad's* whistle wailed in futility, she tore into the side of the *Empress* with bulls-eye precision. She struck one foot below Shelter Deck at a point directly between the funnels. The engines completed five, maybe six, revolutions before impact.

Junior Third Engineer George O'Donovan was on duty in the forward boiler room in Stokehold 2. Coal dust billowed throughout the stokehold before the crunching and tearing of collision ended. Coal dust continued to filter throughout the space for a period of twenty seconds which seemed strangely quiet. There was a nasty smell in the air from the smoke of doused coals. Then O'Donovan heard a thunderous roar behind him. He looked aft and saw a wall of water coming toward him from the starboard coal bunker door. He ordered all the firemen and trimmers out and then ran for the ladder himself.

Kendall ordered Murphy to activate the ship's siren after the collision. This was done by pulling a wire at the port side of the wheel house. The shrill wail of the siren was more than just an emergency warning. It required two specific actions on the part of the crew. Those mandatory actions were to man lifeboat stations and to close all watertight doors. Kendall rang 'ALL STOP' momentarily and then placed the engine order telegraph at 'CLOSE WATERTIGHT DOORS'. He called Chief Engineer Sampson on the loud-speaking telephone to verify the watertights were being closed. Sampson replied, 'We're already doing it!'.

Crew members started hustling about on deck and in spaces below. Second-class Steward Frank Harrison woke up to the unmistakable wail of the siren. He was in charge of Cabins 400 to 430 on the starboard side. His duty was to close Watertight Door 86 located on Main Deck between the second-class boot room and men's lavatory. Like most of the watertight doors it closed horizontally toward the centre of the ship. The gear for Watertight Door 86 was flush with the deck just outside Cabin 400. Harrison pulled his trousers on. He quickly went up on deck to see what caused the crash. By the time he got back to Upper Deck a coating of water had started to conceal the location of the cranking gear. Harrison inserted the key and managed to start closing the door.

James Rankin, who never did get to sleep because of his rash, heard the extension gear of Watertight Door 86 which was being operated by Harrison. Rankin's cabin was one cabin aft of the second-class boot room. He popped out of his cabin and looked down a starboard alleyway next to the boot room. The alleyway porthole was level with the surface of the St Lawrence and water was starting to flow in. The ship had listed nine degrees to starboard within one minute of impact. It was sufficient to jam Watertight Door 86 which had to be cranked shut against the direction of list. Harrison was unable to finish closing the door.

Third Engineer Robert Liddell, in charge of the starboard engine, was concerned when he had to go from full ahead to all back on his engine. It wasn't until he saw water trickle through Watertight Door 90, followed by clouds of coal dust, that he knew the ship was in trouble. Watertight Door 90 separated the after boiler room from the engine room. Liddell ordered the vertically-sliding door shut. Junior Fourth Engineer James McEwen closed 90 but not before a good bit of water had started to accumulate. The five greasers and three engineers in the engine room watched the water's ominous shift toward the starboard bilge.

McEwen ran up to the third-class dining saloon on Main Deck to operate the two horizontally-sliding watertight doors between boiler rooms. The Junior Fourth Engineer groped around in two feet of water. He was unable to locate the deck level pinions. Even if he had, the door on the starboard side would have been impossible to crank shut against its vertical inclination.

Third-class Assistant Steward Joseph Hayes was asleep in Stewards' berthing on Upper Deck. He ran out into the working alleyway and smelled the sick smell that arose from the stokehold. His watertight door assignment was Number 78 on the starboard side. It closed an opening in Bulkhead 5 between the third-class dining room and forward cabins. Hayes could not crank the door shut against the ship's list.

Assistant Stewards Harry Baker and Charley Tunstall were also on Main Deck attempting to work a watertight door. They were trying to close the single door in Bulkhead 4 which protected third-class and steerage accommodation on Lower Deck. This door was not successfully shut. By this time, submerged passengers on Lower Deck were dying one by one as they gave into the impulse to breathe.

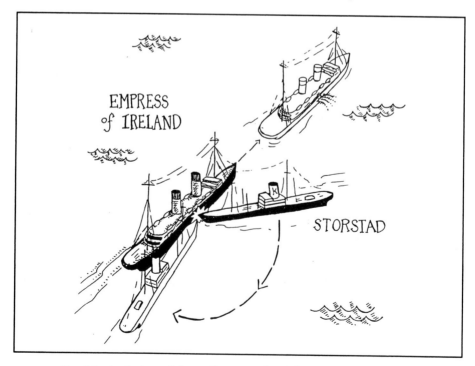

Graphic depiction of the collision angle and moments till separation.
(Drawing by John Andert).

The plating of the *Empress* crushed like an egg shell when the *Storstad* penetrated into her fully loaded coal bunkers. Sparks flew forward and high into the air along the hull. Loitering patches of fog filtered the firestorm generated by steel striking steel. This created an eerie luminescence reminiscent of Toronto's heat lightning earlier in the week. Kendall began a series of five calls through his megaphone directed at the *Storstad's* Bridge, 'Keep ahead, keep going ahead on your engines!'. He wanted to keep *Storstad's* bow in the opening for support in case the *Empress* was mortally wounded.

Captain Andersen had the same instinct for self-preservation as Kendall. He ordered his engines ahead full to try and plug the hole he made in the side of the liner. Hopefully, he could keep his ship in the wound until a damage assessment was completed. Captain Andersen cupped his hands around his mouth and called out 'My ship is going full ahead!'.

The actual angle of collision upon impact, between the forward starboard quarters of the vessels, was most likely 45 degrees. This is based on observations made by the two captains and later supposition by naval architects. Kendall thought it was an angle of seven points while Andersen believed it to be three points. The impact was about 12 feet aft of Bulkhead 5, between the boiler rooms. First contact was made by *Storstad's* starboard bow anchor. Bulkhead 5 may have been breached.

Contemporary newspapers could not resist describing the force of impact using a variety of comparisons. A frequent description said the force of the *Storstad* was equal to 160,000 ton-miles. This was based on her tonnage plus cargo travelling at 10 knots. Another example said the force was equal to a train of 240 standard freight cars hitting a wall at 20 miles per hour. Much of the damage to the *Storstad* was caused by its starboard bow anchor. At rest, the anchor and its twin on the port side projected 18 inches out from either side of the bow. The collision drove the starboard anchor through its hawse pipe and down the starboard side. The anchor flukes peeled back *Storstad's* steel hull plating a distance of 12 feet 6 inches. The anchor points were spotted with blood from an untold number who died instantly.

Seaman Price watched the bow of the *Storstad* slice into the *Empress*. The sea-ladder fell from his hands. Price later described impact as a cut 'as clean as a can opener'. The stem of the *Storstad* reached into the bowels of the *Empress* a distance of at least fourteen feet. As *Storstad's* bow remained clenched in the side of the liner, her longitudinal axis began to rotate 100 degrees toward the stern of the *Empress*. Price, standing at the starboard rail, could see the port side of the *Storstad* rapidly closing the angle formed by each ship's side. Four seconds elapsed during this unwelcome embrace. The fateful couple turned clockwise together toward the south shore and then parted. Captain Kendall thought he saw one of his boilers fall off its cradle when the ships separated. The *Storstad's* nose was twisted to port. Her forecastle was shaved clean right back to her windlass. She assumed a parallel course right down the starboard side of the *Empress*.

Mrs Andersen had joined her husband on the Bridge. She asked her husband what he was doing. He explained that he was trying to plug the hole in the liner's side. He then ordered Toftenes, who had been mute since impact, to inspect the *Storstad's* hold. Saxe was told to muster lifeboat stations.

The hole in the *Empress* was estimated to be 25 feet high by 14 feet wide or about 350 square feet. This was based on *Storstad's* forward loaded draft of 25 feet (below the waterline) times her approximate width forward of her collision bulkhead. The St Lawrence filled the opening in the *Empress* at a rate of 60,000 gallons per second. The height of *Storstad's* bow was 46 feet which accounts for her impaling the *Empress* 21 feet above waterline through Upper Deck. As the *Storstad* withdrew from the hole, she took a memento of where she had been. It was the number plate from the door to Upper Deck Cabin 328. The door was seven feet inboard from the starboard side. Cabin 328 was a first-class 'outside cabin. An imprint of a porthole was left on the *Storstad's* twisted port side along with chips of white enamel.

Mrs Andersen resolved to go down with her husband if need be. 'We are going down?' she asked. 'I think so,' he replied. The Captain's wife held back tears. They had no idea how badly damaged the liner was. To them, the *Empress* seemed to continue on her course as if nothing had happened. They couldn't believe the liner didn't stop to render assistance. Andersen ordered 'ALL STOP'.

Kendall's only chance once the ships had separated was to try and beach the *Empress* on the south shore. He cranked the engine order telegraph all the way forward to 'FULL AHEAD'. He called Sampson on the telephone and said 'Give her all you can!'. The Chief Engineer, sweating and red-faced, reached overhead to operate the engine starting apparatus. The engines kicked once or twice but they would not start. Sampson, who like so many proud engineers wanted to deliver for his Captain, passed on the dejected reply 'The steam is gone'. His options exhausted, Captain Kendall rang up the signal 'FINISHED WITH ENGINES'.

Chief Officer Mansfield R. Steede was asleep in his private cabin just aft of the wheel house on the port side. The senior radioman, Ferguson, also had his quarters on the port side of Boat Deck. Both men were awakened by the blare of ship whistles. Ferguson headed for the wireless room in his night clothes. His junior, Bamford, was looking to starboard to see what bumped into them. Just as Ferguson arrived, Bamford said, 'Here she is!'. They saw the masthead lights of the *Storstad* passing down their side. Ferguson cranked up the wireless transmitter and sent out the message 'MPL here; have struck a ship and may need assistance; by.'

'MPL: was the *Empress's* call sign. 'By,' was short for stand by. Mindful that the wireless operator ashore would be a junior at such an early hour, Ferguson tapped out the preliminary message slowly and deliberately. The junior at Father Point wireless station was Crawford Leslie. The young 19-year-old got the message on the first try and answered without delay. 'Here we are,' Leslie replied. He looked up at the clock which was checked for accuracy every day at noon. Leslie logged the time as 1:45am. He then received another message from the *Empress*. Ferguson told him to get his senior to come to the phones.

Passenger George Smart woke up when he heard a 'double whistle' he described as 'two distressing calls'. His outside cabin was almost all the way forward on the starboard side in perfect position to see the crash. Smart would have seen the impact if he had looked out his porthole. Instead, pyjama clad, he left his cabin to stare out a porthole between cabins. To get a better look, he stepped up on a little box left in the alleyway. He heard Captain Kendall shouting for the other vessel to keep going ahead. He felt that the *Storstad* was so close he could reach out and touch her bow because she was 'straight in against the side of the ship'. The shock of going from sound sleep to crisis distorted reality. Smart was actually 160 feet forward of the collision site.

Toftenes returned to the Bridge. He reported that the bulkheads were intact. The *Storstad* was not about to founder as Captain Andersen expected. She had sprung over twenty plates forward and took on some water.

Mrs Paton woke up before the impact because she thought she heard a bell ringing. She then felt a 'slight shock'. She glanced straight out of her porthole but didn't see anything. She, like many passengers, thought the ship collided with an iceberg. If she had looked down she would have discovered a Norwegian collier gorging on the heart of the liner.

Starboard side of the Empress. *The point of collision is approximately at the X mark.* (Private collection M.J.Rickards)

The shock of collision frightened Alice Bales. She jumped out of bed and cried out to Rose Butler and Miss Willmot, 'Girls, we've struck an iceberg!' Alice had her wits about her. She pulled on a skirt and then grabbed for the life belts stored overhead. She threw them at her cabin mates to get them moving.

The money Alice saved was stuffed into a small linen purse which she wore around her neck. Water started to pour in through the cabin porthole. Alice managed to close it before heading for the stairs.

Will Measures, Teddy Gray, Ernie Aldridge, and Ken McIntyre were asleep in their cabin forward on Main Deck. The ship's whistle must have woken William up because he remembered being awake for the impact. 'It was a gentle bump,' Will recalled, 'like the starting of a train'. He looked out of their porthole which revealed nothing since it was on the port side. He went back to his berth and tried to fall sleep.

Chief Steward Gaade, a light sleeper, awakened to the sound of ferrous metal plates collapsing two decks below on the collision side. He jumped out of bed, threw a dressing gown on, and ran out to the vestibule at the bottom of the main staircase. He encountered Night Watchman William Morl. Gaade asked Morl where she was struck. 'Amidships', was the reply. Gaade told Morl to call all the passengers he could and tell them to get their life belts and get up on deck. Gaade returned to his cabin to get his trousers and overcoat. Morl lit two emergency lamps and started knocking on cabin doors.

First-class Steward Prowse had also started banging on cabin doors to spread the alarm. He repeatedly called on everyone to get their life belts and get out on deck. This commotion aroused Sir Henry Seton-Karr. He thought there was a prankster in the passageway playing a sick joke on slumbering passengers. The same disturbance stirred Mr Merton Darling located in a stateroom directly opposite Seton-Karr. Both men opened their cabin doors at exactly the same moment to see who was responsible for such impertinence. They rushed into the alleyway bumping into each other in comedic fashion.

Stanley Bigland woke up after he heard the crash which didn't sound very menacing. He woke his fellow bandsmen Alfred Keith, Guido Whatmore and Rufus Spooner. 'Something struck us,' Bigland said. Keith opened the cabin door and looked fore-and-aft down the passageway. He saw water spilling in from a porthole at the end of the passageway. 'We've struck an iceberg, Keith announced, get on deck!' Spooner checked the time. He thought the ship had forward momentum. His watch showed 2:10am. The four men raced to get their trousers on.

Miss Grace Kohl, having travelled by liner a fortnight earlier, thought nothing of the slight shake which woke her. She peeked out her porthole and saw the lights of another ship. She assumed they were coming to collect the pilot or that the *Empress* had already dropped him off. Miss Kohl went back to bed.

The crash sounded like a loud firecracker to little Gracie Hanagan, one big 'bang'. A flash of light from the retreating *Storstad* illuminated her cabin. As the ship rebounded from the collision, it shook off the blow and Gracie started to slide toward the porthole she feared. Her father grabbed her and told her it was the pilot boat banging up alongside. Then they heard a violent knock at their door and men in the passageway yelling for people to get out. Gracie turned her head for one last look at her nemesis. Water began to tease the lower lip of the porthole.

Newlyweds Thomas and Mary Greenaway were notified by a steward to get up on deck. Mary Greenaway wasn't nervous at first. She took a moment to throw on a wrap. Just after exiting their cabin, Mr Greenaway became worried about water sloshing in and 'spoiling some of their clothes'. He returned to the cabin to close the porthole. By the time he completed this task, he realized the ship was in serious trouble because she was not righting herself. The newlyweds were separated by the gathering rush in the passageway which pushed Mary along as she called to her husband.

Mr William Hunt of Hamilton, Ontario, looked out his cabin door and saw the crowd of people which absorbed Mary Greenaway. Everyone in the passageway was rushing forward. He asked an open question of those passing by 'What's this all about?'. A crew member gave him the courtesy of an answer 'We've been struck amidships!'.

Mr Hunt, who was identified as a Doctor on the passenger list, gave the matter some thought before joining the crowd. He decided to proceed in the opposite direction, to the stern, believing that the ship would settle headfirst.

Salvation Army Major Frank Morris also surveyed the commotion in the passageway. He said the quick movements of people to the stairs reminded him of a 'school of fish'. Captain David 'Mac' McAmmond shared the outside cabin with Morris. Morris, boomed to his cabinmate: 'Mac, there is something wrong, get up!'. McAmmond thought the ship had run aground because of the 'grinding' noise. He had the inside berth and was able to flip the light on.

The American fathers from Rochester, Minnesota, felt a 'concussion' which was sufficient to wake them both. Herman Kruse suggested to Reinholdt Bach 'We had better go up on deck and ascertain what's the matter.' They knocked on the door to the adjoining cabin housing their daughters. Kruse told them 'We're going up on deck, you had better come along.' The girls threw wraps over their night clothes.

Mr and Mrs Henry Freeman seemed to be waiting for the 'other shoe to drop' after hearing the exchange of whistles. The couple jumped out of their berths upon impact. Mr Freeman grabbed a sweater for his wife and they abandoned the cabin together.

The Irish woman sharing with Mrs Gattrell rushed out of the cabin in her night dress. She asked if all was well. A steward replied 'All's right, ma'am.' Mrs Gattrell also in night attire could locate only one of her shoes. She left the cabin anyway with three children's life belts in hand.

Doctor Grant was in the private quarters designed for the ship's surgeon. He was less than 100 feet forward of Cabin 328 which had been eviscerated by *Storstad's* head stem. The jolt initially knocked him against the inner bulkhead but he fell out of bed on the rebound. Doctor Grant rolled across the deck and came to rest against his sofa.

Ernie Pugmire was one of the first passengers to reach an open deck still wide-awake from olive induced indigestion. He sensed imminent peril but thought about his brother Bert who didn't make the trip. Bert couldn't swim and if the *Empress* went down would Bert have been saved? Pugmire looked over the side and saw water rushing past. He was 'certain' the *Empress* still had forward speed. When Ernie Pugmire looked up he saw Bandmaster Hanagan, his wife, and little Gracie huddled together at the rail. Pugmire took off his overcoat and wrapped it around Gracie to keep her warm.

Reverend Wallet heard a 'horrible, grinding crash'. He felt the ship shake from stem to stern. Wallet, like Mrs Paton, had a stateroom on the starboard side of Upper Promenade Deck. He ran out on deck in time to see the *Storstad* slowly pulling away from the *Empress*. Another first-class passenger stepped out on deck just as the ship lurched to starboard. Wallet watched in horror as the man careened into the bulwark along the edge of the deck. The man groaned in pain. Wallet had seen enough. He went right back to his stateroom with one thought in mind. He would retrieve his life preserver from the closet where he noticed it nine hours earlier.

Clayton Burt woke up when he heard some dishes falling from the cupboard above his sink. The china was upset by the first lurch to starboard. Mr Burt rushed out on deck in time to feel a subsequent dip to starboard. He quickly retraced his steps back to the stateroom. Not removing his pyjamas, he dressed in a blue suit, light overcoat, and street shoes. Mr Burt was not as observant as Reverend Wallet. He didn't know where his life belt was stowed. Burt searched all corners of his room and under the bed but came up empty. He was frantic. He decided to evacuate his cabin and take his chances on deck. A passenger rushed by him with three life belts in hand but left one behind when it got caught on a door jamb. Burt grabbed it and went out on deck.

Chief Steward Gaade had his trousers on and exited his cabin as he slid into his overcoat. He had his second encounter since the crash at the bottom of the main staircase. Several ladies clung to him and pleaded to be saved. Gaade was on his way to his lifeboat station. He braced up and then detached the women. The beleaguered Chief Steward said 'No one will be saved unless you give us a chance to get on deck and get the boats out'.

A number of women and children started to accumulate on the Upper Promenade Deck. Clayton Burt helped some of them get into their life preservers. They were unwieldy appliances consisting of bundles of cork sewn in canvas. A woman without a life belt ran out on deck temporarily leaving her husband behind. She implored one of the ship's officers for instructions. 'There are none,' the preoccupied Third Officer replied, 'It is only a trifle.'

Clayton Burt was incredulous. He intercepted the woman and said 'For God's sake, get a life belt!'

Geographic position of where Empress of Ireland *foundered.*
(Drawing by John Andert).

6 'I Saved Myself'

The woman without a life belt was Mrs Black of Ottawa. Her husband had booked second-class Cabin 446 for their crossing. It was an inside cabin on Upper Deck next to the third-class children's nursery. The couple was on deck earlier than most passengers because John Black peered out in the passageway and saw stewards scurrying about with life belts on. A stronger argument to vacate the cabin could not be made. Incredibly, Mr Black missed his wardrobe cue. He forgot to bring the life belts.

Chief Officer Mansfield Steede was the first of a small parade of characters who went to the Bridge to find out exactly what was going on just after impact. He must have heard Kendall tell First Officer Jones 'Get away, get all hands and get the boats ready!' Bellboy Spencer was told to go below and help wake the passengers in steerage. Steede went to the Marconi shack and told Ferguson the ship would be down in a few minutes and to send the SOS distress signal. Steede did not have an exact ship's position as he had not been on watch.

Sir Henry Seton-Karr and Merton Darling brushed off the indignities of two gentlemen colliding with only their bed clothes to break the contact. Sir Henry had his life belt in hand. Seeing Mr Darling without one, Seton-Karr offered it to Darling. 'Go on man, take it,' Sir Henry roared, 'I will try and get another one.' Darling resisted. Seton-Karr's sportsman's instinct told him time was of the essence. He angrily forced the life belt over Darling's head and started pushing him down the passageway. Darling remembered looking back to see Sir Henry enter his cabin and shut the door.

Grace Kohl who had tried to go back to sleep now found herself toppled out of bed. She hurried out on deck and discovered a rapidly gathering state of confusion accentuated by the angle of the ship. The *Empress* was heeling over like a 'crushed toy'. Grace went back to her cabin where Assistant Steward John Brown helped her get into her life belt.

A firm knock on the door to Cabin 32 was an unwanted but not wholly unexpected surprise to Mrs Ethel Grundy Paton. Thanks to the whistles, Mrs Paton had gotten up and dressed in a blue negligee. She opened the door to a summarily unambiguous greeting from Third Officer Moore: 'If you want to be saved, get out now.' Dresser drawers tumbled halfway out spilling a top layer of stockings and other accessories. Moore pointed his head toward the dislodged drawers for emphasis but said nothing. He left as abruptly as he appeared. Stewardess Helena Hollies rushed in with Mrs Paton's freshly polished shoes. The dutiful stewardess managed to slip them on and button them even though Mrs Paton couldn't sit still.

Laurence Irving and his wife Mabel Hackney emerged from their cabin in night clothes. Passenger Frederick E. Abbott of Toronto was also in the passageway. Irving asked Abbott if the ship was going down. Before Abbott could answer, a lurch to starboard and forward threw Irving into his cabin door. Mrs Irving became frantic when she saw blood streaming from a gash in Laurence's forehead. Irving had to fight her to wrap the life belt over and around her. Mabel was sobbing hysterically with her arms locked in embrace around her love whose only wish was a moment of co-operation. 'Keep cool,' Irving begged. Abbott offered his help but Irving declined 'Look after yourself first, old man, but God bless you all the same.' The Irvings continued to struggle until Laurence finally picked Mabel up and carried her to the main staircase.

Irving was stoic as he began to ascend the stairs in a macabre scene reminiscent of the drama attending Rhett Butler's famous ascent with a struggling Scarlett O'Hara in *Gone with the Wind*. The increasing tilt of the staircase forced Irving to rely on balusters and fretwork for steps. By the time they reached the top of the stairs, Irving dropped to his knees and started to drag Mabel up on deck. The ship's siren stopped wailing. The screams of children mixed with the torturous sound of adult human suffering, echoed from below decks through topside ventilators. The stage was set for the Irvings' last act.

Many passengers in second and third-class were not lucky enough to be personally aroused by ship's company. Those who successfully escaped acted on their instincts immediately.

Mrs George E. Cook of Vancouver, berthing with Salvation Army Officers Hayes and Simcoe had a similar experience. At first she thought the ship struck a rock. She looked in the passageway and saw people rushing the stairs. Some of them were wet up to their thighs! Her survival instinct took over. Mrs Cook ran like a mad woman for the stairs. She wasn't even dressed. A mob mentality prevailed as the list approached a terrifying 30 degrees. People shoved everyone up the staircases toward the Boat Deck whether they wanted to go or not. Tiria Townshend and her Aunt, Wynnie Price, were caught in the rush. Neither of them had their life belts.

When Alice Bales entered the passageway, she had her life belt strung over one shoulder. She almost lost it in the crowd headed for the Boat Deck. A woman blocked her path shouting 'Where is my little boy? I have lost my little boy.' There was nothing anyone could do. Alice finally stepped around the desperate mother. The woman continued her plea 'Someone please find my little boy.'

Will Measures and Ken McIntyre were having trouble staying in their upper and lower berths which were on the high side of the cabin they shared with Teddy Gray and Ernie Aldridge. Will and Ken rolled out of bed when the heel of the ship became too great. Will yelled for Teddy and Ernie to get up. Ernie jumped up and started to put Will's trousers on. The two swapped trousers to end the confusion. Teddy's weight had shifted from his bunk to the inside bulkhead. He propped himself up and started to rub his eyes. Teddy Gray's cabinmates left satisfied that he was coming along when they saw him pulling on his pants.

Herman Kruse, Reinholdt Bach and their daughters stayed together until they reached the stairs. Mr Bach had difficulty with stairs under normal circumstances due to rheumatism. The tilted stairwells were too much for him. He insisted the others go on without him which they did.

John Delamont heard the ship's siren and having travelled by liner in the past knew that 2:00am was hardly the time for a drill. He woke his two sons and had them get into their life belts without delay. He then went to the cabin where his wife and daughter were berthed and was unable to open the door. The door was set ajar on a hook designed to permit air circulation while the door remained locked. All cabin doors on the *Empress* were fitted with this special feature. A stout man, Delamont repeatedly threw his entire mass at the door until it broke open.

First Officer Jones had managed to get Lifeboats 1, 3 and 5 ready for launch on the starboard side. Captain Kendall had thrown the gripes off those boats right after impact. He used his megaphone for the chivalrous cry 'Women to the boats!' Kendall ordered Quartermaster Murphy to get to his lifeboat and prepare it for launch.

Murphy's station was Lifeboat 12 on the port side. He encountered Chief Officer Steede who was already on the port side attempting to launch Lifeboat 8. By the time the canvas was pulled off the port side boats, the ship's list was too great. Even if a boat could be pushed out it would bind along the port side hull plates and rivets.

Chief Officer Steede returned to the Bridge. Captain Kendall went up to him and gave the order 'Send the SOS signal to Father Point.'

Steede replied 'We've already done so.' Kendall asked his Chief Officer to see what he could do to get as many boats out as possible. Steede went back to the port side. Stewardess Hollies saw him climb up on the boat winch near Lifeboat 8. Steede was shouting directions to crew members attempting to muster for the port boats 'It's no good on this side, boys. Go to starboard!' Murphy went to Lifeboat 13 on the other side to see if he could be of assistance. Boatswain Radly was leading the effort to launch 13.

Mrs Paton, fully dressed, bejewelled and covered in fur, made her way to the Bridge, 130 feet forward of her cabin. She found the Upper Promenade swarming with people in a state of 'chaos, horrible in the extreme'. A passenger was calling on others to form a human chain on the port side to counterbalance the ship. Mrs Paton told the man to leave her alone. She climbed the teak stairway leading to the Bridge. Once inside, an officer told her the danger was greatly exaggerated and that the Bridge was not a suitable place for a woman.

Wanting to believe what she had been told, Mrs Paton made her way precariously back down the tilted steps. A man fell into her and knocked her glasses off. The Boat Deck above began to sound to her like a 'bowling alley'. Fire buckets, holding tanks, cargo derricks and port side lifeboats were breaking free from stowage and flying across the deck. First-class passenger Godson, the graduate student who joked about drowning on the crossing, saw a man smashed into the starboard rail by a lifeboat. A shower of soot began to rain down from the belching funnels.

Inside the ship, objects of every description were falling to starboard. Dishes, glassware, pots and pans, luggage, toiletries, brass cleaner and polish all crashed to the low side. General cargo, fresh produce, Royal Mail, silver bullion, and the ship's several pianos systematically broke free and crashed into an accumulation of articles preceding them. This tremendous shift in weight accelerated the starboard list. A river of sand flowed from the children's playground until the once joyful platform was empty.

Chief Engineer Sampson wisely ordered the engine room evacuated before the tilt of the ship made it impossible to escape. He was lucky to get out. He and the last of his evacuees had to crawl 'like flies' along the port side engine columns and hoist themselves up several ladders to reach the outside. A relentless intruder, water eventually found its way to the engine room. It flooded down on the engines and dynamos from above. The electricity surged on and off several times causing the lights to flicker intensely bright for a second and then fade.

Bellboy Charles Spencer never reached the steerage section of the ship. He went as far below as Main Deck to help wake up passengers. He had difficulty picking up his legs to step over the rising water. Spencer saw two of his chums, Baker and Tunstall, continuing their attempt to close a watertight door. Spencer recognized it for the impossible task it was. He turned away and made his way back up the stairs.

Salvation Army Lieutenants Alfred Keith and Stanley Bigland found ice-cold water swirling all around them as they made their way to the nearest staircase. Columns of water 12 inches in diameter shot into the ship through portholes. Three hundred dollars, previously tucked safely under a pillow, now floated freely on the level surface of murky water sloshing around the tilted passageway. The money was ignored in the melee to reach the closest egress. Once up on deck, Keith crawled up to the port-side rail.

Many men, especially the younger Salvationists, pulled women and children up to stairwell landings or midpoints. Once positioned in front, the men would push the women up on to deck or to the next set of helping hands. Ken McIntyre, Ernie Pugmire, John Fowler, Rufus Spooner, Reginald Simmonds, and Assistant Steward J. Hayes were among the many who helped pull others one step closer to survival. Alice Bales' cabinmate, Miss Willmot, credits Mr Fowler with saving her life by pulling her up the stairs with a rope or firehose.

Bert Greenaway successfully climbed the stairs and was about to go to the port side when he encountered Ernest Evans, his wife and baby. The young father was frantic and asked for something to cover his naked child. Bert gave Mr Evans a sweater coat. Evans was so shaken, he kept fumbling with the coat. Bert carefully secured it around the child.

Salvation Army Commissioner Rees, daughter Madge, and wife Ruth escaped from their cabins and reunited on deck. Their son, Harding, was nowhere in sight. Ruth was plump but managed to get up with a little help from those nearby. Madge seemed to be out of touch. 'Oh, this will kill mother,' she complained, as though the imminent foundering was nothing more than a temporary travel inconvenience.

Passengers upon reaching Boat Deck sought to get as far from the water as possible. That is why Alfred Keith and so many others fought to gain the port-side rail. Keith studied the situation. All the passengers had gathered high on the side where lifeboats couldn't be launched. The crew was gathered along the starboard rail where boats were hovering a short distance above the water. Keith decided to follow the crew. He slid back down to the starboard side. He observed davits about to snare a lifeboat still attached. He decided to take his chances in the water. Keith dived in.

Crawford Leslie at Father Point Station called his senior, William James Whiteside, as requested by *Empress* Marconi operator Ferguson. Leslie yelled up to the bunk room for help. Whiteside came down to the instrument room a couple of minutes later and took the headset from Leslie. He heard Ferguson sending out the SOS call sign and the words 'listing terribly'.

Whiteside asked for the ship's position. Ferguson suddenly realized he had no coordinates to transmit. He answered with his best guess '20 miles past Rimouski'. Whiteside asked if 20 miles from Rimouski was correct. Ferguson's power was failing fast. He managed to send the first two letters of 'yes' and the first two dots of the 's' in reply. The spark needed to communicate was gone but there was still enough reserve power to receive one last message. Whiteside told Ferguson that two rescue ships were on the way.

The telegraph key in the Marconi shack must have seemed to Ferguson like a giant light switch. The last 'dot' depressed coincided with a shipwide drain of illumination from sparkling glass globes in the saloon to shielded bulbs in the engineering spaces. Formerly aglow, the *Empress* became a dark and foreign environment.

It takes those unaccustomed to travel by liner a couple of days to find their way about reliably. The vast majority went to bed scarcely remembering how to find their way to dinner when the lights were on. Passengers also did not have the benefit of a lifeboat drill which might have given them a slight edge in finding the nearest way out. Escape from second-class cabins and below was nothing short of miraculous.

The SOS message kicked off a race to rescue the *Empress*. William Whiteside told Crawford Leslie to call Rimouski and get the Captain of the Canadian Government Steamer on the telephone. Whiteside then sent out a 'CQ' (Come Quick) signal to all vessels. Leslie successfully rang up Captain Francois Pouliot of the *Lady Evelyn*. Before Leslie could catch his breath to explain the situation, Whiteside snatched the mouthpiece and put his hand over it. He ordered Leslie to run to Mr John McWilliams' house and wake him up. Whiteside then uncovered the mouthpiece to tell Pouliot the *Empress* was sinking somewhere near Father Point.

John McWilliams was manager of the Great Northwestern Telegraph office at

Father Point. When Leslie reached McWilliams' house, he didn't yell or bang on the door. Leslie cleverly rang the SOS signal on the door bell. McWilliams sat up from a sound sleep and rushed down in his pyjamas to open the door.

'We have a danger signal from the *Empress*,' Leslie reported. 'The *Empress of Ireland* is sinking!' McWilliams asked if the *Lady Evelyn* and the pilot boat had been notified. Leslie advised that the *Eureka* had not been notified as she was not in yet (*Eureka* was not equipped with wireless). Leslie also requested use of telephone line 7 as land line 4 was out of commission. McWilliams switched circuits and continued to think of everything that could be done: 'Have you notified the *Hannover*?' Leslie reported that the *Hannover* did not respond to the 'CQ.' The *Hannover* was a small North German Lloyd ship thought to be in the vicinity on her way from Rotterdam to Montreal.

This dramatic painting is by Canadian artist William Wheeler. It was published in Toronto's Star Weekly *upon the fiftieth anniversary of the tragedy.* (Salvation Army Heritage Centre Museum, Toronto).

Leslie and McWilliams could see the lights of the *Eureka* inbound for the Father Point wharf. The *Eureka* had just returned from recovering a pilot off the *Wagama*, an outbound collier behind the *Empress*. Leslie ran down to meet the *Eureka's* Master — Captain Jean Baptiste Belanger. McWilliams went back in his house to ring the telephone box at the wharf. When the *Eureka* tied up, the telephone was ringing off the hook. It was Whiteside at the Marconi office who actually initiated the call. McWilliams jumped in on the party line. Leslie, in full stride on the wharf, shouted for Captain Belanger to pick up the phone.

Belanger couldn't believe his ears. Whiteside was speaking 'The *Empress* is sinking; go to her assistance; rush!' Captain Belanger replied that the *Empress* had passed Father Point. He realized that he had just been given an explanation for the unusual series of whistles heard while *Eureka* waited to pick up *Wagama*'s pilot.

This was the same Captain Belanger in charge of the same pilot boat which helped capture Doctor Crippen four years earlier. *Eureka*'s Master had furnished the pilot disguise which Inspector Dew used to board *Montrose*. Belanger was returning to the scene of Crippen's capture under equally dramatic circumstances but with hundreds of lives at stake. He didn't pause to hang up the phone. McWilliams could hear Captain Belanger shouting orders to his crew as the receiver swung back and forth 'Cut those lines; let's get away quick; the *Empress* is sinking!' The time was 2:30am.

McWilliams telephoned a piece of critical information to the *Lady Evelyn*. He advised Captain Pouliot that the *Empress* was east of Father Point. The *Evelyn* was still getting up steam and assembling crew. She didn't leave the pier at Rimouski until 2:45am.

Chief Steward Gaade and Purser McDonald were the last of those who made a pilgrimage to the Bridge hoping to hear that emergency measures were taking hold. They had just arrived from their muster station at Lifeboat 1. The boat was launched but not without great difficulty. Amplified by the list, she finally swung free of the Boat Deck, taking six to eight men with her. A couple of men dangled from Lifeboat 1's lifelines until the boat with legs reached water. Assistant stewards threw deck chairs and life rings to those who fell overboard. Their shipmates adequately covered, they began to unfasten additional deck chairs and throw them over the side indiscriminately.

The *Empress of Ireland*'s lifeboats were on radial-style davits. Launching from that configuration was no easy task under the best of circumstances. It required a lot of team work. Two men were required to jump in, ship the rudder, and clear the falls. Two men on deck controlled fore-and-aft lines for lowering. Four to six men provided the muscle which was used to clear away the boat. The aft end would be pushed out first and the aft davit swung out followed by the same procedure forward. Lifeboat drills demonstrated that this could be accomplished quickly. Of course, that was when the ship was level and with a fully manned team used to working together.

The consequences of a hasty launch by an unfamiliar team were quickly realized. One end of a lifeboat fell spilling its passengers into the water. This horrific scene was witnessed by first-class passenger Fergus J. Duncan, a solicitor in the London firm of Kimber, Bull, and Duncan.

Officer Moore was working to free Lifeboat 13 with Boatswain Radley. Chief Second-class Steward Thomas Williams jumped in to free a twisted line. Once clear, Lifeboat 13 swung out suddenly dropping Williams flat on his back. The boat was lowered with Williams safely inside. The idea was to get the boats out as fast as possible and fill them from the water.

Captain Kendall, Purser McDonald, and the Chief Steward must have appeared a peculiar trio on the Bridge as they fought to remain level against the 30-degree list. Gaade asked Kendall if there was any chance of running the *Empress* ashore. 'No,' replied the exhausted Master, 'The steam is shut off.'

A composed Gaade made the inevitable observation 'Well, this looks to be about the finish.'

Captain Kendall, no longer able to punctuate, hoarse from yelling through his megaphone, exhaled the final words of his command 'Yes, and a terrible finish it is too.'

The *Empress*'s normally vertical surfaces continued a clockwise approach to horizontal. Passengers scratched and crawled over whatever blocked their climb to the port rail. Some braced themselves against the exterior wall of Upper Promenade cabins.

Such was the venue for the end of the Irvings. Many passengers later claimed to see the Irvings' final moments but Frederick Abbott's account is the most reliable. He remembers seeing Irving kiss his wife. Perhaps the couple considered Laurence's prophetic last lines from 'Typhoon': 'What is death? Death is nothing but the passing to another life.' Mabel remained clasped around Irving. Abbott jumped over the side.

During the struggle to stay high and dry, there were far more acts of bravery than of cowardice. A common act of heroism was to give up one's life belt to a needy passenger. The most celebrated of these life preserving transfers was Sir Henry Seton-Karr's to Merton Darling. Yet there were many others.

Mr and Mrs Delamont and daughter 'Lizzie' managed to stay together in the climb from below decks to the port rail. Leonard was close behind and soon climbed up the slanting deck to join his family. Their other son, Arthur was separated from the family but reached Boat Deck on his own. Leonard was one of the uncelebrated givers of life. His mother failed to bring her life belt. Leonard took off his and wrapped it around his mother. Anticipating her refusal to accept his life belt, Leonard cut short a potential family squabble. He kissed his mother goodbye and jumped into the water. Mrs Delamont let go with an agonizing scream unique to mothers who have lost children. It was heard above all the rest.

Salvation Army Bandsman Ken McIntyre gave up his life belt to Mrs Ernest Foord of Toronto. 'I'm a good swimmer,' he remarked as he dressed the woman with his canvas preserver. He finished tying the life belt straps as the ship heeled over yet again. Mrs Foord lost her grip, shrieked, and fell 65 feet to starboard. She couldn't be seen in the darkness across the deck. Nothing further was heard from her after the fall. Many women were lost in this manner. Hands grew weak, fingers stretched to the end of their grip, and then an excruciating scream to announce release and its fatal consequences. Sometimes a splash was heard.

Smoking Room Steward Tom Gerrard offered his life belt to first-class passenger George Henderson. The offer was subject to a prerequisite. 'Are you married?' asked Tom. Henderson replied in the affirmative. 'Then you'll need this more than I do,' Tom said, as he handed over his life belt.

Mrs Cook slid across the deck and caught hold of a line. She was half-suspended just above the starboard rail. She could see a lifeboat not far from her. She shimmied down to the starboard rail and then got underneath it. In spiderlike fashion, she crawled upside down until almost directly over the lifeboat. Then she let go and fell in the water. She was immediately seized by frantic persons struggling to stay afloat. They dragged her down. Somehow she freed herself from the frenzy. Mrs Cook was then rescued by the lifeboat she intended to reach. They hauled her out of the water by her hair.

Marconi Operator Ferguson thought he could quell the tide of irrational jumpers. He told those desperate souls that he had radioed for assistance — help was on the way. But many feared the dreaded suction always thought to be associated with the loss of a big ship. Ferguson's calming influence was brief. He lost his hand hold and slid rapidly across the sheer deck.

The *Storstad* had been sitting at 'ALL STOP' and drifting southwest toward Father Point. Captain Andersen thought it would be prudent to get closer to shore just in case there was some unseen loss of watertight integrity. He had an entire load of coal at risk. He ordered 'SLOW AHEAD' and port helm. The head of the ship started a starboard swing toward Cock Point.

The phantom fog, having done its damage, moved on. The lights of the *Storstad* were now visible less than a mile away. Lionel Kent knew it was the vessel which collided with the *Empress* because he recognized her from just after the collision when she was only 50 feet away. A few passengers made the sign of the cross and mouthed 'God bless you,' thinking the *Storstad* was a rescue ship. Salvation Army Major Frank Morris shouted 'Help!' He was joined by others who together started to yell 'Help, Help, Help!' People started to jump for it rather than be taken involuntarily like Bandsman Foord's wife.

One by one, *Storstad's* Bridge watch became aware of an indistinguishable, distant noise. Mrs Andersen's intuition wiped all traces of melancholy from her face. She feared the worst. Her face became stark white with horror. Captain Andersen went forward and listened with Ludwig Fremmerlid from the bow. Off to port, Andersen heard 'cries, like one sound.' He reversed his helm and continued at slow speed. The moaning became louder first; and then more recognizable as individuals begging for help. Andersen vaguely discerned the hull of the *Empress*. She was 700 feet away, pointing away from shore, and hopelessly turning over on her starboard beam.

Mrs Paton completed her descent from the Bridge. When she stepped back on to the Upper Promenade Deck, she slipped and rolled right into Lifeboat 1. She never touched the water. An able-bodied seaman named Fitzpatrick, part of Lifeboat 1's launch detail, was already in the boat.

Louis Gosselin was also spared contact with the frigid St Lawrence. A collapsible lifeboat, possibly a Berthon raft, crashed down next to him at the starboard rail and started to float. He climbed aboard with only the slightest effort and never got wet. Ferguson didn't have the luxury of his own collapsible. He used a deck chair to stay afloat.

Assistant Steward J. McSherry witnessed the last moments of Chief Officer Mansfield Steede's life. Steede braced himself against one of the ventilators. He was removing his boots in preparation for the final plunge. His white combination cap fell off and lodged against a skylight. McSherry retrieved it with great difficulty in a last gesture of deference. Steede thanked McSherry and said 'Look out for yourself.' Then, the violent lurch which undermined the footing of Mrs Paton, Mr Gosselin, and so many others also took Steede. A runaway cargo boom slammed into the Chief Officer killing him instantly. McSherry was flung into the water.

Captain Andersen wasted no time. The emergency signal (rapid short blasts) was sounded on *Storstad's* whistle. He ordered a backing bell and sent Chief Officer Toftenes aft. Third Officer Saxe was told to get all lifeboats swung out and ready for lowering. The *Storstad* turned until her stern faced the port quarter of the wreck. She continued backing until Toftenes shouted 'Don't go any closer.'

Captain Kendall said he was thrown into the water from the port wing of the Bridge. Some reports say that the Captain leaped into the water rather than be taken down on the Bridge. Captain Kendall's own statements reveal that he was in the water before his command went under. Kendall witnessed the ship take her final lurch. The *Empress* rotated to starboard until both funnels struck the water simultaneously. The forward funnel missed Lifeboat 1 by inches. Fitzpatrick and another seaman rowed ferociously to escape the whirlpool of water being sucked down the gargantuan stack. Second Officer Williams disappeared down the barrel of the funnel. The oarsmen on Lifeboat 1 were so focused on pulling away they didn't see the Marconi wires in their path that ran from mast to mast. The lifeboat became imprisoned in the web cast by the death throes of its mothership. Cool heads prevailed. To escape, the oarsmen reversed direction and then dragged the wires over the prow. The freed boat pulled in the direction of the *Storstad*.

Quartermaster Murphy and the officers at Lifeboat 13 were successful. The boat was floating freely. Murphy was floating freely as well after leaping from the rolling ship. He surfaced next to capsized Lifeboat 15.

First-class Steward Jim Prowse was tossed into the water when the ship rolled to starboard. He instinctively swam away as fast as he could but didn't seem to be making much progress. He looked over his shoulder and saw a torrent of small debris getting sucked down a ventilator. Prowse was swallowed by the metal monster all the way up to his torso. He began to inhale more water than air.

The lifeboat which dumped its passengers floated with its forepart still attached to the ship. Menacing davits hovered over the boat ready to snare it on the way down. An able-bodied seaman cried out for an axe. Another man arrived and severed the line with three strokes. He went on to free another lifeboat floating but still hooked to the davits. Mr and Mrs Black jumped — correctly thinking there wouldn't be a better time to catch a lifeboat. A seaman in one of the freed boats pulled Mrs Black inside. Mr Black held on to one of the lifelines. A half-minute later, there was an explosion.

Many passengers were thrown away from the ship by the blast. Salvation Army Major Frank Morris was 50 yards from the ship when he heard a muffled detonation. Clayton Burt described it as a 'loud rumbling noise inside.' 'She began to explode through the portholes,' Morris recalled. A geyser of water was hurled 50 feet in the air. Skylights were shattered. The force of the blast also shot out of the ventilators. That was lucky for Jim Prowse who was blown clear. The explosion was followed by the sound of steam escaping. People assumed the boilers were blowing-up. Scores of people started jumping off the hull.

Newlywed Mrs Thomas Greenaway was 'stunned' by the explosion. She lost consciousness. The next thing she remembered was floating on a deck chair. She was badly bruised and burned. Her ankles were lacerated. Husband Tom was in a different location adrift on a table leg.

Passenger Philip Lawlor of Brantford, Ontario, said the explosion rocked the vessel. 'The shock of the explosion was something fearful,' he recalled. 'People were simply shot out of the ship into the sea.' Lawlor's wife slipped from his grip, splashed into the water, and sank.

Alfred Keith was forced under by the explosion. Water temperature erased all feeling in his arms and legs. He was about to pass out when his head struck part of a mast or derrick. He forced himself up on to the object. Keith's arms dangled over the cylindrical shape keeping his head and shoulders above water. Gracie Hanagan and her father were thrown from the ship. When she surfaced she found a piece of wood to keep her up. Her face was bruised and scratched from banging into wreckage. She held on tight until she saw a man looking over the prow of a lifeboat. Gracie called for her rescue 'Pull me in, Pull me in!'

Eight-year-old Helen O'Hara was 'very glad' that she took swimming lessons at school. She and her father jumped with Helen's arms loosely locked around his neck. They separated before hitting the water. Helen remembered the cold instantly penetrating to her bones. She swam to a lifeboat and held on to a man at the lifeline. Then she climbed over his shoulders into the boat. Her father was never seen again. Mrs O'Hara was later discovered floating on wreckage.

Alice Bales wanted to avoid sliding into the 'maelstrom of water and falling bodies'. She had been clinging to one of the ventilators but climbed over the port rail just prior to the explosion. The reluctant young woman decided it was preferable to jump even though she didn't know how to swim. Alice tied a life belt around her waist. She looked for a hole in the struggling humanity, took a deep breath, and jumped out striving to get as far away as possible. She thought she was jumping to her death.

Passengers Bert Greenaway, John Black, Grace Kohl, and Assistant Steward Percy Gee witnessed a catastrophic tableau amid the backdrop of the liner's demise. Forty or more people, possibly including many of the first-class women, thought themselves safely away in a lifeboat. Mr Black remembered the lifeboat being quite full and somewhat astern of amidships. Unfortunately for its occupants it was in the wrong place when the *Empress* rolled. Black closed his eyes as the ship crashed down. Greenaway and Percy Gee, occupants in the boat, jumped to safety. When Black opened his eyes, the lifeboat and all aboard were gone, squashed by falling objects, perhaps struck by the aft funnel. What was left was beyond recognition.

Doctor Grant recovered from his tumble out of bed. He fought off the disorientation of total darkness and the flip-flop of decks and bulkheads. The Doctor's first thought was to turn on the lights. The brass toggle switch wasn't recessed so it was easy to find next to the cabin door. Grant switched it on and off a couple of times verifying the loss of power. Further groping landed his fingers on the bolt to the cabin door. It was extremely difficult to open against gravity and due to subtle contortions in a door frame designed to remain vertical. The Doctor managed to force the door open and slip out into the passageway. He was motivated to act quickly by the sound of rushing water and screams of trapped passengers.

It was physically impossible to try and climb to a higher deck. Besides, reaching the open decks at that point brought one closer to death if the ship capsized. Grant's only chance was to find an exit from the deck he was on. He grabbed at every possible leverage point using fingers and toes to propel his body up to the port side. He clutched to a carpet which gave him a big boost but it broke free. He lost a few feet of progress and precious seconds. Miraculously, the tenacious young doctor reached an alleyway porthole.

Doctor Grant stuck his head out of the porthole. He was astonished to see hundreds of people sitting, standing, and walking on the port side. Hupmobile salesman Charles R. Clark, in promenade along the riveted plating, paused to tie his shoes! Grant put both his arms through the porthole and quickly discovered that he couldn't clear both shoulders. He yelled for someone to pull him out.

An unidentified man came to his assistance. Grant tucked in his left shoulder and let his left arm fall flat against him. The stranger pulled the right arm and shoulder out first. He struggled to get the Doctor's left shoulder clear and then grabbed underneath both shoulders to extirpate the rest of the body. Grant's shoulders and hips were deeply lacerated but it was a small price to pay for escape from a sinking hull.

There was at least one other passenger who escaped through a porthole. Miss Alise Lee had escorted Mrs Hart-Bennett up to the port-side rail. Neither woman brought her life belt. A sailor was handing out life belts and gave his last one to Mrs Hart-Bennett. Alise asked the sailor if there was time to go to her cabin and retrieve a preserver. The sailor told her yes, if she hurried. Alise located her life belt but not before finding herself trapped in the cabin. She managed to squeeze out of a porthole and then wasted no time escaping. To prevent being trapped again by the sinking hull, she ran down the side of the ship and jumped. She never saw her family friend, Mrs Hart-Bennett, alive again.

Tiria Townshend, Charles Clark, and many passengers walked over portholes toward the bottom of the hull. The portion of the hull which used to be below the waterline was extremely slippery. Tiria managed to climb over the bilge keel and jump. Others rolled over and slid into the murky foam. Ernie Pugmire slipped and cracked his back on rivet after rivet until catapulted up the bilge keel and out over the water.

Helena Hollies and another stewardess named Agnes Ethel Dinwoodie stood together working up their courage to make a go of it. Helena was already freezing. Miss Dinwoodie was warm in the two overcoats she managed to put on before leaving the stewardess's cabin. The pair clasped hands and jumped in.

Mr William Hunt's nonconformity seemed to be paying off. No one was within 50 feet of him at the extreme stern of the vessel. He could gaze down at the bow which was settling first. He remembered seeing passengers huddled together 'like ants' sliding into blackness. A multitude of voices in agony swallowed each other to form one pitiful inhuman howl. Mr Hunt could not hear it. The sound of the stern rearing up and water draining off the port propeller blocked the outcry. His fate only seconds away, Mr Hunt waited until the stern rose four feet out of the water. He threw himself in.

Unknown to Mr Hunt, David McAmmond also went to the stern. He was preparing to step off the taffrail as the vessel lowered him to the water. No jumping would be required. McAmmond seemed to be restaging Charles Joughin's famous exit from *Titanic*. It was a clumsy recreation not true to the original. McAmmond ended up clutching a perpendicular support and dangling over the stern until lowered to the water. Unlike *Titanic*'s Chief Baker who kept his head above water, McAmmond was taken under by suction and then returned to the surface.

Bert Greenaway saw the bow duck under the waves and the stern rise for the final plunge. He remembered the *Empress* 'gave a hiss and a gurgle before sinking.' Clayton Burt and Tiria Townshend watched in awe as the port propeller hung over the water.

Reverend Wallet placed himself in God's hands. Like newlyweds Reginald and Mrs Simmonds, and many others, he sat on the hull plates and waited for the ship to settle beneath him. Mr and Mrs Simmonds embraced. They were terror stricken since neither knew how to swim. In another location, Salvation Army Captain and Mrs Edward Dodd also embraced. Nearby, a stoker sat with his head between his knees praying out loud. Reverend Wallet thought the whole affair surreal. To him, the ship was stationary and the sea rising to take her.

The water parted the length of the ship to make way for the disappearing *Empress*. She sank without completely rolling over — funnels horizontal. The large surface area on the port side of the hull sucked down the parted fluid.

Captain Kendall fought off a wave, perhaps caused by the explosion, which temporarily submerged him. When he surfaced he saw a 600-foot-long furrow where his ship used to be. The gap was immediately filled in by two waves meeting in what Kendall described as 'a long line.' The *Empress of Ireland* was gone. She no longer belonged to him.

A wave of displaced water twenty feet high engulfed Reverend Wallet. He was vigorously treading water while submerged thinking he would never regain the surface. He realized he was coming up when he encountered many pairs of legs kicking madly. He fought his way through. When air finally caressed his wet face it was cold but delicious.

Many lifeboats were successfully deployed by the *Empress* herself. Mr Bernard Weinrauch, from Montreal, climbed aboard a lifeboat near the stern which had toppled down from the port side. It was still tied to the blocks. One man tried biting through the ropes. Two others beat wildly against the lines with oars. Weinrauch thought it meant death for everyone in the boat. 'The *Empress* did us a good turn at the end,' he said, 'instead of drawing us under — she cut the ropes.' The freed lifeboats rode high on the last wave of water to be formed by the hull of the *Empress*.

Mrs Gattrell squeezed into the child's life belt and gently went down with the ship. Before going down, she had given away one youth life belt to a needy mother. The other was snatched out of her hands by a 'foreigner'. Gattrell soon emerged at the top of a wave and clung to some wreckage. It kept her afloat until an oar was extended to her from one of the *Empress*'s lifeboats. Another woman nearby saw this and pleaded: 'Oh Jesus, oh Jesus, save me!' Both were hauled in and seated next to a dead woman. Mr Gattrell went down and never came up.

People swept under by the suction started to pop up all over the wreck site. Corpses bobbed up and down next to those still struggling to stay afloat. Mrs Simmonds surfaced amid wreckage and dead bodies. 'Their faces were awful,' she said, 'it was the most horrible part of it all.' Some of the living used the dead for flotation. Ernest Green, who shared Cabin 587 with Bert Greenaway, was about to succumb to exhaustion when he caught the wrist of Costa Buhler, a Regina passenger. Buhler was floating face down with two life belts on. Green relied on the corpse for buoyancy.

All four remaining members of the Delamont family survived the sinking. Someone without a life belt grabbed Elizabeth by the hair. Mrs Delamont heard her daughter's cries and proceeded to rescue Elizabeth from the dying man's clutches. Elizabeth lost most of her hair during the struggle. Not far away, Mr Delamont used a piece of wreckage for support.

After the *Empress* was gone, survivors remembered darkness lifting as in an early dawn. Perhaps the premature 'dawn' people remember was the green glow of life rings. It was best described by Seaman Price:

The only light came from the flare of some of the automatic life buoys which got free when the ship sank. They made a sort of creepy light over it all. It was like bugs on a pool.

Tiria Townshend came up alongside three men huddled together wearing life belts. She tried to put her hands on their shoulders for support but they pushed her down. She swam a bit underwater to clear and surfaced next to Clayton Burt who was wearing his life belt. Burt helped Townshend get out of an overcoat which was weighing her down and sapping her strength. The pair grabbed for a suitcase which happened by but the wake from their motion pushed it farther away. Tiria, more mobile without a life belt, took a deep breath and swam under the uncooperative luggage. She surfaced and jumped on the case. The two shared it for flotation as they kicked and paddled to the *Storstad*.

HOW THE EMPRESS IRELAND SANK TO HER D

Alice Bales shivered during her plunge. She put her hands over her nose and jaw to concentrate on not inhaling. She hovered deep in the water until the buoyancy of her life belt reversed her descent. The petite young woman shot right back to the surface. She grabbed hold of a man by the arm. Alice pleaded with him 'Show me how to swim!' He shook her off saying he was exhausted and they would both drown. Alice began to imitate his motions. She started pulling herself toward the *Storstad* and was saved.

Chief Engineer Sampson was pulled under and then rose rapidly to the surface. He emerged directly under a capsized lifeboat, striking his head. Disoriented, he groped around thinking he was trapped by wreckage. He swam underneath and away from the overturned boat.

Staff Captain David McAmmond encountered two lifeboats. McAmmond's recollection was of a dark object floating nearby. It was a collapsible. He climbed up on the keel and was eventually joined by three other survivors. The overturned craft seemed quite unstable as it rocked about. They came upon a second capsized boat. Herman Kruse came to the surface under it and immediately helped McAmmond and the others right it. The canvas cover was still in place. A crew member ripped through the canvas and shipped the oars. The keel riders boarded the second boat and began rescuing passengers.

Mrs Delamont and daughter reached an upturned lifeboat. Elizabeth was very weak. Mrs Delamont's endurance waned as her muscles worked to keep Elizabeth from slipping back into the water. While rocking up and down they heard Mr Delamont trying to hail a lifeboat. Mother and daughter made themselves known and soon three family members were reunited on the upside down craft. Their combined cries to the nearby lifeboat were not answered.

Herman and Freda Kruse were reunited shortly after Freda recognized her father in the neighbouring righted lifeboat. 'There is my father,' she said. 'He is saved.' After the two boats came alongside *Storstad*, a third boat carrying Edith Bach arrived. Mr Bach didn't make it.

Several men scrambled into freely floating Lifeboat 13. Quartermaster Murphy was one of them. Lifeboat 13 took a full load of survivors to the *Storstad*. Miss Alise Lee climbed into a tub of some kind and floated until rescued.

Major Morris was scalded on both arms. The 36 (Fahrenheit) water soothed his pain. The Major tried to save Commissioner Rees. He swam over to the Commissioner and pulled him up on his back. The Commissioner held on for a time but was quite weak and eventually slipped away. Morris dived under in two rescue attempts. The Commissioner vanished beneath him.

Stewardess Ethel Dinwoodie was having difficulty staying afloat. The weight of two saturated overcoats was too much to bear. Helena Hollies tried to pull the coats off but couldn't overcome her fellow stewardesses' panic. Miss Dinwoodie gave in to exhaustion. The last sight of Ethel was her face plopping beneath the surface.

Acts of cowardice, self-preservation, and panic occurred repeatedly in the water. John Fowler was surrounded by 'cold, clammy bodies' all fighting for themselves. A large man grabbed Mr Fowler and used him as a personal flotation device. Fowler engaged the man in combat. He had no choice if he wanted to live. Although handicapped by his underwater exposure, Fowler escaped when the frantic man tore off Fowler's life belt.

First-class passenger Robert Cunningham, originally from Edinburgh, Scotland, had a similar experience. He was pulled underwater by the ankle. Someone was using him as a human ladder to claw his way back to the surface. Mr Cunningham was unable to break free. Unexpectedly, the offender's death clutch went limp. Cunningham pulled himself free as the victim sank beneath him.

Salvation Army Bandsman Jim Johnson struggled to reach a lifeboat which had a handful of occupants. As he approached he was warned off. A man in the boat swung at Johnson using an oar like a fly swatter. Fortunately, the man missed. The oar slapped the water. Johnson backed away but pleaded his case arguing that there was plenty of room for one more. He was reluctantly taken aboard.

The *Storstad* lowered three boats plus the Captain's gig. Saxe took charge of the gig and drove his men relentlessly to save lives. On his first trip he dangerously overfilled the gig. There was 'no freeboard left', Saxe recalled, when a woman was found. Exhausted, she had completed half the distance to the *Storstad*. Saxe ignored the protests of others and began to haul her aboard. The boat dipped, people shifted their weight, and imminent capsize was averted.

Captain Kendall and Bellboy Charles Spencer were at opposite ends of the maritime pecking order while afloat. Now both men found themselves on equal footing. They surfaced next to each other, both struggling to keep their heads above water. Kendall encouraged Spencer to stay with it. The pair sought a wooden grating to cling to. Twenty minutes later, Lifeboat 3 happened by with a number of survivors already aboard including Assistant Purser Hayes. 'It's the Captain,' Hayes shouted, 'let's save him.' Kendall and Spencer were pulled into the boat. Kendall took charge of his new command.

Captain Kendall filled Lifeboat 3 with sixty people. He continued the search until his lifelines were fully occupied by frozen arms and clenched fists. Kendall headed for the ship which rammed him passing two of her outbound boats. One of the outbound. boats had three passengers piled across the thwarts. Several *Empress* lifeboats had already reached the *Storstad* and were off-loading survivors. Lifeboat 3 joined them. Kendall ordered Spencer to remain on *Storstad* as he called for able-bodied men to man his boat. Six men joined Captain Kendall to continue the rescue. Sails and provisions were tossed over the side to maximize the capacity of the lifeboat.

When the siren had sounded just after collision, 'Billy Boy' Hughes grabbed his 'monkey' jacket from the bulkhead hook and ran to his boat station in his pyjamas. He had done everything possible to get the boats out under the heroic direction of Chief Officer Steede but now found himself struggling in the water next to fellow stewards John Brown, Billy Hadfield, and Tom Gerrard. Brown, not in the best of health to begin with, was succumbing to exhaustion quickly. Someone called out: 'Take me with you, Billy Boy.' Hughes replied: 'I haven't the strength.' Hughes continued to make strokes toward the distant *Storstad*. He paused and turned to say goodbye to his shipmates using his trademark farewell expression: 'God love you, all.'

The price of 'Billy Boy' Hughes' admission to a lifeboat may have been another man's life. Like Jim Johnson, Hughes was turned away from a lifeboat — but not with an oar. As Hughes attempted to climb aboard a lifeboat, a selfish man already safely inside grabbed him under the jaw and pushed him under the water yelling 'There's no room!' The boat's officer was enraged by the passenger's attempt to play God. 'I'm in charge of this boat, the officer said standing face to face with the offender. 'There's no more room!' shouted the man followed by some venomous expletive. The officer would have none of that behaviour from those in his charge. He knocked the man overboard after pronouncing a sentence of death upon him. The officer then extended an oar to 'Billy Boy' who rapidly pulled himself up and over the gunwale. The passenger summarily discharged was heard to make a few splashing sounds before disappearing in the dark. Assistant Steward Brown was rescued shortly thereafter.

Lifeboat 5 carried a survivor who is better known posthumously than he was during his lifetime. He was an Irish fireman named William Clarke. His notoriety is not based on ships sailed but rather on ships that went to the bottom. Clarke was one of the men ordered out of the stokehold just after collision. Two years earlier, Clarke escaped from *Titanic*'s stokehold. Reporters sought out the lucky Irishman to compare the two disasters. Waiting around for the end was the hard part on *Titanic*, he said. 'There was no waiting with the *Empress*... she rolled over like a hog in a ditch'.

First Officer Jones was working to free Lifeboat 7 when the *Empress* rolled over. Jones was thrown clear and began treading water. Seaman John McEwen successfully launched Lifeboat 9. An unknown male passenger jumped in as the boat was swung out. McEwen took charge of Lifeboat 9 and rescued many people including First Officer Jones. Jones took over and filled Lifeboat 9 until she was riding on the gunwales. The fearfully overloaded craft rowed to the *Storstad*. Across the wreck site, cries for help diminished. A moan was audible here and there. Those without life belts were sinking — the sound of their submergence imperceptible.

Several people demonstrated astonishing endurance. Among them were Ernie Pugmire, Ken McIntyre, and James Rankin who swam all the way to the *Storstad*. McIntyre swam most of it on his back. Rankin was insulated by the coating of salve he smeared on at bedtime. More remarkable was the performance of the history professor from San Francisco. Gordon Davidson swam to shore, a distance of at least three and a half miles, with his life belt on. This was an incredible feat even with the current in his favour.

Captain Andersen saw people swimming up to the stern of *Storstad*. He alerted his deck crew. The *Storstad's* boats made two rescue trips each. The gig made three trips. *Storstad's* crew also manned one of the *Empress* collapsibles.

The *Lady Evelyn* and *Eureka* steamed ahead from Rimouski and Father Point respectively. Both vessels raced to the scene at full throttle encountering fog along the way. Neither Captain slowed; putting more lives at risk. The *Eureka* arrived first sometime after 3:00am. Seaman Price, Chief Steward Gaade, a man, and two women were rescued from a collapsible. In a period of less than eight months, Price had been both hero and victim of disaster at sea.

The *Lady Evelyn* steamed into the vast field of dead bodies and flotsam at 3:45am. She almost added to the death toll as she approached the scene. One of the *Empress*'s lifeboats suddenly took shape directly across *Lady Evelyn*'s bow. It must have seemed to Captain Pouliot like an apparition out of a sea story. A collision was narrowly avoided. As his propeller wash and engine noise subsided, Pouliot could hear a man on the lifeboat yelling. It wasn't an editorial comment about his seamanship. The man in the lifeboat was pleading 'For God's sake, hurry; there are thousands dying ahead!' She launched her two tenders immediately. One of the first survivors discovered was Ernest Green. He was still floating on his deceased human raft.

Lifeboat 13 off-loaded at *Storstad* and returned to the wreck site. Thirty more were rescued and transferred to *Eureka*. The lifeboat was then cast adrift.

One of the increasing number of lifeboats on the scene discovered Mrs Greenaway floating aimlessly by on her deck chair. Her rescuers thought she was dead. Mrs Greenaway was a gruesome sight. From head to waist she was bruised and covered in soot. Her bottom half was burned and bleeding. Magnus Luren, standing tall in the lifeboat, poked at her with an oar asking 'Are you alive?' All she could summon in response was a moan. After she was transferred from deck chair to boat, Mr Luren consoled her 'Don't be afraid little girl, my wife's gone.' Mrs Greenaway answered 'I've lost my husband.'

The Delamonts were rescued and later transferred to the *Lady Evelyn*. Son, Arthur, was among those safely recovered. Leonard, who gave up his life belt to save his mother, was never seen again.

Charles Clark wished he had not stopped to tie his boots before the plunge. The extra weight was almost his undoing. He managed to surface only to be struck about the head and shoulders by wreckage. Bruised but conscious, Clark scrambled on to a piece of timber. One of *Storstad's* boats rescued him. Clark remembered hauling in a woman whose legs were crushed.

Reverend Wallet swam for a lifeboat. He was within inches of grabbing a lifeline when the boat aggressively pulled away. Another boat, the one Clark was in, came along and pulled Wallet in. Wallet's fingers were too numb to grasp the gunwale. The moment his life preserver broke the plane of the surface he felt the magnitude of his soaked weight. The crew put him in the forward part of the boat where he sat panting.

Alfred Keith was weak but able to cry out. He saw the lifeboat carrying Wallet and Clark. Keith sang out 'Help, me!' several times. *Storstad's* crew pulled him in.

Shortly after recovering Keith, Wallet and Clark, the same lifeboat picked up a foreign national who was stark raving mad. They thought the man's panic would subside after being rescued but he continued to jeopardize the boat with frantic behaviour. Once alongside *Storstad*, the man grabbed a line needed to secure the boat and refused to release it. He started to climb up the side of the collier. A crew member cut the rope just above the man's head and he fell back into the lifeboat. The man's continued panic threatened to capsize the boat. A sailor struck the madman on the head with an oar. He was hoisted aboard where he regained consciousness three hours later.

McWilliams had been watching the rescue operation through a telescope mounted in a second story window. He could see the *Storstad*, both rescue vessels, and counted 9 lifeboats. The *Eureka* returned to Father Point. Captain Belanger called for a doctor from among locals who had gathered at the wharf. McWilliams boarded to help the victims. No doctor was available, so *Eureka* immediately left for Rimouski. McWilliams observed the poignancy of the tragedy. Half-naked survivors stumbled over badly bruised bodies stretched out in eternal sleep.

Captain Kendall worked very hard to recover survivors. As Lifeboat 3 came upon victim after victim, a boathook was used to check for signs of life. Captain Kendall saw an *Empress* lifeboat way off in the distance. He ordered his crew to pull for it. It took a long time to close on it. Kendall was disappointed to find it empty and half smashed. By 4:00am only corpses could be found. They floated about peacefully; abiding by the whims of the current and changing tide. The early morning silence of the St Lawrence returned.

The first rescued passenger to come aboard *Storstad* was a Salvation Army woman. She was dressed in night clothes and a corset. She ran to Mrs Andersen and hugged her saying 'God bless you, angel.' The next passenger was carried aboard prostrate and set down where the Captain's wife could attend to her. Mrs Andersen began rubbing the woman's legs after attempting to feed her some whiskey. Mrs Paton came along next. Andersen's wife noticed that she was not soaking wet and wore 'lots of diamonds'. Mrs Andersen, still working on the numb woman's legs, asked Mrs Paton how she managed to escape with all her jewellery. 'I had lots of time,' said Paton.

One of the rescue ships: the Rimouski based Lady Evelyn. *The* Lady Evelyn *is loaded with mail sacks from an inbound liner.*

(National Archives of Canada).

The crew of Lifeboat 3 could do no more. Kendall climbed aboard *Storstad* and immediately checked on the condition of his passengers and crew. He may have been searching for fellow officers. Kendall confronted Andersen on the Bridge 'Are you the Captain of this ship?' Andersen nodded, said yes, and gazed up at the taller Kendall. Kendall started the expected argument with the declaration 'You have sunk my ship!'

He continued with accusation 'You were going full speed and in dense fog.' Andersen countered 'I was not going full speed, you were going full speed.' The pilot, who boarded *Storstad* for her inbound transit, separated the two Captains before the controversy escalated. The pilot cautioned Kendall 'Do not say anything; you had better go below.' Kendall went into *Storstad's* chartroom and collapsed.

Captain Andersen, his wife, and crew pulled every imaginable article of clothing out of their closets and lockers to dress the survivors. Some were naked. Most were wearing undergarments or night dresses. Mrs Andersen handed a scarf to Marconi Operator Ronald Ferguson. He instinctively wrapped it around his neck even though his groin was uncovered. Someone advised Ferguson of his error. He quickly reapplied the scarf where the need was greatest.

Bert Greenaway helped pull Alfred Keith up the rope ladder to *Storstad's* deck. Keith lost his trousers and was blue from head to toe. Another Salvationist rubbed his skin to stimulate his circulation. Keith's teeth chattered as he was escorted to Captain's Andersen's cabin. Several other survivors were already there including Doctor Grant. Someone grabbed the embroidered green cover from *Storstad's* wardroom table and used it to wrap Keith.

Storstad's Captain walked by a shivering woman. He took off his wool overcoat and covered her. Some women were strong enough to remove their wet nightclothes. Curtains were pulled off the hooks to cover these women. The men had less to work with. One male survivor covered himself with newspaper. Another used a single pillowcase to cover his nakedness. Charles Spencer and the only other surviving Bellboy were given canvas sacks. They cut holes for their neck and arms and slipped the sacks on.

Survivors were rushed below to *Storstad's* engine and boiler rooms. Theophile Bartschi, among them, said: 'There was lots of suffering, and it is the sort of suffering that cannot be described.' First-class passenger Abercrombie found the words. He said the engine room was a ghastly inferno far worst than anyone's imagination of hell. He continued in graphic detail:

> *Men and women literally stood naked about the cylinder heads and firedoors in an effort to get their clothes dried and their bodies warmed. Some of them couldn't stand they were so weak. They were supported by others. Over everything played the fiendish light from the furnace and the greasy lamps. I saw one poor fellow not able to stand by himself held against a cylinder head by two stronger men. They knew only they were trying to revive him and paid no attention to his pitiful struggle to get away from the*

steam-hot steel. Finally, I called to them and they took him away. A great section of flesh had been burned off his back.

Captain Andersen opened a well-stocked liquor locker. Mrs Andersen dispensed 'stimulants' to the frozen victims. She offered nips from two bottles of whiskey and a bottle of Benedictine under one arm and poured hot coffee with the other arm. Salvation Army personnel are teetotallers and a few tasted alcohol for the first and only time in their lives. Dr. Grant was roused with some brandy and collected himself.

Doctor Grant called for some pants and was given a pair of trousers several sizes too big. He tied them up with a belt made from a piece of rope. The Doctor did everything possible to relieve pain and suffering. He resuscitated the lifeless, arrested external bleeding, splinted broken arms and legs, relocated shoulders, treated burn cases, and covered the dead. When a delirious man kept interfering in Grant's treatment of Chief Engineer Sampson, Doctor Grant knocked the unknown man unconscious with a blow to the face. After seeing to the Chief Engineer, Grant encountered Captain Kendall.

Kendall sat with his forehead in his palms. The Doctor found him in a state of 'shock' suffering from exposure. Grant offered the Captain some brandy but Kendall refused. He never touched alcohol of any kind. The two men shook hands. Kendall looked at Grant remorsefully. 'Doctor,' he began with a pause, 'there is only one thing I am sorry for... and that is that they did not let me drown.' Grant would have none of it. 'Don't be foolish,' Grant snapped, 'you have done everything you could have done.'

Doctor Grant was undeniably the hero of the disaster. He had taken charge of the situation aboard *Storstad*. The *Lady Evelyn* came alongside. Grant directed that corpses be transferred first, followed by the injured, ambulatory passengers, and finally members of the crew. Doctor Grant ordered Captain Kendall to lie down. Grant tried to remove his wet clothes but Kendall wanted to be left alone. Two out of three newlywed couples survived: Mr and Mrs Reginald Simmonds and Mr and Mrs Thomas Greenaway. They were all non-swimmers. The Dodds were lost. The Evans family and talented artist Teddy Gray, reported to have taken last minute life insurance, all perished. Sir Henry Seton-Karr and Smoking Room Steward Tom Gerrard gave up their lives with their life belts.

The *Eureka* followed by the *Lady Evelyn* steamed into Rimouski with approximately 400 former *Empress of Ireland* passengers and crew. Thirty bodies were already dead when pulled into lifeboats. An additional twenty-two died from injuries and exposure after rescue. All these corpses were laid side by side on the wharf. One deceased mother was still clutching her baby in her arms. Mrs Greenaway, who thought she lost her husband, wept with joy when the two were reunited on Rimouski's pier. Mrs O'Hara stepped on to the pier grateful for the security of land but feeling empty. She thought she had lost her eight year old. Her head lowered, she aimlessly followed survivors walking to the train station. A little girl was yelling 'Mamma, mamma!' At first, Mrs O'Hara believed the voice was in her head. Then she recognized it as her daughter. The two kept moving through the crowd toward the other's voice until reunited. Helen O'Hara was extremely fortunate. She was one of the four children saved.

SS.Lady Evelyn

Ronald Ferguson, aboard the *Lady Evelyn*, identified himself as the senior Marconi operator from the *Empress*. The *Lady Evelyn* had a new Marconi set but no operator. Ferguson managed to get the new installation up and running. A company man, Ferguson requested payment from survivors who wanted to send messages to relatives. Many of these messages were written on anything the survivor could find including toilet paper. Ferguson's refusal to forward telegrams without prepayment created an uproar. It was all a misunderstanding. CPR sent a message through Captain Walsh, CPR Marine Superintendent, to John McWilliams at Father Point which promised free transmission of all passenger telegrams. Ferguson wasn't promptly informed. He began sending anyway.

The people of Rimouski opened their hearts and their homes to the victims. The Mayor of Rimouski helped Canadian Pacific establish two emergency triage stations. One was at the pier. The other was at the Intercolonial Railway Station. Wagons of clothing and blankets were wheeled by hand to the pier. Hot soup was served. Shop owners donated their inventory to help dress the few surviving women and children. Gracie Hanagan was given a new pair of shoes.

Mr Kruse, his daughter Freda, and Edith Bach were well cared for in Rimouski by Frederick Ryder, the American Consul. He opened his home to all the American survivors, clothed and fed them, helped with transportation arrangements for the deceased, and forwarded messages to relatives throughout the world. Mr Kruse arrived at the American Consul's home wearing only a blanket. He was given some trousers so he could return to the wharf to look for Reinholdt Bach. Kruse did not have to study the lifeless pile for long. Mr Bach was easy to recognize but he wasn't wearing the same garments as when he parted company in the stairwell. He had taken the time to get fully dressed and put on his shoes! On Bach's body was his pocket watch and some money undisturbed. Bach's watch stopped at 1:15am. It was still showing Minnesota time (an hour earlier than Quebec).

Special trains were dispatched to return passengers from Rimouski to Quebec, Montreal, and Toronto. The Quebec Central Railway dispatched a private parlour car to pick up Mrs Ethel Paton at Levis and return her to Sherbrooke.

The 7:00am train from Levis (Quebec) derailed 50 miles west of Rimouski. A large contingent of CPR staff and volunteers were on board. No one was injured. It took over an hour to resume the trip to Rimouski. Little Gracie Hanagan boarded the rescue train under the watchful eye of Ernie Pugmire. She was also looked after by Mrs George Attwell, another survivor. She did not know her parents had drowned and expected them to meet her later. The young orphan advised her handlers 'They'll be here on the next boat, you wait and see.'

The lights on the train flickered, reminding survivors of the horror they had experienced after the lights went out on the *Empress*. Gracie was enjoying the attention of reporters who swarmed aboard for interviews. She was happy to be away from that porthole and the sound of rushing water. A reporter from the Toronto *Daily Star* asked the little girl how she was rescued. 'Oh,' Gracie said rather casually, 'I saved myself.'

7 *Rush to Judgement*

The first word of the sinking to the outside world was transmitted from Father Point by wireless. At 3:00am, all stations were advised that the *Empress of Ireland* and *Hannover* collided. The Marconi operators at Father Point thought the *Hannover* was involved because she failed to respond to their CQ signal. Another bulletin said that rescue steamers *Eureka* and *Lady Evelyn* were on the way.

At 3:40am, Father Point reported no sign of either ship. Lifeboats were reported circling around the *Eureka* (actually the *Storstad*). At 4:00am, Quebec received word that the *Storstad* was the ship which struck the *Empress*. The Toronto *Globe* received a wire at 5:00am which said that the *Empress* had foundered. The newspaper immediately called Staff Captain Arnold at Salvation Army Territorial Headquarters.

Much misinformation was spread during the first twelve hours. The Birmingham *Evening Dispatch* reported all saved repeating the early optimism of New York's *Evening Sun* when reporting *Titanic*'s foundering. Salvation Army Headquarters in Toronto received a telephone call at 11:00am reporting everyone saved. As late as 1:30pm, the Salvation Army posted 'All are Safe' on a tote board at their Temple in Toronto. In less than an hour it read: 'As near as we know 900 are lost'.

In Chicago, at CPR's office on South Clark Street, Richard Fisher was waiting to hear if his mother was rescued. 'I wish I had been on board with my mother, said Fisher, 'I'd have seen that she was saved.' A telephone call came in from the Chicago *Daily News* reporting all passengers saved. Fisher threw his hat in the air and started dancing with a friend shouting 'Hurrah, Hurrah!' William Mounsey, whose wife and mother of nine children was on board, said: 'Thank God for that.'

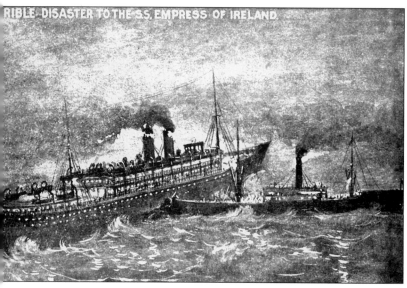

RIBLE DISASTER TO THE S.S. EMPRESS OF IRELAND.

Courtesy 'Les achives Maritimes Armand Therrien'

For a time newspaper reports speculated wildly on all aspects of the story. One story said that smoke from forest fires caused the loss of visibility. Another reported that Captain Kendall was drunk in his cabin at the time of collision. This was a totally inappropriate accusation as Kendall never drank. Kendall was also said to be dying of 'immersion and pneumonia.' The seaworthiness of the *Empress* was also called into question. One account said that the *Empress* was originally ordered from Fairfield by White Star Line but rejected after her sea trials. CPR was said to have purchased the unreliable vessel at a fire sale price.

In Toronto, Mr Mawby began his daily commute to work by train to a factory 18 miles outside the city. The conductor was about to signal 'all aboard' when Mr Mawby asked him to hold one second. Mawby told the conductor he was going to buy the morning paper. 'Better wait and get an extra,' the conductor told him. 'Why?' asked Mawby. 'Because the *Empress of Ireland* has gone down.' The conductor had no idea that Mawby had put his wife and baby daughter on the ship the day before.

Mawby ran to the CPR office. He asked the steamship agent if there was any news of his wife and child. The agent had no specifics; only that 300 or 400 were believed saved. Mawby lost all complexion. The agent tried to be comforting 'Had you friends on board, sir?'

'My wife and baby', Mawby sobbed, 'I guess they would have little chance.' He gave up hope and became reflective 'She was the best little wife in the world. She worked her fingers to the bone making dresses for my little girl.' Mr Mawby's assessment of his family's chances were unfortunately accurate. His wife and baby Katheline, who had just turned two, were lost.

The first rescue train left the Intercolonial Station at Rimouski with 396 survivors. The time was 2:00pm, 12 hours after the sinking. No rail tickets were collected from survivors.

In Montreal, by 7:00pm, Marine Superintendent Walsh walked into Windsor Station with a long list. Here is how Hubert Evans, a reporter for the Toronto *World* described the scene:

> *There is a paper-littered, smoke-filled room in which two weary (CPR) men are sitting. Their faces are haggard and listless, they work as if they had worked without pause for years. About them on the table are dirty coffee cups and remains of sandwiches. Before one of them is a long narrow slip of paper. The other sits at his typewriter. This long paper sheet has several roles. It is a tombstone, an honor roll, a message of hope all in one. It is the official list of passengers aboard the Empress of Ireland when she sank and the list of the saved. Many thousands of persons would give up all their possessions to dispute its verdicts, but from them there is no appeal, save one, and that is to a higher court to which people approach on bent knees and bowed heads. There are no riders to its verdicts; 'saved,' 'lost,' and 'missing' are the only decisions.*

Telegrams were flying back and forth. It was always the same question received at Windsor Station asking who was among the saved. Only the names changed with each new inquiry. The Regina *Morning Leader* cabled to ask about Regina, Saskatchewan, passengers, including Mr A. H. Death. On 30 May, the following reply was received: 'Death, not among survivors'.

Also on 30 May, a telegram was sent to Miss Annie Veronica Williams. It simply read: 'Saved, don't worry. Willie'. It was from 'Billy Boy' Hughes to his fiancée in Liverpool.

CPR offices all over the world were besieged by people who wanted to know if a relative or crew member was saved. Many people made unnecessary inquiries not knowing for sure that their friend or relative had booked on the *Empress*. In London, the anxious, the empathetic, and the curious paced outside CPR's office near Trafalgar Square. The *Daily Mail* introduced the news with the much repeated headline 'ANOTHER *TITANIC* DISASTER'. The Toronto *World* sold 100,000 copies in a special extra with the headline '900 PEOPLE DROWNED AS THEY SLEPT'.

Canadian Pacific's President, Sir Thomas Shaughnessy, immediately exercised damage control. He couldn't believe one of his Atlantic *Empress*es could disappear so quickly. The only suitable explanation would be a giant gash over 300 feet long below the waterline. Early reports incorrectly held that the damage was on the port side. Shaughnessy went before the press at Montreal to offer condolences and reassure the public:

> *From the facts as we have them it is apparent that about 2 o'clock this morning the Empress of Ireland, when stopped in dense fog, was rammed on the port side by the Norwegian collier Storstad in such a manner as to tear the ship from the middle to the screw, thus making the watertight bulkheads, with which she was provided, useless. The vessel settled down in fourteen minutes. The accident occurred at a time when the passengers were in bed, and the interval before the steamship went down was not sufficient to enable the officers to arouse the passengers and get them into the boats, of which there were sufficient to accommodate a very much larger number of people than those on board, including the passengers and crew. That such an accident should be possible in the St Lawrence and to a vessel of the class of the Empress of Ireland, with every possible precaution taken by the owners to insure safety for the passengers and the vessel, is deplorable. The saddest feature of the disaster is, of course, the great loss of life, and the heartfelt sympathy of everybody connected with the company goes out to the relatives and friends of those who met death in the ill-fated steamship.*

The news hit Liverpool in the afternoon on 29 May, beginning with false reports of everyone saved. A woman entered CPR's offices at the Liver Building just as the real story was breaking. She recently lost her husband, a career employee of CPR. She was attending to some matters related to his pension. When she heard that a ship had foundered she immediately demanded to know the name of the ship. 'The *Empress of Ireland*,' someone called out. 'Oh my God,' the woman declared, 'my son is on that ship.' Then she fainted straight away. A stoker's wife, holding her newborn, pleaded with officials 'tell me anything, oh please, tell me anything!'

It did not take long for the woeful truth to spread. The Liver Building was mobbed by relatives and reporters. Never before were so many Liverpool seafarers at risk on a single vessel. No less than 200 families were directly affected. Countless others would lose lifelong friends and acquaintances. The Scotland Road district, home to many stokers, became a neighbourhood of widows and fatherless children.

Mrs Steede went to the CPR office in a very delicate condition having been informed of the sinking but not knowing if her husband was saved. She had a lot on her mind as one of her three children was ill in the hospital. By midnight the crowd increased instead of diminishing. An all-night vigil that would last for three days had begun. As news of specific parties was obtained, a mixture of joy and sorrow could be observed in the great hall. Everyone was tearful. Company officials could be seen offering women a cup of water or administering restoratives. After many anxious hours, the Chief Officer's name was about to be posted on the list of those lost. Mrs Steede was so advised. She collapsed under the strain.

When the rescue train reached Quebec, two ferries were waiting to transport crew (classified as Distressed British Sailors since they were no longer in pay status) and third-class passengers to the Louise Basin. From there, they would board the *Alsatian* which sailed for Liverpool on Thursday, 4 June. The survivors looked pitiful in the assortment of ill-fitting and mismatched garments they were happy to receive at Rimouski. They were too tired and worn out to worry about small matters. As they lined up for the ferry, a Montreal passenger asked onlookers if someone would cash a money order. A couple of Toronto *Globe* reporters gave the man cash and kept the soggy-wet express order as a souvenir of the disaster.

Ken McIntyre also took the ferry across. He went to the Salvation Army emigration station on the wharf. He called New York to tell his father, Colonel McIntyre, that he had survived. The Colonel wanted to know two things: how did he survive and did he still want to go to the International Congress? Ken said he owed his life to his swimming ability and 'Yes!' he wanted to go to London. Arrangements were made to send Ken via New York on White Star's *Baltic*.

First-class passengers and a few from second-class were taken to the Chateau Frontenac along with some of the injured. Among those housed at CPR's expense were Grace Kohl, Tiria Townshend, Alise Lee, F. E. Abbott, Merton Darling, Charles Clark, F. P. Godson, Robert Cunningham, George Henderson, Mr and Mrs Freeman, and Reverend Wallet. Seriously injured passengers were transported to Jeffery Hales Hospital by waiting ambulances.

Jeffery Hales Hospital was the scene of a touching reunion. Newlyweds

Reginald and Mary Simmonds were rescued and transported separately. Each thought the other lost since neither knew how to swim. Mr Simmonds had congestion of the lungs. In another ward, Mrs Simmonds was recovering from shock. She went to her husband's bedside when she learned he was saved. A reporter from the Toronto *Daily Star* interviewed the couple. Mr Simmonds glanced at his wife and said: 'Though we lost everything else, we have each other.'

Many relatives lost more than one family member on the *Empress of Ireland*. In some cases, entire families were wiped out.

Mrs Felstead, who was warned by a little bird; her husband, who refused to make out his will; and their two children were lost. Six members of the Jay family from London, Ontario, were lost. The head of household, Mr John Jay, remained in Canada to work. He waved goodbye to his family for the last time from the pier in Quebec. Mr and Mrs William Forstrom and two children, of Minneapolis, never completed their journey to Norway. All of these family members, with the exception of Mr Felstead, were berthed in third-class. Some may have been trapped below decks as none of the bodies were recovered.

Salvation Army Property Officer, Gideon Miller, first learned of the disaster at 6:00am at Montreal's north end station. He observed the astounding headline of an extra put out by the Montreal *Daily Star* 'EMPRESS OF IRELAND IN COLLISION WITH *STORSTAD* IN GULF OF ST LAWRENCE. ALL HANDS LOST'. Miller and another officer took the night train to Rimouski to assist the living and identify the dead.

An inquest was held, the day after the sinking, by the local coroner in a small Rimouski schoolhouse. A jury was sworn. The coroner's name was Doctor J. Pinault. Captain Kendall, *Eureka*'s Captain Belanger, and Chief Engineer Sampson were among a handful of witnesses called. Sampson gave a statement from his bedside. Kendall was weak and had to be escorted into the proceedings. He was seated next to a window so he could lean on the sill and rest his head against the frame. Noteworthy were Kendall's statements and those of his Chief Engineer. The inquest was conducted in French requiring witnesses to repeat themselves frequently for the benefit of the translator. Kendall said that he first saw the *Storstad* at one ship length away (about 600 feet). He would later testify that the distance was 100 feet. Sampson stated that he left his cabin to go to the engine room when he heard the *Empress* going full astern. He also said that upon entering the engine room, someone told him 'the ship was in danger of being rammed by a big collier.' The jury deliberated for only a moment and moved to continue the inquest in one week.

Gideon Miller attended the inquest. Captain Kendall, seeing the Salvation Army uniform, motioned for Gideon to have a word with him. Kendall asked how many were lost. Gideon explained how he and Lieutenant Colonel Turner examined and counted bodies by lantern light. Over 200 bodies were piled on a heap of coal in a storage shed at the end of the wharf. They found sixteen out of 171 Salvationists. Kendall consoled him with 'We were all keyed up for a happy voyage, little thinking sorrow, death, and disaster were so near.'

The St Lawrence was littered with debris and derelict lifeboats. Air bubbles marked the approximate position of the wreck for several days. The water above the wreck changed colour as machine oil and other fluids leaked out. Specially sworn constables patrolled using automobiles to recover bodies and valuables washed ashore. As many as 14 *Empress* steel boats and collapsibles were recovered and sold for salvage. Two were recovered 25 miles downriver by the steamer *Grampian*. Canadian Pacific made no claim on any of the lifeboats. As with the wreck, it was a matter for the insurance companies. Lifeboat 3, which rescued Captain Kendall, was among those recovered.

The insurance and reinsurance markets fluctuated for a few days. The real concern was not the immediate loss but the viability of the St Lawrence route. The hull and cargo were insured for $2 000 000 and passengers' effects for $10 000. CPR stock dipped a point and a fraction on bad news.

Heads of State from around the world sent messages of sympathy to King George V and Queen Mary. Embassies were directed to make official calls of condolence on behalf of their respective governments. Legislative bodies as far away as New Zealand passed resolutions of grief. President Wilson sent the following:

> *I beg of your Majesty to accept my deepest sympathy in the appalling catastrophe to the steamship* Empress of Ireland *which brought bereavement to so many homes.*

Recovered bodies were gathered in a coal shed on Rimouski's wharf. This image was used on a postcard in remembrance of Empress *victims.*

A special rescue train made up of 8 cars pulled in at Toronto's Union Station in the early evening on Saturday, 30 May. The sleeping car 'Madawaska' had been converted into a hospital. An anxious crowd of 4,000 relatives, business associates, Salvationists, and reporters rushed the platform. Police couldn't handle the crowd and militia were called in to help restore order. The Toronto *Globe* described the madhouse as a re-enactment of *Carpathia*'s arrival in New York using trains. Eatons' and another store opened after-hours to fit survivors with suitable clothing.

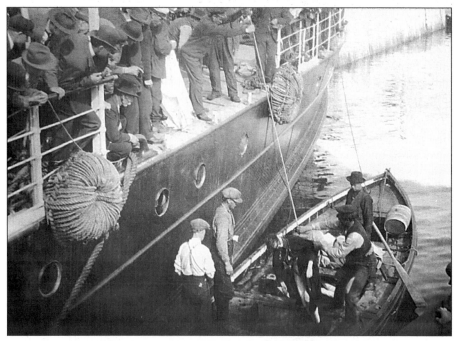

Recovery of the departed by the Lady Evelyn. (Maritime Museum- Pointe-au-Pére).

A total of 188 caskets were loaded aboard *Lady Grey* at Rimouski for the journey to Quebec. The last body loaded was Mr Charles Goldthorpe. Every inch of deck space was needed to accommodate the hastily constructed pine boxes. Some were stacked four deep. Chief Constable McCarthy, the officer who arrested Crippen four years earlier, travelled with the bodies to prevent theft of money and jewellery. HMS *Essex* provided an escort for the 'funeral ship'. The 5:00pm Saturday departure weather was horrendous. Sheets of rain, thunder and lightning pummelled Rimouski. It was so dark that both vessels needed to switch on their interior electric lights. Drenched flags limply streamed at half-mast. The floating cortege arrived early on Sunday, 31 May. HMS *Essex* anchored in the river. She saluted *Lady Grey* as the funeral ship took leave and proceeded slowly into Quebec harbour. It was a bright, cloudless day. Birds could be heard revelling in the morning light. From the moment *Lady Grey* came into view, solemn church bells announced her arrival to this one of many cities in mourning.

Coffins of some of the lost on the deck of the Lady Grey

She tied up at Pier 27 just after 8:00am. A large shed with low ceilings became the temporary morgue. The shed identified the pier with the number '27' painted in tall black letters on two sides. Purple crepe was draped around the entrance and black crepe covered the tables where coffins rested. An Honour Guard of Royal Marines from the *Essex* carried the coffins into the shed. The bearers saluted each victim after laying down the remains. When space ran out on the tables, caskets were placed on the ground. After the adults, a dozen child-size coffins wrapped in white silk were taken to the shed. The caskets of the innocent were so tiny that one Marine carried each child. It took one hour and ten minutes to off-load all the dead. No music was played. All that could be heard were the footsteps of the British Marine Honour Guard.

The story of Emmy the cat comes to mind. She had watched the fateful sailing from atop the shed at Pier 27. Did she take up residence in 27? Was she watching again?

Some bodies were so badly bruised, punctured, scalded, and twisted that identification was impossible. Two parties picked out what they thought were the remains of male relatives. The coroner regretfully advised them to keep searching as they had identified the remains of women. A hopelessly unrecognisable crew member was misidentified as a woman. The Catholic Seamen's Institute kindly took the young man and gave him a decent burial. The pierside shed, now 'Morgue 27,' was the scene of several disputes concerning identification of victims. It is not surprising considering the condition of the bodies.

The temporary morgue at Pier 27

The most well-known dispute involved a 2-year-old infant labelled corpse 118. The baby was first claimed by Mr Frederick W. Cullen, a wealthy buyer from Toronto with the T. Eaton Company. Mrs Cullen, daughter Maudie, and 2-year-old son Albert were travelling to Ireland to escape the summer heat and visit their ancestral roots. They were accompanied by the children's Nanny, Miss Jennie Blythe who had survived the sinking. It was not uncommon for Irish immigrants to spend the summer in the old country. Eight-year-old Fred Cullen stayed in Toronto because he grew tired of summers overseas. Mr Cullen saw his family off in Quebec and immediately began his rail journey back home.

When the train pulled into Montreal Cullen knew something was wrong. Anxiety was high as though war had been declared or a national figure assassinated. Travellers could be heard mumbling: 'It's another *Titanic*'. Newspapers were sold out so Cullen asked what the big news was. He was devastated. An in-law met him at Windsor Station to stand vigil until word of his wife and children was received. The in-law told a reporter: 'I refuse to believe the early reports. Surely help arrived when the boat was out such a short way.'

It soon became apparent that the waiting in Montreal was pointless. Cullen joined the many families travelling to Quebec to try and find their dead. After Mr Cullen pointed out his son Albert to a local minister, he proceeded to look for the bodies of his daughter and wife. While Cullen went from coffin to coffin, a second father, Mr Tracy Harley Archer, came along and insisted that 118 was his son Alfred. Mr Archer, formerly of Regina, Saskatchewan, had also lost his wife on the *Empress*. The minister brought the two fathers together and tried to mediate the affair with the aid of a constable who held up the coffin for closer examination. The child's Nanny readily confirmed the identity of the little bruised body. Ms Blythe checked under the eyelids and opened the mouth. She recognized a tooth which little Albert had been cutting. Archer was not swayed by the Nanny's identification at first. He succeeded in getting the Coroner to register the child as his. Archer was actually torn between the Cullen baby and another corpse labelled 125.

The controversy was finally settled before the Mayor of Quebec. The Mayor granted custody of the remains to Mr Cullen. His decision was based on a comparison of the child's features with those of both deceased mothers. There was no resemblance between the dead baby and Mrs Archer. It is interesting to note that Mrs Cullen, Maudie and Albert were scheduled to sail from Quebec on the Allan Line's *Virginian*. They booked Cabin 18 for the 26 May sailing and retained that booking until the last week in April when it was changed to the *Empress of Ireland*.

Another mortuary dispute involved Tiria Townshend who was searching for the body of her Aunt Wynnie Price. Tiria gazed at the writing on hastily constructed coffins until she found several marked 'femme'. She opened one lid and saw a disfigured form much too short to be her Aunt. Upon opening the next coffin she saw another bruised body roughly fitting her Aunt's description. Several crew members insisted this was the body of Stewardess Lily Leders. William Webber, the travelling CPR Agent, settled the dispute in favor of Miss Townshend when she swore the jewellery on the body belonged to her Aunt.

Reverend Kirkby, Mrs Lyman's father, travelled to Quebec from his home in New York. His daughter and son-in-law were still among the missing. He told relatives 'We are all grieved to the heart, and there is nothing human to console us. I am personally comforted by the knowledge that my daughter, who was noble and self-sacrificing in life, was the same in death.' Reverend Kirkby was referring to his daughter's devotion to the ailing Lyman.

Laurence Irving's body was identified from the initials 'LSI' on his ring. Mabel Hackney's body was not identified. Gideon Miller arranged for rail transportation of his sixteen comrades from Quebec to Toronto. The body of Salvation Army Commissioner David Rees was among those on their final journey. The rest of the Commissioner's family sailing on 28 May went down with the *Empress*.

The *Storstad* arrived in Montreal on Sunday, 31 May, to offload her coal. She was flying the Norwegian flag at half-mast. At 1:47pm, she docked at the Dominion Coal Company wharf where fifty reporters and several government officials were waiting. Solicitors for CPR filed a claim of $2 000 000 against the ship for damages to the *Empress of Ireland*. She was arrested by order of the Quebec Admiralty Court. The Registrar of the Court and an Acting Deputy Sheriff armed with the Writ of Arrest boarded *Storstad* after Captain Andersen held them off for fifty minutes. Captain Andersen asked what authority permitted the men to seize his vessel. 'The authority of the British Empire,' replied the Deputy. The Registrar nailed the document to *Storstad's* chartroom door with his shoe. It read as follows:

The Exchequer Court of Canada, Quebec Admiralty District.
The Canadian Pacific Railway Company against the Steamship Storstad for
damages caused by collision.
George the Fifth, by the grace of God, of the United Kingdom of Great
Britain and Ireland, and of the British dominions beyond the seas, King,
Defender of the faith, Emperor.
To the owners and all others interested in the steamship Storstad:
Action for Two Million Dollars
We command you within one week after the service of this writ,
exclusive of the day of such service, to cause an appearance to be entered
for you in our Exchequer Court of Canada in the above named action and
take notice in default of your doing so that the said action may proceed
and the judgement may be given in your absence.

The Storstad, *her starboard bow crushed and twisted, approaches a*
wharf in Montreal to offload her coal.

The claim prepared by CPR contained seven charges against the *Storstad*. It alleged the following: (1) Failure to maintain course for a starboard-to-starboard passing; (2) Excessive speed and failure to slow and reverse in time; (3) Failure to sound appropriate signals in fog; (4) Bad lookout on watch; (5) Failure to comply with the rules of the road; (6) No competent officers on duty; (7) Improper port order to helm.

The *Storstad's* officers were at a slight initial disadvantage in defending themselves because they had to complete the transit to Montreal before getting down to the business of their defence. This gave the *Empress* and CPR officials a two-day head start which helped fuel a rush to judgement against the *Storstad*. Many newspapers carried stories about how she 'cut the liner down at full speed'. One report described the *Storstad's* bow as the 'assassin's stiletto'. Some accounts said that *Storstad's* crew refused to go to the aid of victims in the water. Others dramatized her arrest in headlines such as '*STORSTAD* IS SEIZED'. Death threats against Captain Andersen forced authorities to provide police protection for several days.

John J. Griffin, one of the solicitors for *Storstad's* owners, said he would fight the seizure of the ship. On 1 June, bond in the amount of $234,000 was posted to release the *Storstad* from arrest. The bond, representing *Storstad's* appraised value, was refused because it fell far short of CPR's claim. On 3 June, a counterclaim was filed in the amount of $50,000 for damages to the *Storstad*. The counterclaim asserted negligent navigation on the part of the *Empress*. Captain Andersen said that the *Empress* had changed course to cross his bow. This constituted a violation of the rules of the road as the *Empress* was the burdened vessel (required to yield) for the *Storstad*.

Captain Andersen and the officers of the *Storstad* issued the following statement when they reached Montreal:

> *The vessels sighted each other when far apart. The Empress of Ireland was seen off the port bow of the Storstad. The Empress of Ireland's green, or starboard light, was visible to those on the Storstad. Under the circumstances, the rules of navigation gave the Storstad the right-of-way. The heading of the Empress was then changed in such a manner as to put the vessels in a position to pass safely. Shortly after a fog enveloped first the Empress and then the Storstad. Fog signals were exchanged, the Storstad's engines were at once slowed and then stopped. Her heading remained unaltered. Whistles from the Empress were heard on the Storstad's port bow and were answered. The Empress of Ireland was then seen through the fog, close at hand on the port bow of the Storstad. She was showing her green light and was making considerable headway. The engines of the Storstad were at once reversed at full speed and her headway was nearly checked when the vessels came together. It has been said that the Storstad should not have backed out of the hole made by the collision. She did not do so. As the vessels came together the Storstad's engines were ordered ahead*

for the purpose of holding her bow against the side of the Empress, and thus preventing the entrance of water into the vessel. The headway of the Empress, however, swung the Storstad around in such a way as to twist the Storstad's bow out of the hole and to bend the bow itself over to port. The Empress at once disappeared in the fog. The Storstad sounded her whistle repeatedly in an effort to locate the Empress of Ireland, but could obtain no indication of her whereabouts until cries were heard. The Storstad was then manoeuvred as close to the Empress as was safe in view of the danger of injury to the persons who were already in the water. The Storstad at once lowered every one of her boats and sent them to save the passengers and crew of the Empress, although she herself was in serious danger of sinking. When two boats from the Empress reached the Storstad, the Storstad's men also manned these boats and went in them to the rescue. Her own boats made several trips and in all about 350 persons were taken on board and everything that the ships stores contained was used for their comfort. Clothes of those on the Storstad were placed at the disposal of the rescued and every assistance was rendered. The statements which have appeared in the press indicating that there was the slightest delay on the part of the Storstad in rendering prompt and efficient aid, do a cruel injustice to the Captain, who did not hesitate to send out every boat he had, in spite of the desperate condition of his own ship. The owners of the Storstad ask of the public that, in all fairness to both vessels and their commanders, judgement as to where the blame for the terrible disaster should rest suspended until an impartial tribunal has heard the evidence of both sides.

Storstad's bow was a graphic picture of the trauma caused by collision. The image of the anchor shoved down its hawse pipe gave one the impression that the *Empress* fought back. A close examination showed traces of where the *Empress*'s deck stringers (girders) cut into the *Storstad*. A six-inch-long rubber pad from below one of the *Empress*'s coaling doors left a mark on the port bow. The upper part of *Storstad*'s bow was twisted in an arc to port. The lower part maintained its longitudinal orientation but was compressed by brute force. This flattening of the lower part may have been caused by striking a boiler.

Thanks to wireless communication, Atlantic liners quickly learned of the tragedy. The Captains of two Allan Line ships handled the news differently. On the *Victorian*, a gag order was issued by the Captain. Wireless operators were not allowed to print the news in the Marconi section of the ship's newsletter or speak of the disaster to anyone. The Captain of the *Calgarian* allowed the news to circulate. Frightened passengers stayed awake during the balance of an eastbound crossing. At 5:00pm on Sunday, 31 May, Captain Hugh David, stopped White Star's *Megantic* near the hastily installed gas buoy marking the *Empress* wreck. The *Megantic*'s orchestra was surrounded by passengers on Shelter Deck. The Captain led the assembly in prayer followed by 'Abide With Me' from the orchestra. Sorrow streamed down lowered faces. Some were so affected, tear droplets spotted the teak decking at their feet. Captain David returned to his Bridge to resume the transit to Quebec.

Storstad's *crumpled bow
showing it twisted to port.*
(National Archives of
Canada).

Two *Empress* passengers gave Canadian Pacific Railway some bad press. Mr F. P. Godson claimed that many second and third-class passengers were trapped behind locked gates designed to prevent commingling with first-class. He also said that the crew snatched up all the life belts for themselves. The few remaining were tied so tightly with binder twine, according to Godson, that they could only be loosened with the 'utmost difficulty'. Godson's charge of a locked folding gate reminds one of the scene in Rank Organization's 1958 *Titanic* film 'A Night To Remember' and James Cameron's 1997 '*Titanic*'. The *Empress* had a gate which separated third-class from second-class on Upper Deck but no other survivor could confirm that it was locked. Another passenger named Langeley came forward and claimed that a Shelter Deck exit door leading out from the second-class main stairwell was locked. The effect of this might have been to hold a large number of people trapped in the second-class smoking room. The door in question opened out against the ship's list.

The other passenger who spoke ill of the *Empress* was Cedric Gallagher, of Winnipeg, travelling first-class with his mother. He said that he and his mother tried to get into a lifeboat but the crew drove them away. This prompted the Toronto *Daily Star* to run a headline which read 'WOMAN DRIVEN FROM LIFEBOATS BY SAILORS'. The article went on to blame Mrs Gallagher's death on this alleged cowardice.

Newspapers ran even more sensationalized, tabloid-quality, stories about the disaster. Foreign nationals and steerage passengers were said to have murdered fellow passengers to clear passage up the packed stairwells. The Toronto *World's* description follows:

> *When the crush became appalling, it is presumed the decks were turned into a carnival of butchery. Jerking knives from waist bands and boots, the foreigners slept half dressed, and stooping low they drove through the terror stricken mass like a pack of demons, thrusting and cutting to make channels to the exits. The horror of this occasion, as yet little appreciated or even suspected by the world, was only cut short by the fatal list of the boat.*

A government medical officer from Quebec refuted the horrific stories about escape from the lower decks in an open letter to the press. Lt-Colonel Pelletier wrote:

> *I have seen wounds of all descriptions on a great number of those corpses, but it was very easy to judge that those wounds were not inflicted with a sharp instrument as a knife would do. Those victims were struck by pieces of iron or wood when the accident occurred, and were killed before they dropped into the water. Others had evident marks of being hit by the explosion. I have not seen one single wound which could be caused by a cutting instrument such as a knife. I have been practicing medicine for twenty-four years, and acted as a coroner for ten years. I have seen victims of railway accidents and mining accidents, of people killed in factories or by explosion, of people killed by knives or by dull instruments, and in this sad case I am firmly convinced that not one of the victims came to death by being stabbed or killed with knives.*

Three days after the *Empress* sank, Mr Frank Dunlevy and relatives held out hope that his wife might still be among the rescued. After all, Mrs Dunlevy had wired Denver on embarkation day confirming that Captain Kendall was personally looking after her. Relatives from Lockeport, Nova Scotia, went to Quebec in search of Mrs Dunlevy. Unfortunately, she was discovered in the morgue. Arrangements were made to bury her in Lockeport.

Sir Henry Seton-Karr managed to escape from his cabin before the ship went down. His body was recovered over 30 miles down river. His death by ocean liner was remarkably tame to friends and acquaintances. People thought the great sportsman would be killed by wild prey or buried by an avalanche. Seton-Karr believed in burial near the site of one's demise. His final resting spot became Mount Hermon Cemetery at Quebec.

The mail posted on the *Empress* at Rimouski started to filter through to addressees. Miss Sadie Bilham received the postcard mailed by her deceased fiancée. Teddy Gray wrote 'I thought you would like this. It is plain, but a novelty.'

Captain Dodd's last dispatch to Salvation Army Territorial Headquarters was received and printed in the *War Cry*. Cecil Attwell received the pathetic message: 'Lovely trip so far'. Cecil was blessed to get much more than a postcard. Both his parents survived the sinking.

Two sailors from the *Storstad* severely damaged the reputation of the ship's company when they were arrested on 2 June. *Empress* passenger Lionel Kent had a large amount in travellers' cheques on his person when he was rescued by *Storstad* sailors. Mr Kent said the documents either fell out of his shirt pocket or were taken while he was in a lifeboat. One crew member tried to cash a $1,000 travellers' cheque with Lionel Kent's name on it. An alert teller at the Merchants Bank of Canada recognized the name of Kent as a survivor from newspaper stories about the *Empress*. The man was arrested at the bank. Authorities went to the *Storstad* to search for additional loot. Captain Andersen willingly permitted the intrusion. The search revealed an additional $990 in stolen travellers' cheques plus $41 in unexplained cash. A second sailor was arrested. Kent was unbothered by the whole affair. He was happy to be alive.

The high death toll and a desire to fix blame for the losses prompted calls for an official inquiry into the disaster. There was no precedent under existing Canadian law to appoint a maritime commission to conduct a formal investigation. Parliament passed amendments to Part 10 of the Canada Shipping Act which allowed the Minister of Marine and Fisheries to appoint special commissioners. On 3 June Minister John Douglas Hazen appointed the Honourable John Charles Bigham, Lord Mersey, to be President of a board of commissioners investigating the loss of the *Empress of Ireland*. The inquest at Rimouski was never reopened having been precluded by the extensive resources of Lord Mersey's commission.

Admittance ticket for memorial services in grief-stricken Liverpool.

On 5 June, Captain Kendall's wife sailed for Quebec on board the Allan Line's fast new *Calgarian*. Her husband would need support during the potentially intense pressure resulting from public inquiry.

On 6 June, the largest funeral in the history of Toronto was held at the Mutual Street Arena. Commissioner Rees and fifteen other bodies lay in state for the service. The Arena was filled to capacity. The overflow crowd lined the streets for the duration of the program. A choir of one hundred children dressed in white robes sang from a specially constructed giant cross in the centre of the arena. Four horse-driven hearses were used to carry the dead to eternal rest at Mount Pleasant Cemetery. The procession of carriages, flower-laden lorries, and marching Salvationists filled Yonge Street for blocks.

Lord Mersey sailed for Canada on 6 June via New York aboard Cunard's *Mauretania*. It was his first ocean crossing. Lord Mersey presided over the *Titanic* investigation by virtue of his position as a High Court judge in the Probate, Divorce, and Admiralty Division. Some said he lacked practical maritime experience as most of his career was spent in commercial law. Mersey would not disagree. Having sat on the *Titanic* inquiry, and possessed of the tenacity to get things done, he seemed a logical choice for the *Empress* inquiry. Of course, the circumstances of 1912 and 1914 were remarkably different. The *Empress* disaster was complicated by another ship, another crew, fog, and nautical rules of the road.

Above left. Lord Mersey at Liverpool landing stage preparing to make his first ocean crossing on route to Canada to head the Public Inquiry into the loss. (British Library) *Above right: Captain Kendall*

Two other commissioners appointed by Minister Hazen were French Canadian Sir Adolphe Basile Routhier and the Honourable Ezekiel McLeod. Routhier was a retired Chief Justice of the Superior Court of Quebec. He was a popular public figure, speaker and author. Routhier was famous for writing the words to 'O Canada'. McLeod was Chief Justice of New Brunswick and Judge in Admiralty for the Exchequer Court of Canada for New Brunswick. The government was represented by Edward L. Newcombe, Deputy Minister of Justice. The commissioners were assisted by four marine and naval experts.

The inquiry was neither a criminal nor civil proceeding. It was considered a fact-finding tribunal. The results were not binding except perhaps in the court of public opinion. Claimants, CPR and the *Storstad* could still fight over liability in the Admiralty Court. The inquiry did require sworn testimony from all witnesses. Notice was served to the officers of both ships advising them that they had a right to present witnesses and defend themselves against charges made during the course of the inquiry. Preliminary statements were taken from passengers, crew, officers, pilots, marine superintendents, and the Marconi operators. Minister Hazen ordered Captain Lindsay, Canadian Wreck Commissioner, to take this preliminary evidence. These statements were reviewed by Mr Newcombe to determine who would be called as witnesses. This process helped speed the investigation but had the appearance of a whitewash. Sir Wilfrid Laurier, opposition leader in Parliament, made a statement to the press questioning the 'advisability of weeding out evidence'. Since the inquiry was non-binding, Minister Hazen was able to successfully defend the expedited process. Counsel for either side could examine the statements in court and call their own witnesses. Lord Mersey did not allow 'fishing expeditions'. Witnesses were expected to have something material to add to the body of evidence.

Canadian Pacific hired Mr Butler Aspinall to represent the company at the tribunal. Aspinall had experience handling maritime cases before British Admiralty judges. He was also familiar with the details of the *Titanic* inquiry having represented the Board of Trade. Aspinall had a reputation for trapping witnesses through gentle persuasion.

The inquiry convened on 16 June in King's Bench Courthouse at Quebec. Captain Kendall leaned on an escort and supported himself with a cane on the way into the courthouse. Kendall did not hold his head up and appeared weak from his ordeal. Captain Andersen was quite alert and seemed ready to defend himself. The two men were seated at the same table. For Kendall, the Quebec courtroom brought back memories. Four years earlier he testified in the same room as the hero of the Crippen case. Now, he was under the microscope. It was his turn to be judged. Would the court find for him or for Captain Andersen?

Before the first witness was called, Lord Mersey noticed that the Amended Shipping Act required the appointed commissioners to take an oath. He questioned Newcombe and the other counsellors but no one knew who had the authority to administer the oath. The question went back and forth among the learned principals until someone consulted the Interpretation Act of the Revised Statutes of Canada for 1906. It read that a judge, notary, or justice of the peace could administer such an oath. Lord Mersey asked Newcombe if he was a justice of the peace. Newcombe replied that it was not an honour he held. Mersey asked if anyone in the room was a justice of the peace. Newcombe generated a few smirks when he sought clarification: 'Do I understand that your Lordship prefers to be sworn before a justice of the peace?' Mersey was a testy old man who had little tolerance for legal shenanigans 'I do not in the least mind before whom I take the oath, but I do mind about this. It seems to be in order, and I wish to be sworn'. The air was finally cleared when someone searched the chambers of the courthouse and found a judge willing to come before Mersey's bench and administer the oath.

Sixty-two witnesses were asked over 8,000 questions in nine days of interrogatory. The official transcript came to 615 pages without exhibits. The key witnesses were Captain Kendall and First Officer Jones for the *Empress*; Chief Officer Toftenes and Third Officer Saxe for the *Storstad*; Marconi operators afloat and ashore; and the pilots (the testimony of these parties was used to describe the events leading up to collision in Chapter 5 of this work). In attempting to reconstruct the collision from time, distances, and bearings, the commission found it impossible to reach any closure. Not only were accounts irreconcilable between ships but witnesses from the same ship were at variance with one another. For example, the length of time the *Empress* allegedly sat motionless varies among crew members from a few seconds to eight minutes. Accordingly, the commission decided to reconstruct the accident based on the probable sequence of events extracted from witness testimony.

Empress witnesses were consistent on one point. They said the *Empress* had crossed the path of the *Storstad* so far ahead of her that there was no risk of collision. The *Empress* then changed course north of the *Storstad* to head downriver on roughly an opposite course. Toftenes said that the *Empress* was not a crossing ship after she changed to the opposite course. The reason Toftenes made the statement that the *Empress* was not a crossing ship was because he believed her to be south, not north, of his position. In the absence of objective detail, the commission jumped on this as a point of agreement from which to build the rest of the story. The commission reasoned that ships on roughly opposite courses were in the best position to pass each other safely. After the *Empress* steadied on her new course, it didn't matter if she was north (starboard-to-starboard) or south (port-to-port) of the *Storstad* because the two ships would pass each other by simply maintaining their course. This simplified the puzzle to one question: which ship changed her course in the fog?

Facing Page: *Conflicting tales of the fatal collision.* (Drawings by John Andert).

The Empress of Ireland *version showing the* Empress *north of the* Storstad. *Chief Officer Toftenes gave the helm order which made this scenario possible but claimed his ship had insufficient momentum to turn into the* Empress.

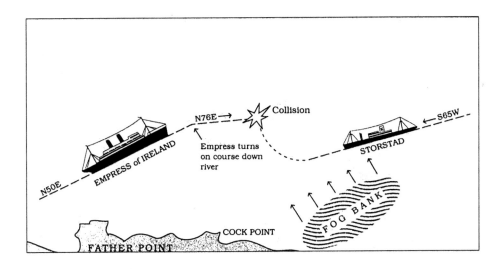

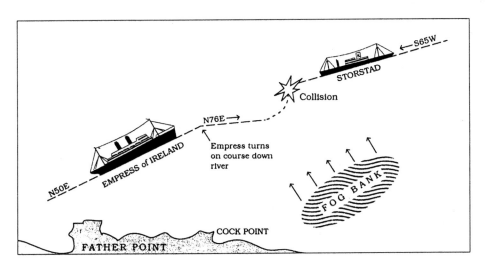

The Storstad *version of events which held that the* Empress *was south of the* Storstad. *Captain Andersen claimed that the* Empress *was underway and turning north to get farther away from the south shore.*

The commission logically concluded that the *Empress* was least likely to have changed course because she had already steadied on a new heading for her outbound transit. Once she entered the fog, not only was there no reason to change course, but any course change would be inviting danger. This forced counsel for *Storstad* to try and prove that mechanical or design deficiencies caused the *Empress* to change her heading.

The attorney handling the tribunal for the *Storstad* was Charles Sherman Haight from New York. He was pre-eminent in the field of admiralty law and a brilliant performer in trial cases. The practice of maritime law was a family tradition. A remarkable coincidence, 42-years later, would fall to his son of the same name. He defended the Swedish built *Stockholm* after she struck the Italian liner *Andrea Doria* amidships on the starboard side in fog near Nantucket. The Italian liner rolled over to starboard and sank eleven hours after impact. Forty-seven lives were lost; most falling victim to *Stockholm's* ice-breaker bow.

Some of the most interesting aspects of the inquiry involve testimony about alleged defects in the *Empress*. Questions were put to Captain Kendall and to naval architects about changes to her rudder. Kendall said he had no knowledge of any change to the rudder. Haight, through the experts, attempted to demonstrate that the rudder represented a defect in design. One naval architect did concede that the *Empress* was designed with an unusually full stern which may have lessened the force of water acting on the rudder's control surfaces. However, the same witness pointed out that the rudder was satisfactory on trials and during its first season of operation. The commission dismissed the rudder as a potential cause of the collision. If there was a design defect, it surely must have been corrected when the rudder was enlarged about a year following launch. It is curious that the issue came up again after being raised and discounted following the accident in October 1909.

At 7:00pm, after completion of day two of testimony, Charles Haight received a call in his hotel room at the Chateau Frontenac. The man on the other end said he was a Quartermaster on the *Empress* and he needed to talk. Haight agreed to see the man at once but didn't know what to expect. Press coverage had supercharged the atmosphere of the inquiry and emotions still ran high. Haight asked his partner, Mr Griffin, to come in and witness what was to transpire. The Quartermaster was James F. Galway.

Galway, at this point, was a free agent. The loss of the *Empress* concluded his employment with CPR at the moment of sinking — one of the harsh realities of maritime life. Quartermaster Galway managed to reach Haight's room unchallenged even though he looked a little out of place at the Frontenac. He began to spin a story that suggested conspiracy. He told Mr Haight that a delegate from the British Seamen's Union advised him of his duty to report certain events. At the same time, Captain Walsh, CPR's Marine Superintendent, was actively pressuring Galway to return to Liverpool. Walsh wrote a letter dated 12 June which offered Galway passage home on the *Montreal* as supernumerary

Quartermaster. Captain Walsh knew that Galway had a complaint to lodge about the steering gear of the *Empress*. He was not aware of the particulars.

Galway was subpoenaed for an appearance the very next morning. He testified that the *Empress* was steering badly on the night of the collision. At the Traverse, a narrow passage immediately east of Quebec, Galway said the ship sheered to port and almost struck a schooner. Later during his watch the gear jammed for several minutes on a port order, he stated. He added that the wheel jammed once on the crossing from Liverpool. Haight was on a roll, he called on three witnesses to back up Galway's story. They were the Second Officer, a sailor, and the pilot from the *Alden*. She was the inbound ship which passed the *Empress* at about 9:20pm.

Alden's Second Officer, Odin Sabje, said that the *Empress* was 'swinging, steering badly down the river.' This was based on his observation of the *Empress*'s red (port) and green (starboard) side lights. Sabje told the court that she did not present her red side light consistently for a traditional port-to-port passing. She went back and forth from red to green and back to red again 'between five to seven times'. CPR's attorney stood to cross-examine.

Aspinall correctly assumed that Sabje had been contacted to secure his testimony. It was, in fact, attorney John Griffin who went to solicit favourable testimony for the *Storstad*. This was not hard to do because the *Alden* was also a Norwegian vessel. Aspinall asked Sabje why Mr Griffin went to visit the *Alden*. The cross-examination ended like this:

> *Aspinall: Can you tell us what it was that induced that gentleman to pay you a visit?*
>
> *Sabje: I heard he was a lawyer.*
>
> *Aspinall: A liar?*
>
> *Sabje: No, a lawyer.*
>
> *Mersey: I don't understand, whom did the witness say was a liar?*
>
> *Aspinall: Not a liar, my Lord, a lawyer.*
>
> *Mersey: Oh, a lawyer.*
>
> *Aspinall: Yes, my Lord. I suppose (addressing Sabje) you pass a great many ships, don't you, going up and down?*
>
> *Sabje: Yes (witness excused).*

The *Alden*'s pilot said that the *Empress* 'twisted all the time, she changed her light three or four times' and that her behaviour 'frightened' him. Cross-examination revealed that the *Empress* was six miles up river when the pilot made those observations. When the two ships were within three quarters of a mile, the *Empress* consistently presented her red light for a steady port-to-port passing. The *Alden*'s pilot also stated that he never slowed further dispelling the suggestion that the *Empress* was crossing back and forth ahead of him. The third *Alden* witness needed an interpreter and was not very credible.

Given Galway's charges and the cloud spun by witnesses from the *Alden*, the commissioners wanted to know more about the *Empress*'s telemotor steering mechanism. Excerpts of testimony about the steering gear are included here because the subject is interesting and to provide a flavour of how the inquiry explored various issues. Percy A. Hillhouse was one of the naval architects who worked on the *Empress* at Fairfield's shipyard. Mr Hillhouse was called to describe the ship's steering equipment and gave the following overview:

Hillhouse: The word telemotor means a mover at a distance, the same as telegraph means writing at a distance and telephone sound at a distance. The instrument is a means of communicating the motion of the hand (helm) wheel upon the Bridge to the steam steering engine at the after end of the ship; it replaces the ordinary system of shafts and bevel wheels. The motion of the hand wheel works a plunger inside of a cylinder and forces a mixture of glycerine and water into one or other of two pipes which travel the whole length of the ship, and at the other end are connected to another cylinder. As pressure comes on one end or the other of that after cylinder, so the steam valve of the steering engine is moved one way or the other, and the steering engine moves (the rudder) to port or starboard. After it is moved a certain distance, it automatically cuts off its own steam, so that if the helmsman puts the wheel over to a certain point and holds it there, the engine will follow and stop after having travelled a distance proportionate to the amount the wheel has been turned. When he releases the wheel, springs at the after end push back the telemotor cylinder, and rotate the wheel back to the original position. On the Bridge, and connected with these two pipes there is a small reservoir tank, the only duty of which is to make up any leakage which may accidentally take place in the telemotor pipes, and on that tank is a little brass gauge, so that people on the Bridge can at any time see whether the telemotor system is properly full of glycerine or not.

Aspinall: With regard to this telemotor system, is it a well known system?

Hillhouse: It is acknowledged to be the best system of steering large passenger vessels and is adopted by all the best lines.

Mersey: Is this system in common use on ocean-going steamers?

Hillhouse: Yes, my Lord.

Mersey: Is it, for instance, in use on Cunard boats?

Hillhouse: Yes.

Mersey: Is it in use on Allan Line boats?

Hillhouse: Yes.

Mersey: Is it in use on the White Star boats?

Hillhouse: Yes, I think so; I do not know for sure.

Mersey: At all events, it is not a newfangled thing that you have in your boats?

Hillhouse: By no means.

Junior Third Engineer George O'Donovan was called as he was responsible for repair and maintenance of the telemotor system. O'Donovan had charge of the steering gear for eight months prior to collision.

Haight: If there is anything wrong in the quantity of glycerine in either telemotor, or if there is by any chance any obstruction, your steering gear is partially or totally out of effective use?

O'Donovan: Partially.

Haight: Well, if the glycerine should leak out from either cylinder, it would be totally out of use?

O'Donovan: No, sir, it just depends on the quantity that leaks out.

Mersey: If it all leaked out, the telemotor would cease to work?

O'Donovan: Quite, sir.

Mersey: And the more that leaks out the nearer you get to that point?

O'Donovan: Yes.

Haight: Have you never refilled (the cylinders) during the eight months you inspected the apparatus?

O'Donovan: I pumped her up twice a trip. It doesn't require refilling; it is full already. There may be a slight leak one way or the other.

Haight: Could you give me an idea of the size of the cylinder next to the wheel?

O'Donovan: About 4-inches, diameter.

Mersey: Who makes these instruments?

O'Donovan: Brown, sir, John Brown, of Edinburgh.

Haight: If you should lose a quart or a quart and a pint of glycerine out of the upper cylinder, would your entire apparatus be out of business?

O'Donovan: Yes.

Haight: Give me the approximate length of the pipe which connects the upper cylinder with the lower?

O'Donovan: About 500 feet.

Mersey: What?

O'Donovan: About 500 feet, my Lord.

Haight: Do you mean that there is a pipe filled with glycerine which runs practically the length of the ship?

O'Donovan: Yes.

Mersey: Is that the usual plan?

O'Donovan: The usual plan, my Lord, as far as I know.

Haight: As I understand you, the man at the wheel who actually obeys the orders from the Bridge, not only pumps the glycerine from one side to the other of the cylinder immediately at the wheel, but is also forcing the glycerine down through the pipe to the cylinder below; and moreover he is also forcing a column of glycerine nearly 500 feet long, which leads back to the stern, to the steering engine?

O'Donovan: *Yes.*

Mersey: *When did you last inspect it (the steering gear) before this calamity?*

O'Donovan: *The day before the sailing.*

Mersey: *Well at all events was it then working properly?*

O'Donovan: *Yes, my Lord. Any leak in the pipes would be shown on the Bridge. There is an indicator on the telemotor which shows if there is any leak in the pipe.*

Haight: *At what hour did you make the inspection?*

O'Donovan: *At eleven o'clock in the morning.*

Haight: *You did not direct your attention at all to the steering gear after you left the dock, when she started upon this voyage which resulted in disaster?*

O'Donovan: *No.*

Haight: *Now when you made your inspection on the day before sailing, will you please state, as precisely as you can, exactly what you did?*

O'Donovan: *Well, I pumped the gear up.*

Haight: *That is you injected some more glycerine?*

Donovan: *Yes.*

Haight: *How much?*

O'Donovan: *She might not take anything at all.*

Haight: *Oh, I know she might not, but I want to know what it did take?*

O'Donovan: *I couldn't say.*

Haight: *Now you had tried the wheel for yourself before you began to pump in?*

O'Donovan: *I did.*

Haight: *And as you tried the wheel you reached the conclusion that she needed to be pumped up?*

O'Donovan: *No I did not.*

Haight: *Then why did you go and pump her up?*

O'Donovan: *It is the usual thing to pump her up in case of the least slackness in the wheel.*

Haight: *What other boats have you been on which were equipped with the telemotor system?*

O'Donovan: This is the first ship I have been on that had it.

Haight: So your experience is limited to this particular ship so far as the telemotor goes?

O'Donovan: Yes, sir.

Haight: What was the difference you noticed between the first time you tried your wheel on this Wednesday before the accident, before you pumped and after you pumped?

O'Donovan: There was none.

Haight: No difference at all?

O'Donovan: None.

Haight: That is all, my Lord.

Galway told the tribunal that he had reported the steering difficulties on the outbound transit to Second Officer Williams. Williams perished so it was not possible to corroborate this story. Galway said he also mentioned the problem in passing to Quartermaster John Murphy who relieved him as well as to Pilot Bernier. Both Bernier and Murphy were called to testify on this point. They both denied that Galway had ever spoken to them about the steering gear. Murphy did agree that once in the prior five years the helm didn't catch. He put his wheel amidships; gave it the ordered helm again, and it caught right away. Pilot Bernier testified that the steering gear worked well all the way to Father Point. The commissioners concluded that allegations of faulty steering gear against the Empress were unfounded. They also reasoned that jammed steering gear would cause the vessel to steer in one direction and not sheer in large arcs from side to side.

Satisfied that the Empress hadn't changed course by human or mechanical failure, the inquiry only needed to show an intentional or unintentional course change on the part of the Storstad to establish the cause of the accident. This evidence was delivered by Storstad's Third Officer. Jacob Saxe confirmed in his testimony that Chief Officer Toftenes ordered a port helm. Saxe added that he put the wheel hard over on his own initiative when the vessel did not seem to respond. Toftenes testified that he was unaware of Saxe's actions to move the helm farther over to hard-a-port. This created the impression that Toftenes was not in control of his Bridge.

All Storstad witnesses were consistent in testimony about the position of the Empress. They all confirmed their belief that she was south — closer to shore. The last-minute turn ordered by Toftenes, and amplified by Saxe, was a logical move to the north which should have given the Empress a wider berth. The only problem was that the Empress was actually north of the Storstad. The commission concluded that the effect of Storstad's hard-a-port helm 'would be to bring her into collision with the Empress of Ireland.' The commission did not accept the following testimony by Saxe who said the port helm did not take effect:

Haight: Where were you standing when you first saw the (Empress's) green light?

Saxe: At the compass.

Haight: Did you then see your heading? Do you know how your ship was then heading?

Saxe: Yes, the course.

Haight: Had the course changed any?

Saxe: No, sir.

Mersey: Do I understand that although you put your helm to port, and afterwards put your helm hard-a port, the course of your ship was not effected in the least, is that true?

Saxe: That is true

Mersey: Well, were you surprised when it didn't answer?

Saxe: No, I was not.

Haight: Why were you not surprised?

Saxe: The engines were stopped.

Haight: How long had they been stopped?

Mersey: Wait a minute: your engines were stopped were they?

Saxe: Yes.

Mersey: What did he (Toftenes) port his helm for? Why did he port his helm?

Saxe: The Chief Mate ordered the wheel to be ported.

Mersey: But why did he order it to be ported?

Saxe: I didn't ask him why.

Mersey: I dare say you did not ask for a reason, but what do you suppose the reason was?

Saxe: I thought it was for the current.

Another issue that the inquiry had to dispose of was the charge that the *Empress* was moving at the time of collision. Ernest Pugmire had told a reporter from the *Detroit News* that the *Empress* was going 10 miles an hour upon impact. Pugmire was subpoenaed to testify at the request of Attorney Haight. Much to Haight's surprise, Pugmire changed his story:

Haight: Did you have an opportunity to observe whether or not the steamship Empress *was in motion when you got on deck?*

Pugmire: I looked over the side.

Haight: And what did you see?

Pugmire: Either the Empress *was moving astern six or seven miles an hour or there was a pretty strong current.*

Mersey: Moving astern?

Pugmire: Moving astern, sir.

Haight: Did you, Mr Pugmire, happen to see an article which appeared on June 1st, in one of the Detroit newspapers?

Pugmire: I did.

Haight: That statement purporting to be an interview with you, just had the facts reversed, then?

Aspinall: My Lord, I object to that.

Mersey: This will not do, you know (addressing Haight); you have asked a question and been given the answer.

Haight: That is quite right.

Mersey: And it is not the answer you wanted.

Haight: Did you, Mr Pugmire, go out onto an upper deck on the same side of the ship that your room is located on?

Pugmire:No, on the opposite (port) side.

Haight: And you went to the rail and looked over?

Pugmire: Yes.

Haight: Now, as you stood at the rail and looked over, which way did the water seem to be moving, to your right or to your left?

Pugmire: To the right.

Mersey: And the stern of your ship was to your left?

Pugmire: The stern of the ship was to my left (witness excused).

Captain Kendall stood and gave testimony on four different occasions. A total of 869 questions were put to him. His longest stay in the box was on the first day of hearings. The inquiry explored two areas of weakness in Kendall's story. The first of these involved Captain Kendall's decision to bring his ship to a dead stop. Excerpts follow:

Aspinall: Seeing a fog bank travelling out from the land towards your ship and towards the other ship, did you do anything?

Kendall: I did.

Aspinall: Did you wait for a time until it got further out?

Kendall: When I saw the Storstad's lights were getting a little misty, I stopped my ship.

Aspinall: At any rate, in view of the fact that it (fog) was beginning to dim the lights which you were seeing, which were the two masthead lights and the green (starboard) light, what did you do on board your vessel?

Kendall: Stopped the ship, and went full speed astern.

Aspinall: What was the reason for that?

Kendall: To take the way off the ship.

Aspinall: What effect had the stopping and reversing of your engines; did it take your way off?

Kendall: It did.

Aspinall: How did you ascertain whether your way was off or not?

Kendall: By looking over the ship's side ...by the foam and the air bubbles on the water.

Aspinall: Is it common practice for seamen to look over the side in fog to see whether or not their ship is stopped?

Kendall: It is.

Haight: You said that when you saw the Storstad's *lights become misty, you stopped your ship?*

Kendall: I did.

Haight: Is it usual, when you consider that you are in a position of absolute safety, to stop your vessel entirely, because the lights look a little misty?

Kendall: A fog bank was approaching me from the land. Not knowing the thickness of this fog I thought it my duty to stop my ship knowing that there was a vessel in the vicinity.

Haight: You have said that you were in a position of starboard-to-starboard so that your boat was in no danger of collision?

Kendall: Quite so.

Haight: When there is only one vessel in the vicinity and that vessel is absolutely in a safe position do you always stop your engines dead?

Kendall: Knowing the position of the Storstad *and knowing the denseness of the fog, I am not in a position to know what the other vessel is most likely to do.*

Haight: You considered that there was no possible danger?

Kendall: I considered I was in a position of safety but not knowing what the other vessel might do when the fog covered her.

Haight: Then, at that time you were not anticipating a possible violent change of course on the part of the other vessel?

Kendall: No.

Haight: Shortly after you stopped you actually saw the Storstad's *green (starboard) light?*

Kendall: Before the ship's way was off her I did not see her light.

Haight: Shortly after you stopped the engines?

Kendall: Then I saw his green light.

Haight: The moment that you saw his green light you ordered your engines full speed astern?

Kendall: Yes.

Haight: Why should you put your engines full speed astern with the vessel green-to-green (starboard-to-starboard) and in safety?

Kendall: The fog would be approaching the ship; I did not know and I preferred to stop until the fog had passed over.

Haight: There is no rule which suggests running full speed astern or stopping dead?

Kendall: I took the way off my ship because she is a ship that will carry a lot of way with the engines reversed.

Mersey: Will you tell me again what was your reason for going full speed astern?

Kendall: To take the way off my ship, my Lord.

Mersey: Why did you want to do that?

Kendall: Because I was in that spot and the Empress of Ireland *is a ship, that when she is proceeding at 18 knots, will carry quite a lot of headway; she will continue running for a mile or two.*

Mersey: Why did you want to stop?

Kendall: Because I saw this thick fog bank approaching from the land.

Mersey: There was no other steamer complicating the situation except *the* Storstad?

Kendall: No other steamer to my knowledge, my Lord.

Mersey: Did you anticipate that she would do something that she ought not to do?

Kendall: I anticipated that she might do anything if she were covered by the fog and the fog came between us.

Haight: You said that the collision as it occurred (in earlier testimony), was only possible because of the Storstad *cutting across and changing her course radically?*

Kendall: Yes.

Haight: Assuming that the Storstad *was originally (as stated by Toftenes and Saxe) on a course of west by south, she had changed her course about seven points before she hit you?*

Kendall: Apparently.

Haight: There is no reasonable explanation that you can give for such a radical change of course as that?

Kendall: I can give no explanation.

Haight: At least you can think of no rational cause for a man who is bound into Father Point changing his course north-northwest and swinging seven points in a fog?

Kendall: I can give an opinion of why he did it.

Mersey: I should like to hear it.

Kendall: My own opinion is that as this man was approaching Father Point he was perhaps on the other side of the fog bank.

Mersey: To the north or to the south?

Kendall: To the south, and he sighted, off his port bow, Cock Point Buoy, which is an occulting light, and he immediately put his helm hard-a port knowing that it marked a shoal.

Mersey: You think he tried to avoid running on a shoal?

Kendall: That is my opinion, by porting his helm.

Haight: When you left Father Point was it clear below?

Kendall: Yes.

Haight: So that at the time the Storstad *could see the shore, Cock Point and Father Point?*

Kendall: Yes.

Haight: It would be pretty hard to be taken unawares at Cock Point Light?

Kendall: I am not supposed to know his actions when he was in the fog.

Haight: You cannot think of any other reason why he should have changed his course seven points?

Kendall: I know of no reason except that.

The second weak area in Kendall's testimony was the closing of watertight doors. Kendall freely admitted that he did not order the doors closed until after the collision as in these excerpts:

Haight: When you first saw the Storstad *through the fog, about 100 feet away, coming out of the fog, you considered the collision inevitable?*

Kendall: I did.

Haight: You did not then close or order closed your watertight bulkhead doors?

Kendall: Not the first order (in earlier testimony Kendall said his first order was to get away all boats).

Haight: Rule 44 (CPR's standing orders) says 'Watertight doors are to be ready to he closed instantly, and every possible precaution taken for the safety of the ship'. Then the first words of that rule are as follows 'in fog or snow speed is always to be reduced, watertight doors to be ready to be closed instantly, and every precaution taken for the safety of the ship?'

Kendall: Yes.

Haight: Now did you consider that you were in fog at the time of collision just before you met with this collision?

Kendall: I was not in fog before, but during the collision I was in fog.

Haight: Was there anything done with respect to preparing to close these doors?

Kendall: Not at that time.

Aspinall grilled Chief Officer Toftenes. He wanted to show that Toftenes was mistaken in saying that the *Empress* was south of the *Storstad*; cast doubt on the Norwegian's assertion that the *Storstad* failed to respond to the helm order issued just prior to collision; and prove that Toftenes disobeyed a standing order to call his Captain when fog appeared. Aspinall challenged the Chief Officer's story and his competence as these excerpts demonstrate:

Aspinall: At what distance were these lights (first sighting of the masthead lights of the Empress*) from you?*

Toftenes: They would be six miles probably.

Aspinall: And about how were they bearing from you? Toftenes: About one-and-a-half-points on my port bow.

Aspinall: And she was on a course crossing yours?

Toftenes: Yes.

Aspinall: And she was, as I dare say you know; travelling a great deal faster than you?

Toftenes: I could not say that then.

Aspinall: But you know, and I think we are all agreed that is the fact?

Toftenes: Yes.

Aspinall: I might tell you that according to her evidence she was travelling at 17 and you were travelling at about 10?

Toftenes: We were.

Aspinall: She proceeded on for how long before you saw her commence to alter her course?

Toftenes: About a quarter of an hour.

Aspinall: In a quarter of an hour, if that is the rate she was travelling at — one quarter of 17 miles: would she not pass over four miles?

Toftenes: Yes.

Aspinall: Do you not think she had got on your starboard bow?

Toftenes: Will you repeat that?

Aspinall: Did you not hear my question?

Toftenes: Not exactly.

Aspinall: If she was one-and-a-half-points on your port bow, six miles away, travelling at 17 knots to your 10, I suggest to you that in a quarter of an hour she would have got across on your starboard how?

Toftenes: She did not.

Mersey: Never mind whether she did or did not, but try to answer the question.

Aspinall: In that quarter of an hour she would travel over four miles at her speed, would she not?

Toftenes: Yes.

Aspinall: At any rate, according to your case, at the end of these fifteen minutes, where was she?

Toftenes: She was about a point on my port bow.

Aspinall: You have been going on the same course?

Toftenes: Yes.

Aspinall: And at the end of a quarter of an hour this other ship travelling seven knots faster than you has only narrowed half-a-point; do you seriously mean that?

Toftenes: That is the fact.

Aspinall: You twice heard her (the Empress) *blow three short blasts?*

Toftenes: I do not know how many times I heard her.

Aspinall: I am not claiming more than two of the three. But you did at least hear her blow three short blasts?

Toftenes: Yes, I heard her blow twice.

Aspinall: The effect of that ought to be to take her headway off, ought it not?

Toftenes: Yes, it would (because it indicates she was backing).

Aspinall: She is a twin-screw boat and has powerful engines. She says that she has taken her headway off.

Toftenes: Yes.

Aspinall: If she had not used her helm and the cause of this trouble was that you did use your helm, and this was a port helm. That is putting the case simply. You heard her sound three short blasts twice and you put your helm nearly hard-a-port?

Toftenes: I did put the helm a-port.

Aspinall: Nearly hard-a-port?

Toftenes: Nearly hard-a-port.

Aspinall: Is it a fact that your head did go to starboard just before this collision happened?

Toftenes: It did not.

Mersey: Put that question again.

Aspinall: Is it not a fact that in consequence of your helm being to port and nearly hard-a-port, your head did go to starboard and that is how this collision occurred?

Toftenes: It did not.

Mersey: I do not know what 'did not' means. Do you mean to say that it did not bring about the collision?

Toftenes: It did not make the ship swing to starboard.

Aspinall: What instructions did your Master give you in regard to fog?

Toftenes: To call him in case fog came on.

Aspinall: Did you give effect to those instructions on this morning (29 May)?

Toftenes: I did call him.

Aspinall: When the fog came on?

Toftenes: Yes, a few minutes after.

Mersey: What is that?

Toftenes: A few minutes after the fog was showing there I called the Master.

Mersey: How long was the fog there?

Toftenes: From the time the fog shut in the lights of the Empress until the collision it would be about ten minutes.

Aspinall: That is from the time it shut him in but I take it that you had seen the fog before that?

Toftenes: A little before that.

Aspinall: We were told by a witness from the Empress that the fog was seen to be coming off shore?

Toftenes: Yes.

Aspinall: Did you see that?

Toftenes: I did.

Aspinall: That would be more than ten minutes before the collision?

Toftenes: Yes, sir.

Aspinall: Why did you not act, obey the instructions of your Master and have called him at once?

Toftenes: I was not so particular about the time of calling him. I sometimes used to wait a few minutes to see if the fog would clear.

Mersey: I heard him say that he thought he would wait a few minutes to see if the fog would clear?

Toftenes: Not exactly that; I said that I sometimes used to wait a few minutes to see if the fog would clear.

Mersey: Why did you not do as he told you?

Toftenes: I did not think it was necessary just then.

Mersey: I understand that your Master, in answer to your summons, did not get on the Bridge until the mischief was done — that is to say until the collision was inevitable?

Toftenes: He did not.

Mersey: And if you had called him as soon as the fog came he would have been there long before?

Toftenes: He might.

Storstad

One gets the impression that Toftenes was sincere in his answers. Perhaps he was too honest and didn't think through the effect his answers would have on his case. Toftenes, for the sake of his defence, could have abandoned his testimony about the *Empress* altering course south of the *Storstad*. He could have testified that the *Empress* was still crossing when the collision occurred. He might have argued that the *Empress* was building up steam and took too long to cross ahead of the *Storstad*. If Toftenes had made these assertions, responsibility for the collision would be very much in doubt.

Lord Mersey wasn't interested in the testimony of passengers. Mr John Black testified about the explosion and about the lifeboat which was crushed when the *Empress* rolled over. When Government counsel Newcombe continued his examination of Black with a question about the *Empress*'s headway, Mersey interrupted and said 'I do not myself think that to multiply this evidence will be to increase our knowledge of the facts.' Mrs Black was set to testify next. Lord Mersey said it was not necessary and that he didn't want to hear from a large number of passengers.

The inquiry adjourned on 27 June, after hearing closing statements from Haight, Aspinall and Newcombe. Haight kept pushing alleged design and mechanical defects in the *Empress*'s rudder and steering gear respectively. Aspinall said that Attorney Haight would have you believe 'the *Empress* was an animal *feri nature* sailing the seas with a rudder whose behaviour made her a more dangerous beast one could hardly imagine.' The shortest but most enlightening closing address was delivered by the Government's attorney.

Newcombe estimated that the two ships should have passed each other one-half-mile apart on roughly opposite courses (11 degrees divergence) if neither ship altered course. He said it is 'absolutely certain' that the *Storstad* did not go one-half-mile north, off her course, to cause the collision. Newcombe did not offer an explanation of who may have changed course. His analysis suggested that both ships must have been in doubt as to their proximity to each other. Newcombe said the two vessels may have been as little as one or two ship-lengths away when the fog shut them out. The collision occurred because both ships lost control of their navigational picture. As for why Toftenes and Saxe believed the *Empress* was south of their position, Newcombe had a reasonable theory. He suggested that when the *Empress* turned to head down river, she must have initially swung too far to starboard. This would show her port side red light until the ship steadied back on the ordered course. Fog took away further opportunity to verify which light the *Empress* intended to show.

Following adjournment, Mersey and the commissioners met daily at the Quebec courthouse to sift through the evidence and work on their findings. Mersey let it be known that he wanted to return to England as soon as possible. Mersey wanted the formal report completed within two weeks.

The Canadian Territorial Staff Band. Only nine bandsmen were saved
(Salvation Army Heritage Centre, Toronto).

Ken McIntyre was the only survivor from the Territorial Staff Band to continue to the Salvation Army International Congress in London. On 15 June, at Strand Hall, thirty-nine chairs were left empty and draped in black in remembrance of the Canadian bandsmen who lost their lives. Ken sat alone in that section.

The 700-strong American contingent sailed on White Star Line's *Olympic*. Commander Eva Booth did not want fear and anxiety to prevail. On horseback, she led a parade from United States Salvation Army headquarters at West 14th and 6th to the Manhattan piers. Four brass bands followed her under orders to play only lively tunes along the route.

Twenty-five Salvationists booked on *Olympic* declined to go. Perhaps some thought they were tempting fate to make an ocean crossing on *Titanic*'s sister after the loss of the *Empress*.

On 2 June, a foreign national was found wandering along the shore between Father Point and Rimouski. The foreigner was a woman believed to be a passenger from the *Empress*. The woman may have been travelling to Sweden and was found naked in a 'daze'. Newspapers said she had been driven insane by the tragedy.

Six days after the sinking, a thirteen-year-old named Eileen Tuggy took a morning stroll along the beach eighteen miles east of Father Point. She discovered the body of a little girl much like herself washed ashore. Local officials immediately had a child's coffin constructed, preserved the body, and sent it to Quebec for identification. When the coffin was opened at Pier 27, a wreath of lilies was found resting on the body with a note which read 'As a token of respect from those who found her.' A bouquet of forget-me-nots and a card had been placed in the child's hands. Written on the card 'Kindly accept my kindest and sincerest sympathy. May she rest in peace. If identified, I would like to know.' It was signed by Eileen Tuggy. The remains were held for days as her identity was in question. The body was thought to be the daughter of Toronto Salvationist Frank Brooks. The coroner determined the remains to be Miss Edith Hart of Mortlach, Saskatchewan, based on her grandfather's identification.

Another interesting story is that of Thomas Parfit. He was reported to be a missing Swift Current, Saskatchewan, passenger booked in third-class. He bought a CPR through ticket for passage from Swift Current to London, England. On 31 May, at 4:00am, Swift Current police found him lying on the street in a stupor. They searched his pockets for identification and discovered an *Empress of Ireland* steamship ticket for her fatal voyage. Parfit's identity was quickly resolved because his brother Edward was a Swift Current contractor known by local authorities. Thomas was also the only Swift Current man ticketed for travel on the *Empress*. He had been visiting his brother but . the two may have parted on bad terms. The cause of Thomas's delirium was never determined except to say that alcohol was not a factor. The police placed him in the custody of the local welfare office.

On 29 June an inquiry was completed at the offices of the Norwegian Consulate General for Canada at Montreal. The inquiry was conducted by W. Maithe Johannesen, First Secretary of the Norwegian Delegation from

Washington, D.C., and two Norwegian captains familiar with navigation on the St Lawrence. The evidence came exclusively from the *Storstad*. No witnesses were called for the *Empress of Ireland*. The results were forwarded to the Norwegian Department of Foreign Affairs in Norway. The Government of Norway exonerated the officers and crew of the *Storstad*.

On 11 July the Mersey inquiry delivered its findings at the Chateau Frontenac. The comprehensive report covered seven areas: (1) Description of the ships; (2) Summary of the stories of each ship; (3) Which ship was to blame; (4) Why the *Empress* sank rapidly; (5) Life saving equipment; (6) Responses to questions posed by Minister Hazen; (7) Recommendations for safety at sea.

The inquiry regretfully concluded that Chief Officer Toftenes was to blame for the collision. This was based on three points: Toftenes' incorrect belief that the *Empress* was passing south of him (port-to-port); Toftenes' and Saxe's turning the *Storstad* north into the path of the *Empress*; and Toftenes' failure to call his Captain promptly upon entering fog. The report went on to say that the St Lawrence River was in no way a contributing factor 'it was a disaster which might have occurred in the Thames, in the Clyde, in the Mersey or elsewhere in similar circumstances.'

Less than one page of recommendations for safety at sea were offered at the end of the report. It suggested that all watertight doors be closed in foggy weather and remain closed until completely clear. It also recommended all portholes be closed from sunset until sunrise. To save life on a rapidly sinking ship, the inquiry suggested easily detachable rafts arranged on the upper decks.

Captain Kendall was the subject of negative comment regarding his decision to stop dead in the fog. The report said that Kendall's actions (reversing his engines) evidenced an 'uneasiness' and a 'consciousness' that he was too close to the *Storstad*. Captain Kendall should have given the *Storstad* a wider berth, according to the findings, but was not required to do so.. The report went further. It expressly deflected blame from Kendall 'We (the commissioners) do not think, however, that his stopping, which was really done for greater caution, can be said to have been an unseamanlike act, nor do we consider his failure to give the wider berth as a contributory cause of the disaster.'

Some of Captain Kendall's testimony was self-serving. He said that he went full speed astern when the *Storstad's* lights got 'a little misty'. When pressed as to why he didn't close the watertight doors upon entering the fog he stated that the fog came up during and not before the collision. Captain Kendall is stretching his credibility here. On the one hand, he claims he sat in the fog for eight minutes. On the other hand he maintains that there was no fog until impact thus evading the requirement to close watertight doors. One can't have it both ways.

An apparent contradiction occurred when Kendall used the same word to describe his ship at standstill as he did to describe the *Storstad* at speed. That word was foam. Alongside the *Empress*, Kendall said it meant no way on. Coming from the bow of the *Storstad*, Kendall intended it to indicate she was going fast. Haight might have made something of this. Perhaps he knew from his maritime experience that this is a difficult call for any mariner especially at night. If Kendall said he threw a woodchip over the side, he would have been more convincing.

Captain Kendall had a greater responsibility to avoid collision in that he was responsible for almost 1,500 lives. He was an experienced man. He knew the St Lawrence River was a busy place. He knew inbound tramp steamers and liners converged on Father Point to pick-up their pilots. He also knew that fog on the St Lawrence could be unforgiving. Kendall seems sincere in exercising his greater responsibility to avoid collision by reversing his engines from a full bell when the fog came on. The only problem with his story is that it sounds unreasonably prudent. A responsible Captain will reverse his engines and risk damage to them to keep his vessel out of danger. But, is it reasonable to reverse your engines, stop dead, and remain on a busy waterway without manoeuvrability for eight minutes in the fog? It is more likely that Kendall's decision to reverse his engines was brought about by imminent collision.

As for watertight door closure, is it reasonable that they were not ordered closed until after impact? Certainly not. One could argue that the Captain might not order them shut during a misty fog because they interfere with the movement of crew between lower deck compartments. In this case, the need was at night when fewer crew members were about. Kendall also had up to eight minutes to think about the safety of his ship. The same prudence that dictated a decision to stop, should have triggered a call to man watertight door stations and close them. Unless... there was no time.

Appendix A contains a chronology of the events leading up to collision. The times are based primarily on the testimony of Captain Kendall and First Officer Jones. It is possible that both vessels maintained speed for a considerable portion of the fog-shrouded ten minutes prior to impact. The *Empress*, like the *Storstad*, may have reversed her engines moments, instead of minutes, before the collision. This is consistent with Chief Engineer Sampson's statement at the Rimouski inquest. Sampson said he went to the engine room when he heard the engines at full reverse. On his way to the engine room, someone apparently told him that a big collier was about to ram the *Empress*. Toftenes' testimony also suggests a compressed time frame. He testified that he heard the *Empress*'s last backing signal just before the collision.

Although this calls into question the veracity of the *Empress*'s story, it doesn't solve the puzzle. The question of what placed the ships in close proximity to each other remains unanswered. Did Toftenes panic at the last moment and turn into the *Empress*? Was the *Empress* a crossing ship which never reached a point north of *Storstad's* path? Before radar, some mariners engaged in the ill-advised practice of turning away from the sound of another ship when in fog. It is a blatant disregard for the nautical rules of the road which require moderate speed and no change of course. Did one or both ships execute such a manoeuvre?

Evidence from logbooks would have been a good source of information to help unravel the mystery. The chartroom logbook of the *Empress* had been placed in a watertight metal container. Captain Pouliot of the *Lady Evelyn* found the logbook which was subsequently introduced as evidence at the inquiry. Unfortunately, entries were recorded through midnight of 28 May and no further. The engineering logbook was never removed from the *Empress*. The logbooks of the *Storstad* were not very reliable. Toftenes completed *Storstad's* chartroom log from scratch notes during the transit to Montreal following collision. The inquiry called some entries into question because they were out of chronological sequence. *Storstad's* engineering logbook did not help her case because it indicated that she went full speed until 2:00am, stopped, slowed, and then collided at 2:05am. Once again, these entries were logged after the fact — a stressful hour after the collision.

The author does not propose to rewrite the history of the disaster. However, it does seem in retrospect that there was a rush to judgement. This was precipitated to some extent by Lord Mersey himself and is reflected by numerous interruptions of counsel and of witnesses throughout the official inquiry. *Storstad* witnesses shouldered the brunt of Lord Mersey's interjection and editorial comment. Sometimes Lord Mersey was impatient such as when two different *Storstad* witnesses requested interpreters and Mersey reluctantly agreed to swear the interpreters in. Other times he framed questions in a manner which presumed *Storstad's* guilt and the *Empress's* innocence. There were several questions put to Captain Andersen about the navigation of the *Empress* which revolved around the editorial phrase... 'why would a man in charge of a vessel like the *Empress*' ...suggesting that the Captain of a liner was less likely to have made an error.

When Lord Mersey stopped to interrupt testimony it created the appearance that the testimony being heard wasn't credible. He interrupted the testimony of Chief Officer Toftenes over a dozen times on different points. Mersey interrupted after Aspinall asked Toftenes to estimate the speed of the *Empress* at the time of collision 'I am getting old and cannot hear what you say. Speak as loud as if you were on the Bridge.' Toftenes said he could not estimate the speed of the *Empress*. Newspaper accounts the following day led with stories about how Toftenes was unable to explain 'DISCREPANCIES OF SPEED'.

Another interruption by Mersey came while Toftenes was attempting to explain how much the range lights of the *Empress* were opening when the *Empress* was first sighted. Mersey decided the information was of little value and added that he could not believe the witness remembered how much the range lights were opening. On another occasion Mersey referred to Toftenes' port helm order as the 'mischief' which caused the collision. This is a curious choice of words by today's usage, but was most likely intended in the old English sense of calamitous outcome as opposed to misdeeds.

Captain Kendall had to handle a few interruptions when Lord Mersey sought clarification but these questions were not laced with a presumption of doubt. Lord Mersey's handling of Kendall as a witness seemed deferential. Perhaps Mersey had a better understanding of the *Empress*'s story from advance statements and did not need to be as aggressive as he was with *Storstad* witnesses. When direct examination by Aspinall revealed that Kendall ordered the watertight doors closed, Lord Mersey interjected with a single question 'This was after, as I understand, the side of the ship was open to the water?' Kendall's reply was affirmative.

It seems out of character for Lord Mersey to have let the matter stand without his customary demand for further explanation. If Captain Kendall had closed all watertight doors before the collision it might have delayed the sinking long enough to save more lives. The editors of a contemporary trade journal seemed to share this view. The 16 July 1914, edition of *Shipbuilding and Shipping Record* concluded an article about Lord Mersey's inquiry as follows 'The general impression in shipping circles is that the limitation of the report let the owners of the *Empress* off pretty lightly...'

The inquiry did not make an exhaustive study of why the *Empress* sank so quickly. Testimony on this area was taken from naval architects and observations were included in the final report. The inquiry concluded that Bulkhead 5 was breached between boiler rooms. A naval architect named John Reid did not necessarily subscribe to that theory because he believed the *Storstad* struck sixteen-feet abaft (behind) the bulkhead. The inquiry did not comment on the possibility that Bulkhead 5 was breached at decks above the boiler rooms. This was possible because Bulkhead 5 was not directly vertical to Upper Deck. It was stepped back at Lower Deck, then vertical to Main Deck; and stepped back again at Main Deck, then vertical to Upper Deck. Accordingly, *Storstad* may have opened Bulkhead 5 at points above the aft boiler room apart from any damage which occurred between boiler rooms.

The *Empress* was designed to stay afloat with two compartments flooded so the damage to Bulkhead 5 should be immaterial. This assumes the ship remains vertical. When the *Empress* began to flood, her longitudinal bulkheads and coal bunkers retained water on the starboard side. The weight of water in one or both boiler rooms caused her to sink until Main Deck was below the water. The retention of water to starboard caused her to list 18 degrees.

Any portholes left open on Main Deck would allow up to 12-inch columns of water to enter freely. Two key watertight doors on the starboard side of Main Deck were not closed: Watertight Door 86 near the second-class boot room; and Watertight Door 78 at the forward end of the third-class dining saloon. This allowed water to build-up along the starboard length of Main Deck, increasing the list; and lowering the ship farther until Upper Deck was similarly affected. The ship could not survive with Upper Deck flooded. The tremendous accumulation of water to starboard capsized her first.

One of the questions which Minister Hazen wanted answered was how many survived by class and gender. Lord Mersey published the following death toll in response to that question. *(Facing page)*

PASSENGER CATEGORY	ON BOARD	SAVED (%)
1st Class - Women	34	11
Men	49	24
Children	4	1
Total	87	36 (41%)
2nd Class - Women	107	13
Men	114	33
Children	32	2
Total	253	48 (19%)
3rd Class - Women	169	17
Men	446	115
Children	102	1
Total	717	133 (18%)
CREW CATEGORY		
ENGINEERING	134	95
STEWARDS	222	114
DECK	59	36
MUSICIANS	5	3
TOTAL	420	248 (60%)
GRAND TOTAL	1477	465 (31%)

Sir Thomas Shaughnessy returned from his summer home in St Andrews, New Brunswick, three days after Lord Mersey delivered his findings.

On 14 July he made the following statement:

> The verdict speaks for itself. It is a source of great satisfaction to the CPR to know that no blame attaches to any of the company's officers, and that Canada's great waterway is equally free from reproach. These are the bright features that emerge from the inquiry into a disaster that cast a gloom over the world, and left many sad hearts.

Attorneys for the *Storstad* were quick to point out that the Mersey inquiry had no legal effect. They did acknowledge that the inquiry's findings would carry 'some weight'. The *Storstad* was sold at auction on 7 July by order of the Registrar of the Admiralty Court. The conditions of sale required the successful bidder to take the ship as is, deposit ten per cent of the purchase price on sale date, and pay the balance within fifteen days.

The auction took place in the same courthouse where Lord Mersey conducted his investigation. Bidding started at $100,000. There were bids and counter bids in amounts as small as $500 until the figure reached $165,000. The bidding stalled. Mr Thomas Hall, the initial bidder, raised the price to $168,000 after which incremental bidding resumed. The hammer fell at a price of $175,000. Mr Charles Cornell, representing a Norwegian concern, was the successful bidder. The proceeds from the sale were held by Admiralty Court pending a legal determination of liability.

As expected, CPR, their underwriters, and a large number of other claimants went to Admiralty court to seek damages. A total of $3,069,483.94 in damages were filed. This consisted of $2,000,000 for the *Empress*; $600,016.43 in lost property; and $469,467.51 for loss of life. The lawsuits were put before Admiralty justice Dunlop of the Exchequer Court of Canada at Quebec. Dunlop essentially accepted the findings of the Mersey inquiry and held the *Storstad* to blame. This decision was issued on 27 April 1915. The Norwegians did not suffer financially because the *Storstad* was the only asset which the court could legally reach. Her liability ended with her sale.

The legal battle continued, however, because Dunlop ruled that claims for loss of life had priority over property claims. Canadian Pacific appealed this ruling to the Supreme Court of Canada and lost. CPR then appealed to the Lords of the Judicial Committee of the Privy Council and won. Their decision, dated 5 December 1919, set aside prior rulings and directed that the $175,000 plus interest recovered from the sale of the *Storstad* be distributed pro rata in proportion to the amounts of respective life and property claims.

Fannie Mounsey's body was never found and no survivors could account for how she died. There was a woman, resembling Mrs Mounsey, who entered a Liverpool institution after the loss of the *Empress*. She also claimed to be 'Mrs Mounsey' and in her half-crazed moments displayed an incredible fear of water. In Chicago, relatives heard about the 'Mounsey' woman and decided to travel to Liverpool to investigate. Perhaps she managed to evade death on the *Empress* or crossed on a different liner only to lose her mind when she learned of the sinking. On 1 May 1915, William Mounsey, his daughter Sarah, and son-in-law Charles Lund boarded *Lusitania* for the journey to Liverpool. Mounsey and Lund went down with the *Lusitania* after she was torpedoed on 7 May. Sarah went on to check out the mysterious woman. 'When I saw her, I was heartbroken,' Sarah said. The deranged woman was not Sarah's mother. She was not Chicago's Fannie Mounsey.

8 Shallow Grave

The completion of salvage operations on the *Empress* immediately following her loss in 1914 was a monumental accomplishment. Initially, CPR and the underwriters had no plans to pursue salvage of her 'treasure'. She was carrying 212 bars of silver valued at $1,099,000, tons of mail, and passenger valuables locked in the Purser's safe. Retrieval of these was an ambitious undertaking not likely to be commensurate with the cost of recovery.

The value of gold, silver, negotiable instruments, jewellery, and contents of mail carried by any ship always increases exponentially when she sinks. The *Empress of Ireland* was no exception. Claims from the estates of deceased passengers poured in. Many claimants had legal representation and were bolstered by the sympathy of a grieving public. CPR was beleaguered.

To steer clear of the looming financial and public relations catastrophe, a decision was made by the underwriters to contract for a salvage expedition. A joint American and Canadian team was employed under the leadership of William Wallace Wotherspoon. Their mission was almost impossible given the technology of the day.

Wreck explorers prior to the turn of the century knew that working underwater, even at modest depths, could kill. Early treasure hunters working for extended periods 40 feet or deeper frequently developed painful tremors shortly after a direct rise to the surface. This condition was called the 'bends' because its victims usually curled up in contorted seizures. Some saw it as divine retribution for robbing the graves of dead ships. In any event, it was accepted by some as a risk worth taking in pursuit of underwater riches.

The dawn of massive public works such as the Brooklyn Bridge resulted in many labourers getting the bends from working in underwater caissons. Caissons were pumped free of water and slightly pressurized to permit the excavation and installation of deep bridge footings. The premier architectural firm of the day, John A. Roebling and Sons, was responsible for construction of the Brooklyn Bridge. The chief engineer on the project, Washington Augustus Roebling, spent so much time in caissons that he suffered depth induced paralysis. Many of the caisson workers he supervised suffered the same fate.

In a curious twist of fate, Roebling's son, Washington A. Roebling II, lost his life on another engineering marvel in 1912. At the age of 31, W. A. Roebling II, jumped from the rail of *Titanic* as she took her final plunge. He was never seen again.

The senior Roebling's depth-induced affliction was a call to action for scientists because he was important enough to raise public consciousness about the mysterious malady. Nitrogen in the lungs at pressure is dissolved in a diver's blood. The nitrogen accumulates in the body and is absorbed faster as pressure increases with greater depth. Decrease the pressure rapidly and dissolved nitrogen reverts to its gaseous state filling the body with bubbles. This process is somewhat analogous to what happens with a bottle of champagne. The liquid in a corked bottle under pressure is free of bubbles. Decrease the pressure by uncorking and the champagne becomes a bubble generator. In human beings, the bubbles lodge in joints, hands, and knees, causing spasmatic disease.

In 1878, scientist Paul Bert showed that nitrogen bubbles could be avoided if the diver gradually came up to the surface. The nitrogen would escape slowly through the lungs without forming an overwhelming expansion of life-threatening bubbles. Decompression as a diving procedure was born. However, more study was needed to perfect the process.

Enter then Lieutenant G. C. Damant, Royal Navy, who helped refine the process to involve stages. Each decompression stage would be calculated to allow nitrogen gas to escape but at an ascending pressure level great enough to prevent large bubble formation. Later, as Commander Damant, he would be assigned to recover the gold lost on *Laurentic* in 1917.

At the time of the *Empress*'s loss, the science of diving had progressed to give divers a better understanding of the physiological consequences of their work. Decompression tables were published to help divers plan their ascent. Divers could visit the outer hull of the *Empress* with a fair degree of confidence. Salvage operations, however, were still in their infancy. It was cumbersome to perform manual labour underwater in the diving outfit of the day. The equipment looked like costume on loan from a Jules Verne movie set especially the diving bell helmet with round view glass. After putting on a rubber and canvas suit, weighted boots, and breast plate, the diver was crowned with a copper helmet. This hardened headgear was bolted to the rest of the outfit. Mobility was reduced by an umbilical cord consisting of surface-supplied air hose and tender line. There was no reliable underwater torch invented yet which could burn through cables or other obstructions inside the hull. The most effective tools at the time were the underwater drill and dynamite. Successful salvage of the *Empress*'s riches seemed doubtful, if not impossible. It would require teamwork plus a brand of individual fortitude reserved for a few. To begin the odds-defying task, the exact location of the *Empress* would have to be determined.

The government steamer *Druid* had already installed a gas buoy north-east of the wreck. HMS *Essex* was given the mission of marking the exact location of the hull. This involved far more than just dropping over the side and installing a buoy. Divers needed to know how the ship was oriented on the bottom. To 'map' the exact position of the hull, diver Wilfred Whitehead crawled along the length of the port side from stern to bow. Members of the dive team on the surface followed Whitehead's bubbles and used them as a basis for longitudinal orientation of the hull. Bearings were also noted for future reference. Whitehead's bubbles showed the *Empress of Ireland*'s bow to be pointed north-east confirming Captain Andersen's last observation from the *Storstad*.

All access to the *Empress* had to be through deck hatches or openings on the port side since she leaned to starboard about 45 degrees at that time. It was conceivable that a diver could have looked over the starboard rail and proceeded down to examine the damaged side. Whitehead's team deemed this foolhardy as they believed the giant liner was poised to roll another 45 degrees to starboard without notice. Even if Whitehead had permitted exploration of the starboard side most or all of the damage was probably hidden by virtue of the ship's starboard inclination.

Whitehead's fears about the stability of the wreck were well founded. On 24 July 1914, powerful surges of current caused the formerly lifeless leviathan to move. To everyone's surprise, especially Whitehead's, the *Empress* rolled to port not starboard. Like a proud lady, she was trying to right herself for an imaginary run to the surface or perhaps just getting comfortable in her new surroundings. She came so close to righting herself that her masts were reported to be visible. This is entirely possible given her keel to mast-tip height of 177 feet. The Ministry of Marine and Fisheries rightfully saw this development as a potential menace to navigation and ordered the masts blown off with dynamite. The *Empress* eventually settled back to starboard so the masts were never removed. The forward mast remained intact until it broke above the crow's nest in 1985.

Preparing to dive in the very unwieldy diving suits of 1914.

The starboard declination of the hull was a minor factor complicating salvage when compared to overall environmental conditions facing Wotherspoon's team. The St Lawrence was virtually opaque under water so divers were lucky if they could see 10 feet in front of them. Current at the site reached peaks of strength where it was physically impossible to descend to the wreck. The flow of current was also subject to unnerving changes in direction due to a perpetual tug of war between opposing Labrador and Gaspe currents. Water temperature was just two or three-degrees above freezing, quickly numbing hands and fingers so critical to underwater tasks. A thermocline played havoc with buoyancy and visibility which can be radically inconsistent above and below the layer. These adverse environmental conditions still plague divers today. The modern technical diver, however, is not encumbered with a heavy, unwieldy canvas suit.

A diving team aboard the Marie Josephine - (Courtesy Merlin Films)

The copper diving bell helmet used by Wotherspoon's divers had a spring-loaded exhaust valve which permitted air to escape into the sea. This was the source of bubbles observed from the surface in tracing the position of the hull. The surface-supplied air in the helmet is maintained at a pressure a little bit above depth pressure. This offsets the tremendous forces pushing against the body and allows the breast plate to expand during inhalation. If this delicate balance is upset so that the diver's internal pressure is lower than sea pressure, a calamity called the 'squeeze' results. This is how the *Empress of Ireland* took her first diver. Lost on 20th June 1914, he was Edward Cossaboom, from New York, one of Wotherspoon's crack team.

Every diver below the surface had a handler on board the *Marie Josephine*. The *Marie Josephine* was an old tramp schooner known for hauling fish and cargo up and down the St Lawrence. She was refitted with air tanks, two air compressors, hose, valves, gauges, and tons of equipment to support salvage operations. *Lord Strathcona* towed her to the wreck site. The handler's job was to keep the diver's umbilical cord — his lifelines, semi-taut. Down below, Edward Cossaboom had walked so far forward on the hull that his lifelines descended as a leisurely arc from the surface. Cossaboom lost his footing and was swept off the *Empress*'s bow by a strong current. The slack lifelines allowed him to plunge freely to the bottom.

Using the 65 foot width of the *Empress* as a guide, Cossaboom suddenly experienced the pressure of an additional 65 feet of water. The blood volume of his arms and legs was squeezed up into his heart and lungs until his chest exploded. By the time he reached bottom, the flexible canvas suit allowed sea pressure to strip the flesh from his bones. His organs and tissues were pile driven into the one part of his suit which didn't flex — the copper helmet. Prior to his fall,

Cossaboom had sent the bodies of two *Empress* victims to the surface. After 30 minutes, his handler was unable to hail him so two divers from the Wotherspoon team were dispatched to rescue him. They returned empty-handed probably not having looked for their dive mate on the bottom. The salvage team was out of fresh divers so an *Essex* diver volunteered to look for Cossaboom. The *Essex* diver was successful in locating what was left of the fallen salvage diver. When Cossaboom was hauled to the surface, he resembled a jellyfish with copper armour and dangling canvas tentacles.

As grotesque as Cossaboom's fatality was, it did not bring a halt to salvage attempts on the *Empress*. The dive team had to face far more gruesome mortality throughout the *Empress* on a scale unparalleled in diving history. Passageways and overheads were crammed full of waterlogged, deformed corpses. One by one, bodies were pulled out of their ocean-liner coffin and hooked to lines for the trip to the surface. It was a grisly business made more horrendous by crustaceans drawn to the new bounty contained within the cavernous hull. Some of the bodies were consumed sufficiently to forever preclude identification. Once the critical passageways were clear, divers searched other areas of the ship including some cabins. This involved crawling along pitch black, tilted corridors with no idea what to expect beyond the range of an anaemic underwater lantern. Divers would slowly peer around the edge of a cabin door and often find themselves rushed by a hideous corpse. The face of the dead seemed to dart for the diver's helmet as though to plant a kiss in gratitude for their release to the surface. Some faces revealed magnitudes about a moment frozen in time. They shared a wide eyed look of horror capturing the very last seconds of entrapment before water totally replaced the air in their lungs. Many must have shared a last gasp of prayer and a belief in divine providence... not understanding why, yet not questioning their historic final passage.

Bodies which were not recognizable and could nor otherwise be identified were interred in a mass grave along the banks of the St Lawrence at Pointe Pouliot. On one day alone, 22 June, 47 unidentified corpses were laid to rest at this spot. An additional 21 unidentifiable bodies and 20 known dead were buried shortly thereafter. A tall grey, granite monolith was erected over the tomb as a permanent memorial to these lost souls. The names of the 20 known dead are engraved on the memorial together with a tribute to the unknown laid to rest. Canadian Pacific provided the monolith and maintains the site to this day.

The process of hoisting bodies one by one from underwater was emotionally as well as physically draining. It was not possible to recover all the bodies especially those deep within the hull so hundreds of corpses remain permanently entombed. Although Canadian Pacific had committed to recovering as many bodies as possible, it was a token effort. The economic reality of the situation made the salvage of mail, money and silver a priority.

The salvage of mail bags was more pleasant work and gave the divers personal motivation to continue. Raised mail bags also demonstrated their productivity to naysayers. The recovered postal cargo comprised 318 bags of mail containing letters, parcels, newspapers and registered documents. After drying on benches in a Rimouski warehouse, each letter was stamped 'Recovered by divers from wreck of SS *Empress of Ireland.*' The value of money orders and other financial instruments amounted to $90,842. 01. All salvaged mail was returned to the Dead Letter Office in Ottawa.

This office returned salvaged letters to the sender wherever there was a legible return address (three months had passed since they were posted). Amazingly some originators wrote back to the Postmaster General to complain. One woman from Armstrong, British Columbia, wrote 'Two letters recovered from the wreck of the *Empress of Ireland* have recently been returned to me. As in each case the address on the envelope is perfectly legible and the postage duly paid, I am at a loss to understand why they were not forwarded to the respective addresses.'

Some of the salvaged and returned letters from the Empress of Ireland.
(Courtesy Merlin Films.)

Eventually, salvage of the silver bullion was also completed. Every bar was accounted for. There was a rumour that some of the silver was stashed in the wreck for later unauthorized recovery by the divers.

The Purser's safe was the primary target of the salvage expedition. Canadian Pacific imposed one qualification on recovery of the safe. The safe had to be retrieved unopened and undamaged otherwise litigants would claim their valuables were compromised. If the door of the safe was breached, claimants would say their valuables were lost or substituted with items of lesser value leaving the company little recourse except to settle on unfavourable terms.

Wotherspoon's team did their homework to prepare for their monstrous final lift. They studied blueprints and memorized details like the number of rivets between portholes to fix locations on the hull. They also studied the layout of the *Empress of Ireland*'s twin sister, *Empress of Britain*. On 3 July 1914, the dive team boarded *Lady Evelyn* at Rimouski and steamed until alongside the *Empress of Britain*. It was 2:30am. Salvage divers measured the Purser's safe and noted the dimensions of various routes out of the hull from the port side of Upper Deck. The safe was enormous. It was a giant rectangular box, fives times taller than its width, approximately the size of a telephone booth. The visit aboard *Empress of Britain* was brief. After less than an hour she was underway and the divers were returning on *Lady Evelyn*.

To begin the recovery of the Purser's safe, divers located a cargo hatch which was almost directly over the ship's office. Chains were secured to the port rail above this location. L-shaped angle-irons suspended from the chains served as a work platform. A pneumatic drill was used to bore holes delineating a 6-foot by 12-foot area around the hatch. The original plan was to saw between the holes until an opening was achieved. Given that the divers were dealing with an existing hatch, dynamite was the next logical step. A substantial opening was blown in the ship's side. Modern day technical divers use this opening to get inside the wreck appropriately referring to it as the 'explosion hole'.

The Purser's safe is raised on August 20, 1914.

Most of the labour which created a vertical exit point for the safe was performed by the explosive. The next step involved dexterous manual underwater labour which was hard to effect inside a dark hull at freezing temperatures wearing a cumbersome diving outfit. Two teams were used to provide the labour necessary to free the *Empress*'s safe. The first dive team unbolted the safe from the bulkhead behind it and attached preliminary rigging to haul it out of the purser's office. The second team went down with sledgehammers to demolish any potential obstacles which might impede the path to the exit hole.

Using all their might, the second team pushed the giant safe on to its side. Word was passed to the surface to start the winch. The steel cable tightened and slowly pulled the safe down a passageway to its manmade port of freedom. The cable was re-rigged for the journey to the surface. The final lift commenced with divers using crowbars to align the safe to the exit hole. The safe twisted back and forth at the end of the cable repeatedly banging against the hull as it progressed upward. On the surface, the steam powered winch huffed and puffed under tremendous strain. Steam engine noise masked the more alarming pinging and grinding of cable fatigue. The *Marie Josephine* dipped to the side as everyone on board focused their attention on the spot where the cable disappeared below the water. An interminable wait, then, an immense shower of water as the safe broke the surface on 20 August 1914. The deed was done.

The triumphant salvors were about to dance an Irish jig when they noticed something as the safe twisted serenely over the water at the end of the boom. The harness chain and steel cable which embraced the safe had slipped perilously close to the top edge. If the rigging edged its way up much farther, the safe would drop off the end of the cable leaving an empty harness dangling at the end of the boom. Fortunately cool heads prevailed. The boom was gingerly swung over the deck. The winch slowly lowered the safe to the deck. Now, the deed was done. The salvage team had beaten the odds and successfully completed all aspects of the expedition under extremely unforgiving conditions. They were entitled to cheer, sing and dance.

Soon, Canadian Pacific would also have something to cheer about. Observers from the Canadian Government sealed the door of the safe. Arrangements were made for the *Lady Evelyn* to transport the safe to Quebec. The safe was kept at the Bank of Montreal on St Peter Street until the day finally arrived to show its contents to what seemed like a worldwide audience. It was Saturday, 22 August 1914. Barristers, litigants, executors, relatives of the deceased, insurance examiners, company officials, and reporters crowded into a room where the *Empress of Ireland*'s safe was centre stage. The official parties to the event were Angus M. Campbell, CPR's travelling auditor; William Q. Stobo, Secretary Treasurer of the Canadian Salvage Association, Ltd; Arthur Nash, Manager of the Quebec offices of the Bank of Montreal; and Reginald Meredith, Notary Public for the City of Quebec.

A locksmith with expertise in 'safecracking' was hired to perform the honours. He would drill for a few seconds and then pause to examine his work. With the dramatic flair of a perfectionist, the locksmith used a special cloth to brush metal shavings clear of the drill site. After a long morning the drilling stopped. The disquietude of the assembly was palpable as shoulders competed for space and heads jockeyed for the best view. The one-sided handle in the centre of the door freely cranked to the right disengaging the interior latches. A mechanical click echoed through the anxious room. A hard tug on the pull handle and then whoosh as the safe rushed to expel its stale air. Showtime had arrived.

The crowd was stunned by the sight of a virtually empty, capacious Purser's safe. There were a few canvas bags and three more locked compartments to be opened. The process of opening the locked compartments was delayed when the locksmith went to an alcove and opened his lunch pail.

Many in the crowd expected the safe to be brimming with cash and jewellery. They must have imagined an overflow of riches which would cascade out upon this momentous opening. After a long lunch break, the locksmith resumed his duties. Two of the three compartments were opened. At 5:00pm, the locksmith packed up his things. The third compartment would have to wait until Monday, 24 August to be opened.

There was cash, travellers' cheques, and negotiable paper in the safe but the sum total barely reached one-half-per cent (0.5%) of the amount claimed. Claims against *Titanic* were also exaggerated, totalling well over twice the cost of the ship and her fittings. The liability proceedings against White Star were still ongoing during and after the loss of *Empress of Ireland*. Canadian Pacific officials must have been relieved to watch embarrassed claimants whose liability cases evaporated as quickly as stale air from the Purser's safe.

The *Empress* lay peacefully undisturbed for fifty years following Wotherspoon's initial salvage expedition. She was relocated on 17 July 1964 by five divers assisted by Aubert Brillant who volunteered the use of his vessel *La Canadienne*. The five members of the dive team were Robert and Claude Villeneuve, Jean-Paul Fournier, Fernand Bergeron, and André Ménard. The first artefact recovered was a wooden block and pulley assembly recovered from the forward cargo handling area. Another choice find was the ship's 10-inch brass warning bell originally located on the Bridge.

Today, the *Empress* lies in a shallow grave which is visited regularly by sport and technical divers, especially during the months of August and September. Diving the *Empress of Ireland* became extremely popular in 1990 with the advent of organised expeditions. Now, every summer, she is reticent hostess to divers from all over the world.

The *Empress of Ireland* rests on her starboard side at an angle of about 60 degrees. Sediment has filled in almost the entire starboard side on an angle running from the keel to a point inboard of the starboard rail. The starboard side of the wheel house is touching the clay bottom. At low tide the distance to the port side of the hull amidships is about 70 feet. Her starboard side at the bow is down 150 feet or more. The bottom of the stern came to rest slightly higher than the bow at 120 feet below the surface. Current has furrowed out the area immediately under the stern permitting divers to swim under her counter and sounding platform. Two blades of the starboard propeller and the rudder are visible.

The hull is perfectly intact retaining its original shape and volume from keel through Shelter Deck. The superstructure of the *Empress* has crushed together leaving only crawl spaces between decks. The superstructure has also settled sideways, sliding off the hull to starboard, onto the channel floor. There is a small debris field which fans out about 25 feet to starboard. The debris runs from the wheelhouse bulkhead forward to just aft of the second funnel. The debris field is largely comprised of superstructure or items from the superstructure. There are no large components scattered on the bottom as in *Titanic*'s debris field because the hull never fractured. Spared unsightly dismemberment and evisceration, the *Empress*'s machinery remained in place, forever entombed within the darkest reaches of the hull.

Canadian technical diver Stephen Brooks began diving on the *Empress* in 1983 and has completed many dives since. He has reached areas not previously explored such as the second-class pantry and parts of steerage. In 1986, Brooks discovered a lifeboat outside the immediate debris field. It was sitting upright, facing east, about 100 feet from the starboard side of the wreck. The stern of the lifeboat appeared to be torn off.

The *Empress* is in better overall condition than either *Titanic* or *Lusitania*. Her remaining exterior features are readily discernable because she is not bleeding a profuse river of external rust like *Titanic*. The high port side of the *Empress* is littered with tunicates. These sea creatures obscure the port side in places to the point where first-time divers think they missed the wreck and hit bottom. One diver described tunicates as a 'stomach on a stem' and warned that they give off a ghastly smell when exposed to air.

Most remarkable is that the *Empress* has not lost much of her woodwork to natural causes. *Titanic*'s planking is completely gone. *Empress* woodwork has been spared ingestion by marine life. It is so well preserved that loose wooden decking from the superstructure has been harvested by commercial salvors. Wooden railings are still intact and clearly visible except for occasional barnacles. In the superstructure, a complete oak door including door knob is suspended on its side having turned to horizontal as the decks compressed. So clean and free from encrustation, the rich grain of the oak reminds one of how the *Empress* was appointed during her Edwardian heyday.

The commercial salvage of the *Empress*'s teak decking began in June 1993. Seven divers working for 3091-5243 Quebec, Inc., removed approximately 5,000 feet of teak planks ranging in length from 8 to 22 feet. The divers were directed by Michael Tadros, owner of the 127 foot northern trawler *Gesmer 1* which served as dive platform and on-site base. The recovered planking was warehoused for future use.

The funnels of the *Empress*, as one might expect, are no longer visible. One can see where they attached but the stacks must be buried in the mud. Outboard from the collapsed superstructure are the remains of two lifeboats. These are believed to be two of the Englehardt wood and canvas collapsibles which were nested below each steel boat. Collapsibles, sometimes called surf boats, resemble a standard wooden whale boat except that the sides are missing. In storage, they look as though something squashed them flat. To properly deploy a collapsible, canvas covered steel frames are pulled up adding 25 inches to the craft's sides. A diver can stand on the St Lawrence seabed and look right down into the *Empress*'s collapsibles. Lathe planking and stringers can clearly be seen. Also visible are copper airtight tanks (approximately 2 feet x 2 feet x 3 feet) which were used for buoyancy. These copper air compartments are in excellent shape except for one which has been dished inward by damage and pressure. In general, copper seems to hold up well in shipwrecks. In Ballard's *The Discovery of The Titanic*, copper kitchen pots appear as new, barely having lost their original shine.

The *Lusitania*'s hull rests 300 feet below the surface just south of the Irish coast off Old Head of Kinsale. Like the *Empress*, she is relatively free of feature-obscuring veils of marine growth. Also like the *Empress*, she sank quickly, within sight of shore and then settled on her starboard side. The *'Lusi'*, however, is in the worst condition of the three contemporaries: *Titanic*, *Empress of Ireland*, and *Lusitania*. Her hull has collapsed to half its original beam. What is left is torn open between the position of the third and fourth funnel as though giant hands snapped the hull in two. She is draped in cobwebs of fishing net which hazards her exploration and adds to her foreboding, macabre appearance. Unlike the *Empress*, her superstructure is totally obliterated.

The 90-foot ship *Morrisburgh*, under the direction of Captain Brian Erb, served as dive platform for an expedition to recover one of the *Empress*'s manganese-bronze propellers. Technical assistance was provided by Donald Tremblay of the Rimouski Marine Institute. Each propeller was 20 feet 6 inches in diameter, had four blades, and weighed twenty tons. On 28 September 1968, divers succeeded in freeing the port-side propeller after blasting a hole in the stern. The propeller was hoisted near the surface and towed by *Morrisburgh* at a speed of 1 knot to Rimouski. During transit, the *Morrisburgh* almost foundered when the propeller struck bottom. One of the propeller blades hit a rock, snapped a cable and was lost.

The *Morrisburgh* eventually reached Rimouski where she off-loaded her burden. More than 3000 people showed up to view the 62-year-old propeller which was sold to a scrap dealer who paid $5000 for the giant screw. The sum of $5,000 was a disappointing reward for all the effort expended.

In 1980, oceanographer Jacques Cousteau and his son Jean-Michel Cousteau, explored the St Lawrence Seaway aboard their research vessel *Calypso*. Side-scanning sonar was deployed to search for the *Empress of Ireland*. The *Calypso* carried a distinguished passenger, Ronald Ferguson, an *Empress of Ireland* survivor from Chelmsford, England. Ferguson, now deceased, sent out the *Empress*'s SOS distress signal as lead Marconi Operator.

The *Calypso* dive team, joined by local diver Philippe Beaudry, conducted an underwater examination of the *Empress of Ireland*. A visit to Captain Kendall's cabin yielded a few interesting artefacts. The Captain's ink well, a straight razor, and glass clock face were recovered. The discovery of the clock face was fortuitous in that Beaudry recovered the clock itself years earlier. A video entitled 'St Lawrence, Stairway to the Sea' produced by the Cousteau Society has a short segment documenting the *Empress of Ireland* exploration. It is distributed through Time-Life Video, Alexandria, Virginia.

Philippe Beaudry became enthralled with diving the wreck of the *Empress*. He made hundreds of dives and retrieved many artefacts. He founded the Rimouski

Maritime Museum (Musée de la Mer de Rimouski) in May 1980 and served as its first President. The museum was later reorganized as a joint public-private enterprise known today as Musée de la Mer, Pointe-au-Pére (Maritime Museum, Father Point). Beaudry plans to sell 401 items from his collection of artefacts to an American businessman for the princely sum of $1.5 million. Among the items are one of the ship's 24-inch brass fog bells, the Captain's stateroom telephone, assorted glass and china, unopened wine bottles, a telemotor, and ironically the starboard side navigation light which featured so prominently on the night of the collision. On 16 June 2000, the Canadian Cultural Property Export Review Board placed a moratorium on Beaudry's proposed sale in an effort to keep the *Empress of Ireland* artefacts in Canada.

A video entitled 'Lost Not Forgotten', was released by Canadian Dan Lindsay in 1996. This 22 minute production includes historical photos, underwater footage, and computer animation by Norman Pickthall. It is available from SeaView Imaging of Brantford, Ontario.

American technical diver John Moyer has made about 30 dives on the *Empress* since 1990. He describes it as 'fantastic', among his top 2 or 3 wrecks to explore. Moyer is also an expert diver on the *Andrea Doria*. Moyer has extensively explored the rich-rich first-class areas of the wreck including the alcoves of the main saloon; and third-class pantry. In the music room, the grand piano can be seen toppled over on its back.

Gary Gentile, American author and technical diver, has made 40 dives on the *Empress* since 1990. He has recovered a wide variety of artefacts including examples of all three classes of china, a full bottle of champagne, the brass button from a steward's jacket, and a Rube Goldberg-inspired copper hard-boiled egg timer. He has encountered human bones on the wreck including skulls but, like most divers, leaves these undisturbed. Gentile describes a dive on the *Empress* as dismal, 'like a night dive', complicated by the build up of mud and silt. The clay mud in the wreck has accumulated on the starboard side where many artefacts came to rest when the ship rolled over. Gentile said one of his most exciting finds was when he stuck his hand into the clay sediment of the first-class children's saloon. He felt a series of ridges and from previous experience knew he had a great find. Adrenalin pumping, he carefully pulled out his treasure — an arm's length stack of first-class china.

John Reekie, technical diver and owner of Alternative Dive Products, has made about 100 dives on the *Empress* since his first dive in 1989. He says that he is probably the only person on the planet who has been in *Empress of Ireland*'s engine room since she sank. He descended into the wreck through an opening in the deck and swam aft until he reached what appeared to be a shaft. At the end of this passageway was a narrow opening. This opening may have been one of the two watertight doors in Bulkhead 6 at the forward end of the engine room. Another possibility is that this narrow egress may have been a channel for steam pipes. Reekie gingerly negotiated his body through the silt-choked opening to find he had arrived in the engine room.

Looking aft, to his left, John Reekie could see the top of one of the giant reciprocating engines. It was hard to distinguish because it was filled in with tons of sediment. Looking forward, he discovered the unmistakable brass engine order telegraph in perfect shape. The letters spelling out engine orders could still be seen on the white faced indicator. Reekie was not looking for the last order shown on the indicator so he does not recall what was showing. The brass base was still bolted in place but the entire engine order telegraph was oriented in the wrong direction. It should lean to starboard in the same direction as the ship. John was surprised to find it leaning dramatically over to port. One possible explanation is natural decay. Years of deterioration undermined the deck and the weight of the telegraph shifted the instrument from its original position. Another theory is that the interior of the engine room was reconfigured by the explosion.

Reekie observed conditions deep inside the engine room and hold. He described them as 'scary' like 'your worst nightmare'. The bowels of the *Empress of Ireland* are in an advanced stage of decay. Yellow, brown and black rusticles ooze from the ship's pores. Two to three foot long 'hairs' hover like tentacles in search of foreign invaders. Loose electrical wires drenched in silt form menacing spider webs which when disturbed pull down gobs of debris. Partitions which used to define rooms and passageways are gone. Limited visibility blurs what little is left to recognize. Darkness hides a presence which seems to be standing watch.

Among the artefacts recovered by John Reekie are spoons, dishes, port holes 511 and 518, and a jar of peaches. He can also take credit for one of the most unusual finds — a set of moose antlers. This was a trophy to commemorate Sir Henry Seton-Karr's travels through the Canadian wilderness. Reekie donated the antlers to Musée de la Mer, Pointe-au-Pére, where they are on permanent display.

Several years after Reekie, Canadian Technical diver Dany St-Cyr also explored the engine room. He went further and penetrated the dark reaches of the ship's emergency steering station at the extreme stern. St-Cyr said one visit to the engine room was enough to satisfy his curiosity.

Terry German, a Canadian technical diver and video producer, recalled his feelings the first time he was about to descend to the *Empress of Ireland*. He thought it would be 'hell on earth'. An eerie descent in murky, cold water was suddenly interrupted by a massive, 'mind-blowing' hull. In subsequent years, Terry has explored the deeper third-class areas of the wreck. One such journey graphically revealed the enormity of life lost on the *Empress*. Terry was reaching to recover several bottles when falling debris uncovered the skeletal remains of dozens of third-class passengers. Many were children. Fragments of leather clothing formed a loose shroud over some of the victims.

To commemorate the 80th anniversary of the *Empress of Ireland* disaster, on 29 May 1994, divers Terry German and Kim Martin of Toronto placed a plaque on the hull. (see next page)

The plaque reads:

> ## *EMPRESS OF IRELAND*
>
> In memory to all those
> Promoted to Glory from The Salvation Army
> and the rest of the 1012 passengers
> who lost their lives on May 29, 1914
> Honouring the 80th anniversary
> May 29, 1994

Divers German and Martin presented the Salvation Army with recovered wine bottles and a gold pocket watch which now reside in the Salvation Army Heritage Centre Museum in Toronto, Ontario. The museum has a permanent exhibit dedicated in honour of Canadian Salvation Army personnel who were 'promoted to glory' in the loss of the *Empress of Ireland.*

One of three service anchors manufactured by Halls Patent Anchor Company Ltd. This was a 'Sheffield' 7 ton anchor. (Musée de la Mer, Point-au-Pére).

Epilogue

No passengers were believed to have boarded the *Empress of Ireland* at Father Point. Any travelling CPR Agent would have disembarked with Pilot Adelard Bernier and at least one did. Accounts differ on the name of the Agent who disembarked at Father Point. It may have been David Reid Kennedy Jr, from Montreal. He was a career employee of Canadian Pacific who worked his way up from baggage handler to District Agent. The other name mentioned as the disembarking Agent is William Webber. Mr Webber assisted relatives with identification of the dead at Quebec. CPR officials at Windsor Station in Montreal first learned of the sinking by telephone. This call came from the Agent or Agents who left the ship at Father Point. Some reports held that Captain Kendall notified CPR by telegram using only two words 'Ship gone.'

Cunard's *Aquitania* sailed on her maiden voyage from Liverpool on 30 May, with no publicity. This momentous event was completely overshadowed by press coverage of the tragedy on the St Lawrence.

Sir Arthur Conan Doyle, author of the Sherlock Holmes mysteries, was in Montreal on a lecture tour immediately following the tragedy. Journalists asked him to solve the mystery of the fog-shrouded collision. Sir Arthur, unprepared and slightly embarrassed by the serious question, offered no clues.

Hundreds of letters poured into the Canadian Government following the loss of the *Empress of Ireland*. Some of the suggestions from citizens and industry were noteworthy. The Illinois Malleable Iron Company of Chicago asked if cabin doors could be made detachable for use as small rafts. An individual wrote repeatedly with a plan to give all steamship passengers the equivalent of military dog-tags to speed identification in the event of accident. Several letters suggested an electric buzzer in all cabins which the Captain could activate if immediate evacuation was required. The Maytham Improved Ship Construction Company of Buffalo offered a new hull design consisting of a series of watertight hoppers. If struck forcibly, the hull could split yet both pieces remain afloat. Some volunteered to dive the *Empress* having seen discussions of salvage in the newspapers. There were also salvage proposals such as connecting cables from a giant land-based winch to the hull in order to drag the wreck ashore. One woman wrote to Minister Hazen to request a spiritual investigation into the disaster. She claimed a 'fallen angel' blinded the steersmen on both ships.

Writers were very careful not to criticize the St Lawrence River on which Canadian colonization and growth depended. Some were so cautious, they closed letters with phrases such as 'the writer is a Canadian, and of course, interested in everything that affects Canada'. Another concluded with 'I hope you attribute it (the presumption of offering suggestions for safety on the St Lawrence) to the zeal and interest of a true Canadian'.

On 5 June 1914, John McWilliams, General Manager at Father Point Pilot Station, wrote a letter to Minister Hazen to offer his suggestions on preventing accidents near Father Point. He pointed out that the *Eureka* would have been at the scene 40 minutes sooner if she had had wireless. She would have left the outbound collier she was servicing immediately upon receiving the SOS instead of returning to Father Point. He also recommended that colliers be required to keep a pilot on board for their entire St Lawrence transit. This would eliminate delay and potential collision at Father Point. The Quebec Board of Trade also recommended round-trip carriage of pilots.

Specific tracks for outbound and inbound steamers were considered by the Lighthouse Board. Deputy Minister of Marine and Fisheries Johnson believed the matter was best left to the various shipping interests. CPR's Captain Walsh supported an inbound track five to seven miles north of Father Point and an outbound track closer to shore. This was to be accomplished by mutual understanding without Government edict.

The belief that the second-class exit door was locked continued to plague Mr Langeley. On 29 June 1914, he sent a telegram to Minister Hazen requesting that salvage divers examine the door. His message was brief and concluded with 'I am of the opinion they were locked'. It is not known if any attempt was made by the salvage team to investigate this further.

After about one month of leave, CPR gave Captain Kendall a shore position as Marine Superintendent at Antwerp. The same edition of the *Shipbuilding and Shipping Record* which commented on the *Empress* getting off lightly added '...we are glad to hear that Captain Kendall has been given a good shore job by the Company'. If he had been dwelling on the loss of the *Empress*, World War I soon displaced those emotions. Kendall acted like a hero in his wartime escape from Antwerp during August 1914. He rescued two Canadian Pacific ships: *Montrose*, the famous carrier of Crippen and his girlfriend; and *Montreal* whose engines were being repaired. Coal was transferred from the *Montreal* to *Montrose* as the latter's bunkers were empty. Kendall, assuming command of *Montrose*, towed the *Montreal* safely to England. It was a narrow escape with a swarm of refugees boarding Captain Kendall's self-made evacuation fleet at the last possible moment.

Montrose was purchased by the British Admiralty, filled with cement, and used to block the entrance to Dover Harbour. In December 1914, she broke free and drifted on to Goodwin Sands where she eventually broke up.

Captain Kendall fulfilled the obligation of his reserve commission throughout the war. For most of the war he served on the Allan liner *Calgarian* as second-in-command. Early in the war, *Calgarian* escorted four new submarines built by Vickers at Montreal across the Atlantic. On 1 March 1918, the German submarine U-19 fired three torpedoes at *Calgarian*, off Rathlin Island, in the channel between Northern Ireland and Scotland. Forty-nine of *Calgarian*'s crew were killed. Captain Kendall slid down a rope into a passing trawler and was saved. *Calgarian* sank.

In *Adventures on the High Seas*, Kendall relates an interesting coincidence following the loss of *Calgarian*. He was waiting for a train to Portsmouth where he would receive new orders. A man on the train kept looking at Kendall until he could stand it no longer. The man asked Kendall his name and received 'Kendall' in reply. The man asked if he was the Captain Kendall who had caught Dr Crippen. Kendall said he was. 'That's damn funny,' the man said, 'I'm the one who executed him. I was the Governor of Pentonville Prison.'

Captain Kendall became CPR's Marine Superintendent in Surrey after the war. In 1939, he retired. Kendall died in a London nursing home on 28 November 1965, at the age of 91. Almost his entire London *Times* obituary recalled his capture of Crippen fifty-five years earlier. The *Empress of Ireland* wasn't even mentioned.

On 9 June 1914, McGill University presented Doctor James Frederick Grant with a diploma to replace the one which went down with the *Empress*. Grant was nominated by McGill University for the British Medical Association's Silver Medal for Distinguished Merit on 19 June. The outbreak of war relegated this nomination to the back burner and no action was ever taken to reinstate it. Canadian Pacific Railway gave Doctor Grant a shore assignment as Chief Medical Officer at Vancouver. He retired from that position in 1938. The heroic ship's surgeon predeceased Captain Kendall by 32 years at the age of 59. His death certificate identified duodenal ulcer as the cause of death complicated by manic-depression. Doctor Grant's obituary in the Victoria *Times* said he is best remembered for the part he played in saving many lives following the loss of the *Empress of Ireland*.

Marconi operator Ronald Ferguson spent his entire career in radio following war service in the Royal Flying Corps. He was employed by the Radio Communications Company, one of the precursors of the British Broadcasting Company (BBC). In 1927, he returned to marine radio with the British Wireless Marine Service and later as General Manager of Marconi International Marine. In 1934, Ferguson accepted an assignment to manage the unprofitable Egyptian State Broadcasting system in Cairo. He was awarded the OBE and Egypt's Order of the Nile for returning the Egyptian operation to financial health and for his service there during World War II. He retired from Marconi International Marine in 1961 but continued on as a member of its Board of Directors for several years. Like Captain Kendall, Ronald Ferguson had a long life. He died on 28 July 1985, at the age of 91.

Chief Steward Augustus Gaade became the CPR Shore Steward for Liverpool. It was a position assigned to him before the last sailing of the *Empress*. Voyage 96 was to be Gaade's last trip.

William 'Billy Boy' Hughes went on to marry his sweetheart Veronica about a year after the tragedy. The couple had six children together. Hughes was one of many surviving crewmen who sailed home on the *Alsatian*. He remembered being unable to sleep on the crossing so he polished silverware each night until safely at Liverpool. He later remarked that cleaning the silver was therapeutic like cleansing away a 'secret crime'. Hughes had a long and successful career with Harrisons & Crosfield of Canada, Ltd, importers, after surviving a gas attack during World War I.

Steward Jim Prowse lost all desire to cross on the high seas. He stayed in Canada where Canadian Pacific gave him a job as waiter at the Chateau Frontenac in Quebec. He later became Maitre'd at the Royal York in Toronto.

Mrs Paton resumed life at 'Rockmount', her residence on Moore Street in Sherbrooke. She and her husband continued to take a leading role in Sherbrooke social life. Mrs Paton was extremely active in the welfare of World War I servicemen and veterans. Her principal affiliations included the Canadian Patriotic Society, Canadian Red Cross, and Imperial Order of the Daughters of the Empire. She died ten years after her husband on 17 December 1956, at the age of 82. Her obituary in the Sherbrooke *Daily Record* recalled her experience on the *Empress of Ireland* and praised her for the assistance she gave to the injured and traumatized.

One year after closing the *Empress of Ireland* proceedings in Quebec, Lord Mersey found himself sitting on yet another famous maritime tribunal. Once again, the circumstances were remarkably different from the prior investigation. Mersey's *trifecta* of lost liners concluded with an investigation into the loss of *Lusitania*. Lord Mersey focused the inquiry's blame on Germany and not on the ship's Captain, William Turner, or her owners, Cunard Line. Mersey died fourteen years later at the age of ninety. Butler Aspinall, who represented Canadian Pacific Railway at the *Empress* inquiry, also served as counsel for Cunard at the *Lusitania* inquiry.

Gordon Davidson published his doctoral thesis 'The Northwest Company' in 1916. His reported swim to shore is one of the most remarkable feats of all *Empress of Ireland* survivors. He was wearing his life belt but it is hard to believe he could have swum almost four miles in water temperature just above freezing. Perhaps he utilized a raft or some wreckage?

Henry Herbert Lyman's legacy continues today in the Lyman Entomological Museum and Research Laboratory. It was established following the reading of Lyman's will which left $40,000, an insect collection, and five cabinets of butterflies to McGill University. The original collection was housed in the Peter Redpath Museum at Montreal. It was relocated to the Macdonald Campus by Curator Vernon Vickery, Ph.D., where it has continued to grow in size and recognition. Today, the collection contains over 3 million specimens.

Salvation Army Officer Alfred Keith rose to the rank of Lieutenant Colonel. He retired in 1959. In 1975, at the age of 83, he recalled his experience in a Reader' Digest story by F. J. Woodley. Keith remembered being taken to the Hotel St Germain in Rimouski for breakfast on the morning of 29 May 1914. He was still wrapped in the *Storstad's* table cover. The cloth cover was donated to the Salvation Army Heritage Centre Museum in Toronto, by Keith's family.

Ernest Pugmire rose to become National Commander of the Salvation Army in America. He dropped dead from a heart attack on West 14th Street, just outside Salvation Army Headquarters in New York, after forty years of Christian work.

Each year, on the Sunday closest to 29 May, the Salvation Army of Toronto holds a memorial service in Mount Pleasant Cemetery. Little Gracie Hanagan, later Mrs Grace Martyn, attended the service almost every year without exception. Each year she placed a wreath at the foot of the Salvation Army's *Empress of Ireland* monument. The granite monument was erected in 1916 based on Major Gideon Miller's design. Sculpted by Emanuel Hahn, it consists of a cross rising above the waves. At the base are the names of those interred. Grace Martyn's fear of running water haunted her for the rest of her life. Even the sound of a bathtub filling stirred frightful memories. Grace died at the age of 88 on 15 May 1995.

The *Storstad*, having been purchased by Norwegian interests, eventually rejoined the Klaveness Line. Captain Thomas Andersen's maritime reputation with Klaveness hadn't tarnished. He was reassigned to *Storstad*. On 8 March 1917, *Storstad* was torpedoed and sank off the coast of Ireland. Andersen and his crew survived.

The Canadian Government Steamer *Lady Evelyn*, formerly the *Deerhound* at Blackpool, Great Britain, was sold for $180,000 in 1922 to the Union Steamship Company of Vancouver. She was named after Earl Grey's daughter as he was Governor General of Canada in 1907 when the ship was acquired by the Canadian Government. Union Steamship Company officials did not change her name and adopted the prefix 'Lady' for future vessels.

Crippen's house at Hilldrop Crescent was destroyed by World War II bombing. Wolf Mankowitz and Monty Norman produced a musical entitled 'Belle — or the Ballad of Dr. Crippen' in 1961. It lasted six weeks. The shovel Crippen used to bury Belle's remains is kept in the Black Museum at New Scotland Yard.

A play entitled *Empress of Ireland*, written and directed by Marion Kelch, was staged by the Czar Theatre Guild at Czar, Alberta, during February 1993.

In 1998, a salvage company had planned to intrusively remove what was alleged to be a substantial quantity of Nickel ore from the cargo holds of the *Empress*. Individual citizens, the Salvation Army, and Musée de la Mer lodged protests with the Provincial Government to prevent demolition of the hull and disturbance of human remains contained therein. On 29 April 1998, Quebec's Culture Minister Louise Beaudoin announced the Government's intention to make the *Empress of Ireland* a protected historic site. One year later, this action became official and the wreck was also declared an underwater heritage site. Canada's Coast Guard installed a new buoy several hundred feet south of the wreck which warns prospective visitors that the *Empress* is a protected wreck. Divers may continue to make recreational dives to the site but are not allowed to remove anything without a permit.

On the 85th anniversary of the sinking, 29 May 1999, a 92-minute documentary premiered in Rimouski. Entitled '*Journey To Oblivion*', it was created by Merlin Films of Montreal, Michel T. Prévost, Producer. First broadcast in French, and later remade for English-speaking audiences, '*Journey To Oblivion*' is the first comprehensive documentary entirely devoted to the *Empress of Ireland*. Written and directed by Alain Vézina, it is an emotionally moving remembrance of the tragedy as well as a thorough history of the liner. Computer graphics were skillfully used to dramatize the events leading up to collision. There is extensive underwater footage of the interior and exterior of the wreck. The once thought impenetrable engine room and emergency steering station can be seen. '*Journey To Oblivion*' was selected for screening by a number of international film festivals including: Montreal World Film; International Maritime and Exploration, Toulon; Baie-Comeau; and the International Underwater Film Festival, Antibes, France.

Musée de la Mer at Pointe-au-Père, Quebec, inaugurated its $1.2 million *Empress of Ireland* Pavilion on 2 June 2000. In this new building, visitors can experience a 3-dimensional, multi-media program which recreates the last voyage of the *Empress*. The Pavilion also contains an exhibit on other Canadian Pacific ships.

On 12 July 2000, the Public Broadcasting Service premiered Dr Robert Ballard's '*Lost Liners*' documentary in the United States. The *Empress of Ireland* was profiled together with the liners *Titanic* and *Lusitania* in this 120-minute production by Partisan Pictures of New York. '*Lost Liners*' chronicles Ballard's visits to the great liners 'that didn't make it'. The film begins with Dr Ballard on the St Lawrence en route to the wreck site of the *Empress*. The narrator cues Ballard's reflections by saying that 'this visit will be his last'. Ballard continues: 'Clearly, before I could end this journey and hopefully move on to some other phase in my life, I had to come to the *Empress of Ireland*'.

The story of the *Empress of Ireland* is unknown to many and forgotten by others. Some historians say World War I overshadowed the peacetime loss of one liner. This conclusion is supported by events which were quickly unravelling in Europe. On the day the *Empress* sank, President Wilson's advisor in Berlin, Colonel Edward House, cabled the White House to advise that an extraordinary state of 'militarism' predominated which might some day lead to 'cataclysm'. On 28 June, Archduke Franz Ferdinand was assassinated at Sarajevo. By 4 August Germany crossed into Belgium igniting the cataclysm. British and Canadian citizens woke up the next day to find themselves at war. In April 1915, Canadian troops in Belgium suffered through the first German gas attack at Ypres. On 7 May 1915, the vulnerability of large liners to attack by U-boats was driven home by the loss of *Lusitania*.

World War I ended with the popular will to forget the events of 1914 and war years thereafter. The U-boat war, slaughter in the trenches, and the evil of gas warfare were horrors to be forgotten. It was the fate of the *Empress of Ireland* to sink at a time when the world was poised for the future and ignoring the past.

Exploring why the *Titanic* is remembered may also provide some insight as to why the *Empress* was forgotten. Part of the *Titanic* legend was born out of the image of men, especially those of wealth and power, stepping aside while women and children filled the lifeboats. Chivalry composed a very dignified shipwreck.

The tilted deck of the *Empress* made it impossible for gentlemanly displays of decorum. Survival of the fittest prevailed without an orderly allowance for gender or innocence. Some *Empress* survivors credited God's will for their rescue; others said they were dealt a lucky hand.

Survival of the fittest can be a very graphic picture. Newspapers carried stories about passengers clawing their way out of the *Empress* and pushing others under the water to stay afloat. Although some of this was pure sensationalism, the instinct to live certainly resulted in behaviour which was unimaginable to a civilized society. In short, it was not the stuff legends are made from but rather an episode to be swept from memory.

The images we commit to memory come from clear, vivid events. The *Titanic* observing a towering block of ice too late to avoid collision is an unfortunate but easy sequence to grasp. The same is not true in the case of the *Empress of Ireland*. The mechanics of the tragedy, such as who turned when and what was required by the nautical rules of the road, were difficult to understand. An irrefutable explanation for the loss of the *Empress* never seemed to emerge from the fog which enshrouded her moments before death. The public was left with a complicated and contradictory story which imparted blame to the *Storstad*. There was no enduring visual image for historical recollection or public reinvention.

People share a fascination with unexpected interruptions in the longevity of others. This is another reason why the *Titanic* legend endures. People enjoy the fantasy of a ship with slightly over two hours to live because of the vicarious contemplation of one's fate. What if we knew we had but two hours to live? How would we behave? Passengers on board the *Empress* had little time to think about reaching a lifeboat or immersion in ice-cold water. Their fate was decided in minutes instead of hours. Some on Lower Deck may have had only seconds, if they even woke up at all.

The difference in length of time it took for the two liners to sink affected how survivors assimilated the tragedy. *Empress* survivors were almost instantly confronted with confusion and darkness. This unexpected trauma, comparable to today's high-speed automobile accidents, became a simultaneous blur which was difficult to sort for memory. It must have been especially difficult to recall coherently how one went from sound sleep to a life and death swim in the St Lawrence. The drama aboard *Titanic* unfolded slowly allowing survivors to commit much to memory before trauma took hold. *Titanic* also had a greater number of survivors to retell the tale.

Lowell Cote, grandson of 'Billy Boy' Hughes believes that the *Empress of Ireland* was 'lost in the wake of *Titanic*'. There was no historical room for another passenger liner catastrophe and so the *Empress* never became well known. Interest in *Titanic* also waned for years, overshadowed by world war before and after the Depression. Steven Biel in *Down With The Old Canoe* writes that *Titanic* was just a shipwreck until Walter Lord's *A Night To Remember* launched her on the way to icon status in 1955. Interest in the *Empress* was non-existent from 1915 until dives on the wreck in 1964. Following her rediscovery, there were a few blips of interest when *The Tragic Story of the Empress of Ireland* by Logan Marshall was reprinted by William Tantum IV in 1972 and when *Fourteen Minutes* by James Croall was released in 1978.

If not for *Titanic*, would the peacetime maritime tragedy of the century have been the *Empress of Ireland*? Perhaps not when one considers factors other than passenger lives lost. The *Empress of Ireland* had the drama and the Edwardian sets but was short on cast. She carried socialites and peers of contemporary celebrity but Laurence Irving is believed to be the only passenger who commanded international recognition. Contrast this with *Titanic* passengers whose names were synonymous with Edwardian excess like Astor, Guggenheim, Widener, and the Duff Gordons. Lacking a 'wealth' of millionaires in her saloon, the *Empress* would not have clearly signalled the end of the pre-income tax era. Consider, however, that these wealthy passengers would be unknown to many had *Titanic* missed the iceberg. *Titanic*'s survival might have made Irving, Seton-Karr, Lyman, Paton and Dunlevy the venerable of ocean liner disasters.

Some people believed the ostentatious aboard *Titanic* got what they deserved. This lot would probably not wish the same fate to befall the *Empress of Ireland*. In eight years of service, the *Empress* had earned many admirers in all social circles. She carried many immigrants to new lives in Canada and the United States. She might have served as an auxiliary cruiser or troop carrier in World War I.

The *Empress of Ireland* is noteworthy for her contribution to maritime history as well as for the compelling story of her loss. Study of the 29 May 1914 collision by naval architects and underwriting classification authorities resulted in changes to future ship design. Raked or overhanging bows, which project forward above the waterline, replaced vertical cutwater bows in new construction. In the event of a collision like the *Storstad* striking the *Empress*, an overhanging bow absorbs impact first, before damage occurs below the waterline.

A final thought about why she is the forgotten *Empress*. Perhaps it is because the *Empress of Ireland* destroyed any remaining belief of invincibility of ships at sea. She carried enough lifeboats for all (having learned the lesson of *Titanic*) but sank mercilessly, taking over a thousand lives with her. In May 1914, the public did not want to be reminded of the perils of ocean travel, much as we seem impervious to an ever-increasing number of downed airliners today. People allowed the *Empress of Ireland* to fade from memory because she was a more graphic and irreconcilable reminder of our frailty at sea than *Titanic*.

In 1912, *Titanic* could be rationalized as an unfortunate incident, never to be repeated. Faith in travel by liner was magically restored when Board of Trade regulations were revised to require lifeboats for all. The loss of the *Empress of Ireland* 18 months after the effective date of those regulations, shattered hopes for safety at sea.

When the *Empress of Ireland* did sink, in the blink of an eye, there was nowhere to go. There was no quick fix to reassure us. Lifeboats for all meant nothing. The Detroit *Free Press* reported that people were 'queerly stunned' and disposed to accept the collision as an act of God.

It was unthinkable that an accident could be caused by an excess of caution on the part of experienced seamen. The St Lawrence River was beyond reproach. The *Empress of Ireland* was a safe ship. There was nowhere else to go. The *Storstad* became a convenient scapegoat. She didn't do the 'mischief' all by herself.

It took *two* steamships and *two* crews to collide.

Canadian Pacific Railway memorial located on the south shore of the St. Lawrence between Romouski and Father Point.

APPENDIX A - CHRONOLOGY
EMPRESS OF IRELAND

Official No. 123972 — Hull No. 443

28 November 1904
Naval Architect Dr. Francis Elgar completes waterline sketch for transatlantic liner in anticipation of CPR's order.

14 December 1904
CPR President Thomas G. Shaughnessy orders two twin-screw steamers from Fairfield Shipbuilding & Engineering at £375,000 each to be delivered 18 months following contract execution. Classification standard Lloyd's 100 A-1 (Note 1).

17 January 1905
Fairfield's Board of Directors ratify the CPR contract. Signatories are Chairman William G. Pearce and Managing Director Alexander Gracie.

20 January 1905
Lloyd's and 15 other companies insure Hull 443 based on contract price. Lloyd's assumes 51 percent of the risk.

10 April 1905
Empress of Ireland's keel is laid at Fairfield's Berth No. 4.

27 January 1906
Launch day. Mrs Alexander Gracie, wife of Fairfield's Managing Director, christens the ship.

17 March 1906
Fairfield ships *Empress of Ireland* model in 13 foot case to Milan Exhibition via Antwerp.

5 June 1906
Progressive and coal consumption trials at Firth of Clyde yield maximum speed of 20.002 knots, 81.8 revolutions per minute, 18,683 Indicated Horse Power.

7 June 1906
Full speed 12-hour endurance trial at Firth of Clyde yields sustained speed of 19.64 knots, 80.5 revolutions per minute, 17,774 Indicated Horse Power.

12 June 1906
Departure from River Clyde for delivery to CPR in Liverpool. CPR orders £4,611 in extras bringing the total price to £379,611.

29 June 1906
Maiden voyage from Liverpool to Quebec via Moville, Ireland, in rough

weather. Frank Carey is first Master. The Moville to Quebec crossing is completed in 6 days, 15 hours.

1 August 1906
Fastest westbound crossing from Moville to Father Point in 5 days, 10 hours, 30 minutes.

18 September 1906
Fairfield engineers draw plan to enlarge existing rudder. The new surface area is 21 percent greater.

31 January 1907
Empress of Ireland model returns to Fairfield. S.S. *Paris* carries model to Bordeaux Exhibition in April. Later, Fairfield presents model to CPR for their Toronto office.

14 October 1909
Collision with a submerged object which pierces hull on inbound St Lawrence transit. *Empress* arrives in Quebec under her own power on 15 October with water in forward hold. John V. Forster is Master.

16 October 1909
Rescue from Quebec Harbour conflagration.

26 October 1909
Commissioner of Wrecks Inquiry into accident of 14 October.

16 September 1910
Fastest eastbound crossing from Father Point to Moville in 5 days, 10 hours, 58 minutes.

6 October 1911
Duke and Duchess of Connaught sail to Canada in specially appointed suites.

11 July 1913
Empress takes position No. 13 in the flotilla of merchant and naval vessels reviewed by King George V and Queen Mary upon the opening of Gladstone Dock in Liverpool.

1 May 1914
Henry George Kendall relieves James A. Murray as Master in Halifax.

23 May 1914
CPR Safety Officer completes lifeboat drill at dock in Quebec with satisfactory results.

28 May 1914
Return leg of Voyage 96 from Quebec to Liverpool begins at 4:27pm.

29 May 1914
Empress of Ireland founders.

30 May 1914
Coroner Inquest at Rimouski.

16 June 1914
Commission of Inquiry convenes in Quebec. Lord Mersey presiding.

27 June 1914
Commission of Inquiry adjourns.

7 July 1914
Storstad sold at Admiralty auction for $175 000.

11 July 1914
Commission of Inquiry issues final report.

20 August 1914
Purser's safe is raised.

22 August 1914
Purser's safe is opened in Quebec.

27 April 1915
Exchequer Court of Canada finds *Storstad* to blame for collision.

8 March 1917
Storstad is torpedoed and sinks.

17 July 1964
Divers relocate wreck of *Empress of Ireland* after 50 undisturbed years.

28 September 1968
Port propeller is raised.

CRASH CHRONOLOGY
Events of 29 May 1914

1:20am
Pilot Adélard Bernier disembarks according to Captain Kendall and First Officer Jones. Pilot boat *Eureka* records him aboard at 1:30am.

1:35am
Chief Officer Toftenes and Third Officer Jacob Saxe of *Storstad* first see lights of *Empress of Ireland.*

1:38am
Jones first sees the lights of *Storstad.*

1:41 am
Empress of Ireland changes course according to Jones. Kendall places the time at 1:35am.

1:45 am
Fog impairs visibility. Kendall reverses his engines. Crawford Leslie, Marconi operator at Father Point, records first call to standby received from *Empress of Ireland* based on his office clock (Note 2).

1:47am
Empress of Ireland is dead in the water according to Kendall.

1:50am
Leslie records SOS signal from *Empress of Ireland.* William Whiteside, Senior Marconi Operator at Father Point, hears the trailing end of SOS message using Leslie's headset (Note 2).

1:55am
Storstad makes a last minute turn to starboard and impales the starboard side of *Empress* (Note 3).

1:56am
Empress of Ireland transmits first signal to standby according to Ronald Ferguson, Senior Marconiman.

2:0lam
Empress of Ireland transmits SOS as lights dim and all power is lost.

2:05am
Captain Belanger of pilot boat *Eureka* hears the conclusion of three sets of whistles: one long; two short; and three short. He remarks to his Quartermaster that it sounds as though something is wrong (Note 4).

2:09am
The *Empress of Ireland* rolls over to starboard. Her funnels strike the water simultaneously.

2:10am
The *Empress of Ireland* disappears 9 hours and 43 minutes after leaving Quebec.

2:12am
Lady Evelyn first learns of sinking by telephone.

2:30am
Eureka learns of sinking and leaves Father Point for wreck site.

2:45am
Lady Evelyn leaves Rimouski for wreck site.

3:15am
Eureka arrives at wreck site (Note 5).

3:45am
Lady Evelyn arrives. Launches two boats (Note 6).

Notes:

1. Lloyd's 100 A-1 is a high standard of marine survey conducted during progressive phases of construction.

2. The time logged by Father Point Station is 10 to 11 minutes earlier than *Empress* time.

3. Kendall's timeframe places the *Empress* dead in the water for eight minutes prior to collision. There is a great variance in testimony on this point: Marconi Operator Bamford said 'a few seconds'; Quartermaster Murphy said 'two minutes'; and Engineer Brennan recalled 'four minutes'.

4. The whistles heard by Belanger were most likely the *Storstad* standing-on; the *Empress* dead in the water; and the *Storstad's* backing signal as she tore into the *Empress*. Belanger's observation is consistent with impact at 1:55am since *Eureka* time is 10 minutes later than *Empress* time. Leslie's log entry suggests impact twenty minutes before Belanger heard the last whistle. This is curious because *Eureka* set her clocks daily according to Father Point Marconi office time. Possible explanation: Leslie's log was completed incorrectly due to excitement of the moment; Belanger's recollection is faulty even though he testified that the deep throated whistle of the *Empress* was unmistakable.

5. Estimate according to Captain Belanger.

6. Estimate according to Captain Pouliot.

The Salvation Army Monument at Mount Pleasant Cemetery, Toronto.

Ship's Officers of the Empress of Ireland
pictured on board. Captain Kendall is front row left.
Courtesy Salvation Army Archives

APPENDIX B - PASSENGER MANIFEST

FIRST CLASS

ABBOTT, MR FREDERICK E. (Rescued)
ABERCROMBIE, MR JAMES R. (Rescued)
ADIE, MR PERCY JAMES. (Rescued)
ADIE, MRS PERCY GAUNT. (Rescued)
ANDERSON, MR ALBERT BRUCE
AVERDIECK, MR PERCY CLIFFORD
BARLOW, DR ALFRED ERNEST
    ALBERT
BARLOW, MRS FRANCES E TOMS
BLOOMFIELD, LIEUT-COL WILLIAM
    READ
BLOOMFIELD, MRS ISABELLA
    LOUISA CLARKE
BLOOMFIELD, MISS HILDA ISABEL
    READ
BOWES-LYON, MR CHARLES
    LINDSAY CLAUDE (Rescued)
BRANDON, MR VERNON GETHING
BURROWS, MR A J. (Rescued)
BURT, MR CLAYTON R. (Rescued)
CASH, MR JOHN HARWOOD. (Rescued)
CASH, MRS MARY KATE WHITE
    (Rescued)
CAY, MRS CATHERINE BEATRICE
    CHEAPE
CAYLEY, MR FREDERICK J
CLARK, MR CHARLES R. (Rescued)
COX-EDWARDS, MR JOSEPH FRANCIS
CRATHERN, MISS WANETA
CULLEN, MRS MAUDE YOUNG
CULLEN, MISS ISOBEL MAUDE
CULLEN, MASTER ALBERT EDWARD
CULLEN (NURSE) MISS JENNIE P.
    BLYTHE. (Rescued)
CUNNINGHAM, MR ROBERT A.
    (Rescued)
DARLING, MR MERTON DENNIS A.
    (Rescued)
DICKSON, MR PETER
DUNCAN, MR JAMES FERGUS.
    (Rescued)

DUNLEVY, MRS GRACE FISKE
FENTON, MR WALTER. (Rescued)
GALLAGHER, MRS ROBERT
GALLAGHER, MR CEDRIC. (Rescued)
GAUNT, MISS DORIS. (Rescued)
GODSON, MR F P. (Rescued)
GOLDTHORPE, MR CHARLES
GOSSELIN, MR LOUIS A. (Rescued)
GRAHAM, MR WALTER DOUGLAS
GRAHAM, MRS ELIZABETH
    HUMPHREYS
HAILEY, MRS ELIZABETH RHODES
HART-BENNETT, MRS ELLA MARY
    TUCK
HENDERSON, MR GEORGE W.S.
    (Rescued)
HIRST, MR ALFRED E. (Rescued)
HERXHEIMER, MR WALTER
    SALOMON
HOLLOWAY, MRS CHARLOTTE E.
    OLIVER
HOWES, MR FRANK WILLIAM
HYAMSON, MR LIONEL ALEXANDER.
    (Rescued)
IRVING, MR LAURENCE SYDNEY
    BRODRIBB
IRVING, MRS MABEL LUCY
    HACKNEY
IRVING (MAID) MISS MABEL HILDA
    HAGGERSTON
JOHNSTON, MR DAVID
KARR, SIR HENRY SETON
KENT, MR LIONEL. (Rescued)
KOHL, MISS GRACE. (Rescued)
LEE, MISS AILSE. (Rescued)
LINDSAY, DR. MURDOCH
    ALEXANDER
LYMAN, MR HENRY HERBERT
LYMAN, MRS HENRY KIRKBY
MAGINNIS, MR ALEXANDER
    GORDON
MALLOCH, MR CHARLES. (Rescued)

MARKS, MR GABRIEL JACOB
MARKS, MRS MARION ALEXANDER
MILLER, MISS CATHERINE
MULLINS, MR ALBERT EDWARD
MULLINS, MRS KATE EMILY PIERCY
              (Rescued)
MULLINS, MISS EILEEN
O'HARA, MR HENRY ROBERT
O'HARA, MRS MAY L GREENE.
              (Rescued)
O'HARA, MISS JOSEPHINE HELEN.
              (Rescued)
PALMER, MR WALLACE LEONARD
PALMER, MRS ETHEL COURTNEY
              SHORT
PATON, MRS ETHEL SABINA GRUNDY.
              (Rescued)
PRICE, MRS FANNY WYNN PLUMLEY
RUTHERFORD, MR FREDERICK J
SEYBOLD, MR EDWARD. (Rescued)
SEYBOLD, MRS SUSANNA BRICKER
SMART, MR GEORGE BOGUE. (Rescued)
STORK, MRS M N REEVES
TAYLOR, MR JOHN THOMAS
TAYLOR, MISS DOROTHY
TAYLOR, MISS HELEN. (Rescued)
TOWNSHEND, MISS TIRIA VERE
              FERRARS. (Rescued)
TYLEE, MR CHARLES D
TYLEE, MRS MARTHA HATTON
WAKEFORD, MR A J. (Rescued)
WALLETT, REV JOSEPH WEBSTER.
              (Rescued)
SECOND CLASS
ALDRIDGE, MR ERNEST WILLIAM
ARCHER, MR TRACEY HARLEY
              (Rescued)
ARCHER, MRS MARY RUTH
              CONGDON
ARCHER, MASTER ALFRED CECIL
ASSAFREY, MISS ALMA FEDORA
              MAUDE
ATKIN, MISS MARTHA

ATWELL, MAJOR GEORGE (Rescued)
ATWELL, MRS MARY (Rescued)
AXTON, MRS H
AXTON, MASTER
BACH, MR REINHOLDT
BACH, MISS EDITH (Rescued)
BALCOMBE, MISS DOROTHY AMY
BALES, MISS ADA ALICE (Rescued)
BARBOUR, MRS SEBENA
BARBOUR, MISS EVELYN
BARBOUR, MISS FLORENCE (Rescued)
BARRIE, MR WILLIAM S.
BAWDEN, MISS BESSIE
BAWDEN, MISS FLORENCE
BAXTER, MISS MARY
BEALE, MR EDWARD
BEAUCHAMP, MRS RUTH
BECKSTEAD, ADJT. JANE ETTA
              ELIZABETH
BERRY, MISS ETHEL
BIGLAND, LIEUT STANLEY
BIRKETT, MR HENRY
BISHOP, MR THOMAS GEORGE
              TETLEY
BLACK, MR JOHN W. (Rescued)
BLACK, MRS ROSE LETCH
BLACKHURST, MRS ADA RATCLIFFE
BONYNGE, ENSIGN GEORGE
BOYNTON, MRS F E BRIGGS
BROOKS, MR FRANK P. (Rescued)
BROWN, MISS ALICE
BROWN, MR OVERAND
BUHLER, MR COSTA
BULPITT, MR R G
BUNTHORNE, MR ALEX
BURGESS, MRS S
BUTLER, MISS ROSE
BYRNE, MR EDWARD. (Rescued)
BYRNE, MRS E
BYRNE, MISS GERTRUDE
CAUGHEY, MR ALBERT EDWARD
CAUGHEY, MRS HELEN HUGHES

CHIGNELL, MRS ELIZA
CLARKE, MRS LAVINIA
CLARKE, MISS NELLIE
COLE, MRS A
COOK, MRS ANNIE.E J RAMPLING
   (Rescued)
COURT, MISS EMILY. (Rescued)
CREIGHTON, MAJOR DAVID LAW
CREIGHTON, MRS BERTHA JANE
   DIXON
CRELLIN, ROBERT W. (Rescued)
DALE, MRS MARY PARKER
DALE, MISS
DANDY, MR JAMES F. (Rescued)
DARGUE, MRS JOSEPH
DAVIDSON, MR GORDON CHARLES.
   (Rescued)
DAVIES, MR WILLIAM. (Rescued)
DAVIES, MRS ETHEL GOUGH
DAVISON, MRS DAISY BARLING
DAVISON, MISS DOROTHY
DEATH, MR A H
DE BOW, ADJT. EVERETT
DE BOW, MRS EVERETT McKIM
DODD, CPT. JOHN EDWARD
DODD, MRS VIOLET HOWSON
DUNN, MRS JENNIE ELLIOTT
EASTES, MISS FLORENCE
EDWARDS, ADJT. GEORGE
ELINSLIE, MRS JANE
ERZINGER, MR WALTER. (Rescued)
EVANS, MR ERNEST
EVANS, MRS.
EVANS, MISS C
FARR, MISS KATHLEEN HELEN
FARR, MISS NANCY
FARR, MISS DOROTHY
FARR, MISS BESSIE
FELSTEAD, MR GEORGE PHILIP
FINDLAY, MAJOR HUGH
FINDLAY, MRS
FINDLAY, MR JOHNSON McWILLIAM

FISHER, MRS MARGARET SMITH
FISHER, MASTER WILFRED
FOARD, MR HERBERT E.
FOORD, MR ERNEST
FOORD, MRS ERNEST WARD
FOORD, MISS ALICE MARGARET
FREEMAN, MR HENRY. (Rescued)
FREEMAN, MRS. (Rescued)
GODDARD, MR JOHN ARTHUR
GRAFTON, MRS SARAH C
GRAY, MR EDWIN P
GRAY, MRS MADELINE SHIRT
GRAY, MISS MARY WINIFRED
GREEN, ADJT. HARRY
GREEN, MRS ADJT. MARY J
GREEN, MR ERNEST. (Rescued)
GREEN, MISS JESSIE
GREENAWAY, MR BERT. (Rescued)
GREENAWAY, MR THOMAS H. .
   (Rescued)
GREENAWAY, MRS MARGARET
   E. DALZELL. (Rescued)
GREGG, MR JAMES
GREGG, MRS.
GRIFFIN, MRS GRACE WITHNELL
GRIFFIN, MISS WINNIEFRED PAULINE
GROOM, CAPT. SYDNEY
HAKKER, MRS HARRIET
HAKKER, MISS JUDITH
HALLIDAY, MR CHRISTOPHER H.
HANAGAN, ADJT. EDWARD JAMES
HANAGAN, MRS EDITH COLLISHAW
HANAGAN, MISS GRACE. (Rescued)
HART, MR WILLIAM
HART, MRS EMMA ROACH
HART, MISS EDITH
HART, MASTER WILLIAM
HAYES, STAFF CAPT. EMMA
HEATH, MR HUGH LENTER
HEATH, MASTER JACK RUSSELL
HEPBURN, MRS MARY K. MEREDITH
HEPBURN, MISS BARBARA MEREDITH

HEPBURN, MASTER OWEN
       MEREDITH
HOGGAN, MRS ROSINDA BLAKEY
HOLCOMBE, MISS FLORENCE L.H.
HOPE, MISS CHRISSIE.
HORWOOD, MR WILLIAM
HOWARTH, MR WILIAM
HOWARTH, MRS
HOWARTH, MASTER MELVIN
HUDSON, MR R.W.
HUMPHREYS, MR WILLIAM J.
HUNT, DR. L.WILLIAM (Rescued)
HUNT, MISS ELEANOR DE VERE
HUNTER, BRIGADIER JAMES
HUNTER, MRS JESSIE TULLOCH
HUNTER, MASTER
HUNTER, MISS
JOHNSON, MR JAMES. (Rescued)
JOHNSTON, MR GEORGE A.
JONES, ENSIGN EMILY
JONES, MR THOMAS
KAVALESKY, MR IVAN
KEITH, LIEUT. ALFRED. (Rescued)
KNUDSON, CAPT. HANNAH
KRUSE, MR HERMAN. (Rescued)
KRUSE, MISS FREDA J. (Rescued)
LANGELEY, MR J.W. (Rescued)
LANGLEY, MISS MARY ANNE
LAW, MR ERNEST.
LAW, MRS MARGARET RILEY
LAW, MASTER
LENNON, MR JAMES JOSEPH. .
       (Rescued)
LONGLEY, MR LEONARD
LONGLEY, MRS LEONARD DAY
LONGLEY, MISS MARION
MAIDMENT, COL. SYDNEY C.
MAIDMENT, MRS HETTIE PECKHAM
MALONE, MR ROBERT
MARDALL, ENSIGN OLIVER PINNOCK
MATIER, MR ALEXANDER A.
McALPINE, MR AL

McAMMOND, CAPT DAVID FOSTER
       (Rescued)
McGRATH, CAPT. JAMES
McINTYRE, MR KENNETH. (Rescued)
McLEAN, JOHN McQUEEN
MEACHER, MR GEORGE
MEASURES, MR WILLIAM H. (Rescued)
MOIR, MRS EUPHEMIA PRIOR
MORGAN, MISS LILY
MORGAN, MR JOSEPH
MORGAN, MR WILLIAM
MORRIS, MAJOR FRANK
MORRIS, STAFF CAPT. ARTHUR
MORRIS, MRS DAISY C. COOMBS
MOUNSEY, MRS FANNIE SEWELL
MYERS, CAPT. JAMES PATRICK
NEEVE, MR ERNEST EDWARD
NEWTON, MISS JENNIE
NONELEY, MISS ALICE
NUTTALL, MRS CHRISTINE McCOLL.
NUTTALL, MASTER RALPH
NUTTALL, MASTER TOM
OSLENDER, MR T. (Rescued)
PANTLING, MRS S.
PATRICK, MR JULIAN. (Rescued)
PATTENDAN, ENSIGN BERTRAM
PATTERSON, MR JOHN
PATTERSON, MR ROBERT
PATTERSON, MISS SARAH SMITH
PERKINS, MR RICHARD
PERRY, MR WILIAM HENRY
PETURSON, MR H. (Rescued)
PETURSON, MRS. (Rescued)
POTTER, BRIGADIER WILLIAM SCOTT
POTTER, MASTER WILLARD
POTTS, MRS H.
PRICE, ADJT. HANNA
PRIESTLY, MISS ALICE
PRIESTLY, MISS MARTHA
PRIOR, MRS EDITH AUGER
PUGMIRE, ENSIGN ERNEST. (Rescued)
REES, COMMIS 'NR DAVID MATTHIAS

REES, MRS RUTH HEPHZIBAH BABINGTON
REES, CAPT. HARDING WILLFORD
REES, MISS ANNIE INA
REES, CAPT. RUTH MAYBURY
REILLY, MR JOHN
RICHARDS, MR GEORGE CLEMENT.
RICHARDS, MRS SARAH ROWBOTTOM
RICHARDSON, MR WILLIAM JOHN.
RICHARDSON, MRS
SAMPSON, MR SAMUEL JAMES
SCHONGUTT, MISS H.. (Rescued)
SCOTT, MR JOHN M.
SEARLE, MISS EVA R.
SHATTOCK, MR WILLIAM NOAH
SIMCOE, MAJOR MRS ANNETTA WALLIS
SIMMONDS, MR REGINALD FRANK. (Rescued)
SIMMONDS, MRS MARY MAHONEY. (Rescued)
SMITH, MRS LEWIS
SOUTH, MR HAROLD NEVILLE
SOUTH, MRS ELSIE VRON
SPOONER, CAPT. RUFUS T.. (Rescued)
SPOOR, MR ROBERT
SPOOR, MRS MARGARET CALPIN
STAGE, MISS ISABEL
STAINER, MISS E.
STILLMAN, MR A.E.
STITT, ADJT. FITZWILLIAM
STITT, MRS CLARA CORFIELD
SWINDLEHURST, MISS AGNES
TAPLIN, MRS ELIZABETH TURNER
TURPIN, MAJOR RICHARD. (Rescued)
VEITCH, MISS B.
VINCENT, MR JOHN
VINCENT, MRS CLARA SEARSON
WAKEFIELD, MR WILLIAM H
WALKER, BRIGADIER JOHN HENRY W.
WEINRAUCH, MR BERNARD. (Rescued)

WHATMORE, CAPT. GIOVANNI GUIDO
WHITE, MRS MARY MITCHELL
WHITE, MISS AMY
WHITELAW, MRS BELLA HENDERSON.
WILLMOT, MISS E.. (Rescued)
WILSON, CAPT. GEORGE. (Rescued)
WOLTER, MRS AGNES ISABELLA LISTON
WOOD, MISS MARY
WOODS, MRS SARAH
YATES, MR HARRY
YATES, MRS MARY TAYLOR
ZEBULAK, MR JOSEF

THIRD CLASS

ADAMIAK, KASPER. (Rescued)
ADAMIEC, FRANK
ADAMOVICH, JOVO
ADAMOWICZ, JOSEPH
AERTJENS, EMIEL
AFANASSIEF, MISS FRANCES M.
AINESWORTH, MRS EDITH
AINESWORTH, MAUDE N.
AINESWORTH, ERIC
AINESWORTH, JACK
ALBORG, JOHANN
ALEXEJEW, LEONTY
ALEXOFF, DEMITER
ALLGROVE, MRS FLORENCE
ALLGROVE, MISS EVELYN
ALLGROVE, MISS VERA
ANDERSON, MRS ALVIN
ANDERSON, A.
ANDERSON, J
ANDERSON, JOHN. (Rescued)
ANDERSON, OLAF. (Rescued)
ANDREWS, H.
ANTONUK, NIKOLI
APPLETON, CHARLES
ATKINSON, JOHN. (Rescued)
BABEZUK, B.
BABEZUK, MRS

BABEZUK, MARY
BABISKI, WASILI
BAIE, SIMA
BANGER, MARY
BARARI, MEDREA
BARTSCHI, CHRISTIAN
BARTSCHI, THEOFIL. (Rescued)
BASTA, ANDREW
BEDNARZ, JAN
BEFARA, NAZZARINO
BEKOEFF, TETARI
BELL, DAN
BELLUCCI, DANTI
BELLUCCI, LUCIANI
BELSER, KATHERINE
BENARI, PETE. (Rescued)
BERARI, ILIE
BERCSAN, SANDOR. (Rescued)
BERGMAN, REINO
BERGMAN, SENJA
BERNABIE, ANTON
BERNOSISS, LUIGI
BERRY, DANIEL
BEVAN, W.G.. (Rescued)
BIRCH, MRS ELLEN GERTRUDE
                          TURNER
BIRCH, MTR. JOHN REUBEN HENRY
BIRCH, MISS ELSIE ALICE
BJORDAL, PEDER. (Rescued)
BLACKBURN, MISS M.
BLACKHAM, ARTHUR JAMES
BLOMQUIST, MARCUS AUGUST
SYLVESTER
BLOMQUIST, MRS ELISABET
KATARINA
BLOMQUIST, OLOV SIGFRID
BLOMQUIST, ERIK WALFRID
BOARDMAN, CHARLES
BOARDMAN, MRS CHARLES
BOKIC, MILE
BOLANIAN, ZACHARIE
BOLTON, GEORGE HENRY

BOLTON, MRS GEORGE HENRY
BOLTON, MASTER GEORGE
BOLTON, INFANT
BONNE, JACOBUS
BORSIK, FRED
BRAET, VICTOR. (Rescued)
BRAGA, EGILDO. (Rescued)
BRAGA, MRS CAROLINA. (Rescued)
BRAGA, MISS JOSEPHINE
BRAITHWAITE, MRS MARTHA ELLIS
BRAITHWAITE, MASTER
BRAITHWAITE, MASTER
BRENDI, NAZZARINO
BRISCHUK, D
BRISTOW, CHARLES. (Rescued)
BRISTOW, MRS CHARLES
BRISTOW, CHARLES JNR.. (Rescued)
BRITTON, JOSEPH
BRONCHIN, JULES
BRONKEN, MRS LENA
BRONKEN, MISS ELLA
BROOKS, MRS HETTY (Rescued)
BROOKS, MISS DOLLY
BROOKS, HARRY
BROWN, ARCHIE. (Rescued)
BRYAN, MISS C
BRZOZOWSKI, JAN. (Rescued)
BUCCARELLI, JOHN
BUCHACS, LEONTY. (Rescued)
BUCK, MRS MARY JANE STALEY
BURROWS, WILLIAM THOMAS.
                          (Rescued)
BURROWS, MRS CHARLOTTE
BURROWS, MASTER WILLIAM JOHN
BURROWS, MISS MAY
BUTACS, DIMITRIE
CARLSON, ANDREW
CARTER, HAROLD HEWITT.
CHMILEWSKY, A.
CHOMICZ, MOISEJ
CHOU, MRS AMELIA MOTT
CHURCIA, PAVA

CLARK, STEPHEN
CLARK, MRS ALLAN
CLARKE, THOMAS
CLAUSEN, DAVID. (Rescued)
CLEMENTS, ROBERT H.
CONSTANTIN, DELIMAN. (Rescued)
COOPER, PERCY DANIEL
COSTCA, GEORGE
COSTE, DALAHEA. (Rescued)
COTTERILL, LIZA OAKLEY
COX, MISS HENRICA MARIA
CRAWFORD, MRS MAY ICESON
CRESWELL, JOSEPH
CRESSWELL, MRS FANNY
CZELISOK, VALENTI
DAB, MRS ELIZA
DAVIES, MRS E
DELAMONT, JOHN. (Rescued)
DELAMONT, MRS ELIZABETH.
         (Rescued)
DELAMONT, MISS LIZZIE. (Rescued)
DELAMONT, LEONARD
DELAMONT, ARTHUR. W (Rescued)
DELLIMORTI, FRANCESCO
DEVESON, F.
DEVESON, MRS F.
DISKI, PHILIP. (Rescued)
DIXON, MRS POLLY.
DOWKER, GEORGE
DOWKER, MRS ALICE
DRANSFIELD, GEORGE. (Rescued)
DREHA, JOHN
DUDKA, ROMAN
DUFFY, MRS W
DULEVICH, STEFAN
DUMA, ALEXANDER
DURRANT, MRS JOSEPH
DURRANT, JAMES
DUTTON, MRS KATHLEEN
EDWARDS, CHRISTOPHER
EKQVIST, ARVID. (Rescued)
ELLIOTT, ERNEST

ELLIOTT, MRS ELLEN FLORENCE
ELLIOTT, MSTR. FREDERICK ERNEST
ELLIOTT, MSTR. GEORGE BRUCE
ENGEL, JULES
ENGSTROM, JOHN
ERICKSON, ERIK J.
ERICKSON, NELS L. (Rescued)
ERIKSEN, ANTHON
EVANS, RUSSELL
EVENSEN, ARTHUR. (Rescued)
EVICH, DEMENTI
EVINSON, ELI
EVINSON. MRS FANNY LEVI (Rescued)
EVINSON, MASTER JULIUS
FALNI, DAVID
FANT, MICK
FARKAS, GEORGE
FAULKNER, JAMES
FAULKNER, MRS MARY ELLEN
FELL, MISS EDITH
FELSTEAD, MRS LOUISE LAST
FELSTEAD, MASTER WILLIAM
FELSTEAD, MISS GLADYS
FERGUSON, A.C. (Rescued)
FISHWICK, EDMUND
FLACK, PERCY FLYNN. (Rescued)
FLACK, MRS EDITH FRANCES
         HARRALD
FLIFLET, MRS JOSEPHINE
FORSTROM, WILLIAM
FORSTROM, MRS WILLIAM
FORSTROM, WALDO WILLIAM
FORSTROM, TANE
FOWLER, BENJAMIN JOHN. (Rescued)
FRANSEN, OSCAR
FRASER, FRANK
FREGORICZUK, WASIL
FURNISS, S.G.. (Rescued)
FUSS, VAVROSHENETZ. (Rescued)
GAGULOFF, NALUK
GARBUZEW, EWDOKIM
GARD, JOHANNES. (Rescued)

GARNETT, WILLIAM
GARNETT, MRS MARY HEWARD
GASIEFF, STEPAN
GASSELSEDER, FRANK
GATTRELL, MR.
GATTRELL, MRS E.N. (Rescued)
GILES, WILLIAM J.
GILL, MARTIN. (Rescued)
GLOVER, F
GODDEFROY, L.
GOFF, MISS AGNES
GOGOFF, TASKO. (Rescued)
GORALSKI, FELIX
GOSS, JOHN
GOSS, MRS
GOSS, MISS VIOLET
GOSS, JOHN JNR.
GOSS, JOSEPH
GRASA, ANTONIE
GRDISA, NICK
GREEN, MRS FLORENCE ROBERTS.
GREENFIELD, MRS AMY RUTH
GREGOVICH, JOHN. (Rescued)
GRIFFIN, MRS VIOLET JANE BOAZ
GRINEVICH, ALEXANDER. (Rescued)
GUPKA, RIPRIJAN
GUPPY, MISS NELLIE
GUSTAFSON, JOHN
GUSZCZO, ADAM. (Rescued)
HAKALA, MARY
HALASCH, WASILJ (Rescued)
HALL, MISS EDITH
HALL, HENRY
HAMALAINEN, VILHO. (Rescued)
HAMMER, MISS EMMA
HANNUNEN, EDWIN
HANNUNEN, MRS AINO. (Rescued)
HARKONEN, REINO. (Rescued)
HARRISON, HUGH
HARVEY, MISS CARRIE
HATISCHKY, TANASKA. (Rescued)
HAVERINEN, MISS KREETA

HEDGECOE, GEORGE. (Rescued)
HEIKKILA, ANTTI
HEIKKILA, HILJA
HEIKKILA, VIENO
HELLER, ABRAM. (Rescued)
HILL, MRS MARY E. CLEGG
HOAD, MRS KATHLEEN
                MAVOURNEED LANE
HOAD, MISS KATHLEEN EMILY
HOBBS, MRS MARY ANN
HOBBS, MISS LOUISE
HOKLEY, EDWARD
HOLMBERG, EDWARD
HOLMI, LIISA
HOPPER, FRANK
HOPPER, WILLIAM
HORWITZ, MOLLIE
HOWANICZ, ALBERT
HOWARTH, MRS RICHARD MORGAN
HOWARTH, MASTER LEONARD
HOWARTH, MISS EMMIE
HOWELL, MRS A
HOWELL, MISS LILIAN
HUNT, MRS BEATRICE
ILIE, BORIS. (Rescued)
ILIEFF, PAVELL
INGLETON, MISS VIOLET
ISPAS, ALEXANDER
IVANE, M
IVANE, W
JACK, MRS SARAH COUTTS
JACK, MASTER DAVID
JAKSIC, MILE
JAKSIC, VASO
JAY, MRS EMILY
JAY, MISS QUEENIE
JAY, MASTER CLIFFORD
JAY, MASTER FREDERICK
JAY, MISS EMMIE
JAY, MISS STELLA
JEFFREY, MISS MARY ANN
JEFFRIES, MRS MARY E HOULT

JEFFS, MRS KATE HALIDAY
JEFFS, MASTER ERNEST
JELISAVAC, SIMO (Rescued)
JENSEN, MRS ANNIE
JOHNSON, ALIDA
JOHNSON, ANDREW. (Rescued)
JOHNSON, J
JOHNSON, MRS
JOHNSON, MISS TILLIE
JOHNSON, W
JOHNSON, EDWARD
JOHNSON, MRS
JOHNSON, ULF
JOKINEN, FRANK
JONES, MISS NELLIE
JOUKAINEN, SIMO. (Rescued)
JOVITY, MRS GYULA
JOVITY, MILAN
JUNIPER, MRS ANNIE
JUNIPER, CHILD
JUSSILA, KALLE
KADIEFF, HANGER
KALLIO, MISS HILMA (Rescued)
KAMINSKI, JOSEF (Rescued)
KANGAS, EINAR
KANGAS, JOHN
KARANES, MICHAEL. (Rescued)
KASPAROWICZ, JOSEPH
KEELEY, THOMAS
KERNEY, HARRY
KERR, PETER
KERR, MRS MINNIE RUSSELL
KERR, MASTER GEORGE
KERR, MASTER WILLIE
KERR, MISS CATHARINE
KERR, MISS MAGGIE
KERR, MISS SARAH
KESANIEMI, MATTI
KESTILA, IVAR
KICZAK, WOJCIECH. (Rescued)
KILSBY, CHARLES.
KINOS, EINO

KIRTLEY, MRS ELIZABETH. (Rescued)
KIRWIN, MRS AMY SELLERS
KIRWIN, MASTER JAMES
KITSON, HERBERT
KITSON, MRS MARY LONG
KITSON, MISS MONICA
KIVISTO, HILMA
KIVISTO, LAURA
KIVISTO, TOIVO
KLEMENS, JOSEF
KLEVA, WASILJ
KLIMCHUK, ISTAFI
KLUKACZ, ADAM. (Rescued)
KNISZ, ANDREJ
KOIVISTO, ARVI
KOIVISTO, MARTTI
KOIVISTO, PAULINE
KOIVISTO, TOM
KOLOMETZ, MITROFIM. (Rescued)
KORGA, JAN. (Rescued)
KOSKINEN, HELVI
KOSKINEN, J.
KOSKINEN, MILJA
KOSKINEN, MRS MANDA
KOSTOFF, DELCHO
KOWALSKI, JAN
KOYNYTO, SAVELI (Rescued)
KOZLOWSKY, STANISLOW
KOZORIZ, KUZMA
KRAVETZ, LARION
KRAWCZENKO, ANTON
KRUCHINSKY, ANDREJ. (Rescued)
KRUTIN, JAN
KRYCZUNIAK, IVAN
KUBELESS, FRANTZ
KUCHOJ, MIKE. (Rescued)
KUJALA, JACOB
KUPRECZENKO, JOHN
KUTZI, GRIGOR. (Rescued)
KUUKARI, VICTOR
KWARCHEK, FEODORE
LAHTI, HERMAN

LAJESIC, JOVAN (Rescued)
LAMMI, MATTI. (Rescued)
LAMPINEN, LIISA
LANCA, JOSIP
LANGENICZ, PETER
LARSON, ANTON
LARSON, MRS JOHN A.
LARSON, NELS
LASKEY, FRED
LAWLOR, PHILIP (Rescued)
LAWLOR, MRS ELLEN GARTHWAITE
LAWLOR, MASTR. HERBERT (Rescued)
LAWS, ROBERT
LEBEDOWICZ, IVAN
LEE, MRS ETHEL DURHAM
LEEKS, MASTER WILLIE
LEHTO, MATTI
LEIKAS, ANSELM
LEJCZUK, MARCIN (Rescued)
LEVCHIK, OLEF
LEVETZ, ARCHIV (Rescued)
LEWANDOWSKI, B.
LIEZNER, HRYE
LILEK, T.
LINDQUIST, JONAS. (Rescued)
LINDQUIST, MRS MARTHA. (Rescued)
LIVANOFF, PETER
LONE, ALICK
LONE, CLARA
LONE, HANS
LONE, RENA
LOS, HARRY
LUBNJEWSKY, ADAM
LUBNJEWSKY, JACOB (Rescued)
LUCHOVICH, LUKA
LUKIJANEC, MATY (Rescued)
LUNG, ILIA (Rescued)
LUPINE, NAZZARENO (Rescued)
LUREN, MAGNUS. (Rescued)
LUREN, MRS MAGNUS
LUZENSKY, IGNOTTY
MADSEN, MRS PETER

MAGYAR, TOMA
MAKELA, JOHN
MAKI, MISS MANDI
MAKI, MATTI
MAKI, MRS ORVOKKI
MAKINEN, OSCAR
MALASCHCUK, FOMA. (Rescued)
MALOBASA, DANE
MANDRYK, HARRY
MANDRYK, SYDOR
MARAZEWICZ, TERENTY. (Rescued)
MARIAN, JUON
MARIN, JOVAN
MARINI, GUISEPPE
MARINKOV, GYMO
MARKKULA, MISS SOFIA
MARKKULA, AINO
MARKKULA, MISS TONIA
MARKKULA, ARVO (Rescued)
MARKKULA, EERO
MARTIN, MRS EMMA SMITH
MASIC, STEVE
MASON, MRS J.
MASON, HOWARD
MATTYOS, N.
MATTSON, MRS IDA
MATTSON, SULO
MAULE, MRS FRANCES
MAWBY, MRS E. M.
MAWBY, MISS KATHLINE
MAWHINNEY, GEORGE
MAY, MARK
McGACHEN, MRS MAUD ANFIELD
McGACHEN, MISS GLADYS MAUD
McGACHEN, MISS MARJORY MARY
McGACHEN, INFANT
McVEIGH, JAMES HENRY
MEZIN, DIMITRI
MIHEKOVIC, TOMO
MIKULICZA, GEORGE
MINARDO, LUIGI
MINCY, PETRU

MITCHELL, SYDNEY
MITEFF, GAIRO
MITOFF, ALEXI
MOOREHOUSE, FREDERICK
MOROSUK, MOISEI
MORRELLI, PAOLO (Rescued)
MORTON, LOWTHER
MORTON, MRS RUTH SPRUSTON
MORTON, MISS JANE
MORTON, MISS KATHLEEN
MOSE, H.N (Rescued)
MOSKELLI, K.
MOTKI, MIKE
MULLEN, ROBERT
MURCSAN, T
MUZICHUK, NIKITA (Rescued)
NAULLS, MRS L
NAULLS, WILLIAM
NELSON, GUSTAF
NEVALAINEN, OTTO
NIKULA, JOHN
NIKULAIE, ILIE
NILSSON, SIGFRID (Rescued)
NINUTEAR, PAVELL (Rescued)
NIRNY, ILIA
NISSILA, FRANK. (Rescued)
NISSILA, SANNI
NIVALA, JOHN
NIVALA, LIZZIE
NIVALA, ROY
NIXON, MRS ETHEL JEFFREY
NIXON, MASTER LESLIE
NIXON, MISS EMMA
NOBISKI, PIOTR (Rescued)
NOVIKOV, SPEREDON (Rescued)
NURMINEN, MANU (Rescued)
OAKLEY, G.
OLECKI, ONUFREJ
OLSEN, GUSTAV
PAC, VAVYENCE
PACCOZZACHI, GUISEPPI
PAJIN, NIKA

PARKER, MISS T.
PARKINSON, MISS LETITIA
PARRISH, MRS ALBERT
PARRISH, MASTER HARRY
PARRISH, MISS FLORENCE
PARSK, MARIA (Rescued)
PASZKOWICZ, IWAN (Rescued)
PATERSON, ALEX
PAWLOWSKY, PETER
PERKINS, MRS LOUISA TOMS
PERMIAKOF, IVAN
PERYER, MRS J.
PETERSON, G.
PETTERSON, GEORGE
PETROVICH, SIMON
PETRUS, METRO (Rescued)
PHILLIPS, MRS RACHEL PASS
PHILLIPS, MASTER HUBERT
PHILLIPS, MISS ETHEL
PIERMATTER, LORENZO
PIERPOLI, DOMENICO (Rescued)
PIIRAINEN, ERIK (Rescued)
POLIC, ISIDOR
POLIC, STEPAN (Rescued)
POLKLUF, JOHN
POMPEY, CEASAR
POMYCHONSKI, IGNACY
POP, GEORGIA (Rescued)
POP, VERALIN
PORRE, HILMA
POWDELESKI, MR.
POWDELESKI, MRS.
PRAKSI, FRANK (Rescued)
PRATT, MRS M.HOLDER
PRATT, MISS F.
PRESOINTTI, WALDO
PRINCE, WILLIAM
PRINCE, MRS WILLIAM WILSON
PRINCE, MASTER GILBERT
PUKAS, IWAN
PYKARI, JACOB (Rescued)
PYKARI, KALLE

RAASAKKA, ANTTI
RADBURN, MRS MARY NICHOLLS WILSON
RANTALA, KALLE (Rescued)
RASK, PETER (Rescued)
RAVEN, L. R.
REBALJCHENKO, FEODOR (Rescued)
REEVES, MRS ROSE WRIGHT
REEVES, MISS DORA
REED, LAURA
REID, CHARLES
RIGBY, MRS SARAH A.
ROBINSKY, ADRIAN
ROBSON, GEORGE LISLE
ROGOZIN, ALEXEY
ROGOZIN, ANASTAZIA (Rescued)
ROGOZIN, WLADIMIR
ROMAN, PETRA
ROMANIUK, JAKOW (Rescued)
ROMANYSZIN, IGNATZ
ROMANYSZIN, PAWLO (Rescued)
ROSS, THOMAS
RUDDY, JOHN
RUSSELL, WILLIAM
RUSSELL, MISS SARAH
RYAN, ALFRED
RYAN, MRS ALFRED
RYCZKO, CHARYTON
SAARINEN, DAVID
SAARINEN, ERNESTI
SAARINEN, HILMA
SAGRAFENO, AURELIO
SALO, JOHN (Rescued)
SAMUELSON, CARL
SAMUELSON, CHRISTIAN (Rescued)
SANDEN, MISS T.
SCHAKALIDA, WASYL (Rescued)
SCHWAZ, JOHANN
SCOTT, THOMAS U.
SCOTT, MRS MARGARET PEVERLEY
SCOTT, MASTER THOMAS A.
SEJMON, DYONIZY

SESCHINSKI, JOSEF
SHEDLOOK, STEVE (Rescued)
SHROPAS, J.
SHURNAK, MARTIN
SIDOROWICZ, JAKIM
SIKORSKI, LUCJAN
SIMCZESIN, JAN (Rescued)
SIMPER, ALFRED
SIMPER, MRS
SIPKA, NIKOLA
SIVULA, MATTI
SKOCIN, JOHN. (Rescued)
SLYEPOVIC, S
SMART, ARTHUR THOMAS. (Rescued)
SMEDBERG, R
SMEDBERG, MASTER C.
SMEDLEY, MISS ROSE
SMITH, MRS I
SMITH, FREDERICK J.
SMITH, MISS MAUD
SOKAR, S.
SOPAN, JANOS (Rescued)
SPOONER, RALPH
SPOONER, MRS MARGARET. SNR.
SPOONER, MRS MARGARET. JNR.
SPURGEON, MRS KATHLEEN BRITTON
SPURGEON, MISS KATHLEEN
STALEY, DANIEL
STALKUSS, ANTONIE
STAROWOITOW, ALFANASI
STEELE, MISS LILY
STEELE, MRS R.J.
STEELE, MASTER JAMES
STEELE, MISS NORA
STEVENSON, CHARLES A.
STEVENSON, MRS
STEVENSON, MRS MARGARET
STONE, MRS GEORGE
STRECHA, GRIGORI (Rescued)
SUNDBERG, M
SUNI, MATTI

SUNICH, PETER
SUVELEAN, GEORGE
SVNIESUK, A
SWAN, CHARLES BARRON (Rescued)
SWANSON, AMANDUS (Rescued)
SWANSON, MARTIN (Rescued)
SWIDER, STANISLAW
SYDONIK, PETRO
SZABO, JOHN
SZAMBARGO, W
SZILAGY, NIKOLAE
TAAVETTILA, MRS HILMA (Rescued)
TAAVETTILA, ALLAN
TAAVETTILA, ANTTI
TALBAKKA, ALEX (Rescued)
TALES, MR MATTHEW
TANKIS, DEMETRE. (Rescued)
TARRY, ALBERT R.
TARRY, MRS ANNIE MOBBS
TARRY, MISS HILDA M
TAVENER, JAMES
TAVENER, MRS
TAVENER, CHILD
TAVENER, CHILD
TAYLOR, JAMES T
TAYLOR, MISS FLORENCE
THALIX, NESTOR (Rescued)
THALIX, SOFIA
THIRKETTLE, DUDLEY
THOMPSON, MRS T
TIITUS, JACOB
TIPURICZE, JOAN
TODOROVICH, MLADRU
TOME, LUIGI
TORIKOFF, GRIGORI
TOWLANDER, MRS
TREHERNE, ALLAN
TRIF, KOSTA (Rescued)
TUFFLEY, LAURA
TURKICH, AMBROSE
TURNBULL, ALBERT REGINALD
TURNBULL, MRS CAROLINE ELLEN

TURNER, JOSEPH
TWORKOWSKI, DOMINIK
UDIN, AARON
UGOLINI, JOHN
VAGRE, ADELE
VAGRE, AMERIGA
VAGRE, AMERIGO
VAGRE, ANGELO
VAGRE, LUIGI
VAISANEN, DAVID
VALHOTT, KRANCHO
VALHOTT, MICO
VALIMAKI, TUOMAS (Rescued)
VAN CASTRE, VICTOR (Rescued)
VAN DE MOERE, VICTOR (Rescued)
VANNER, THOMAS EWART
VARNEY, MRS LOUISA
VARNEY, MISS VIOLET
VERNIER, MR C
VERNIER, MRS C
VERNIER, JEAN
VERNIER, LOUIS
VERNIER, EDOUARD
VERNIER, RENE
VERNIER, JOSEPH
VERNIER, MARGUERITE
VIITA, KALLE (Rescued)
VINQUIST, C J
WALKER, JAMES (Rescued)
WALKER, MRS JAMES
WALKKY, HILDA (Rescued)
WARWICK, CHARLES RALPH
WASZKO, PAWLO
WATSON, MRS MARY ELLEN
WEIR, MISS VIOLET
WHITE, MISS JESSIE
WHITE, MRS LENA
WHITE, MISS MAY
WHITE, MRS MARY JANE KNOX
WIDLASKI, HARRY
WIKTORSKY, STANISLAW
WILCOCK, HENRY

WILKES, CHARLES
WITIAZ, FONIO
WOJTOWICZ, MIKE
WOLCZUK, JAKYM (Rescued)
WOODWARD, MR WALTER
WOODWARD, MRS
WOODWARD, MRS S.
WOODWARD, MISS MAY
WOODWARD, MISS
WOROBIEN, MARIA
WOROBIEN, NIKOLAI
WOROBIEN, TIMOFEI

WORRALL, HERBERT HORACE
WREN, MRS JANE
YULIK, IWAN
ZALEVA, MARCZIN
ZOLOTOROW, WASILI (Rescued)
ZOUK, GEORGI (Rescued)
ZOUK, MRS MARIA
ZOUK, MASTER WLADISLAW
ZOUK, MISS JOSEFA
ZROTAM, TOADER
ZSUFFA, A.
ZUK, KIRILIO (Rescued)

A Canadian Pacific postcard from the Empress of Ireland,
'Hands across the Sea'

APPENDIX C - CREW LIST

NAME	POSITION	RESCUED/LOST
Absolon, Victor	Bedroom Steward	Rescued
Ainge, Edward	Linen Keeper	Lost
Anderson, J	Trimmer	Lost
Baker, Samuel	Bell Boy	Rescued
Baker, Harold	Assistant Steward	Lost
Bailey, George	Fireman	Rescued
Bamford, Edward	Marconi Operator	Rescued
Barber, John	Fireman	Lost
Bell, Robert	Deck Boy	Lost
Bent, James	Seaman	Lost
Bishop, Thomas	Assistant Cook	Rescued
Boyd, E	Fireman	Lost
Braime, Edward E	Bedroom Steward	Lost
Braithwaite, Isaac	Baker	Rescued
Bray, Manny	Kitchen Porter	Lost
Brennan, Robert Henry	Junior 2nd Engineer	Rescued
Brown, John	Assistant Steward	Rescued
Brown, Patrick	Trimmer	Rescued
Brown, William	Seaman	Rescued
Bruin, Thomas	Seaman	Rescued
Burns, Charles	Assistant Storekeeper	Rescued
Burrows, Thomas	Bedroom Steward	Rescued
Byrne, John Patrick	Bedroom Steward	Rescued
Caley, Frederick J	Junior 9th Engineer	Lost
Campbell, J	Fireman	Rescued
Campbell, M	Trimmer	Rescued
Canepa, William	Assistant Steward	Rescued
Carroll, John	Seaman	Rescued
Chadwick, John	Assistant Steward	Rescued
Challis, Montague E	Assistant Steward	Rescued
Chance, William George	Staff Steward	Lost
Cheetham, John M	Assistant Saloon Steward	Lost
Clague, Robert Henry	Assistant Steward	Rescued
Clandon, H	Cook	Rescued
Clare, William	Assistant Steward	Lost
Clarke, J	Seaman	Rescued
Clarke, J J	Trimmer	Rescued
Clarke, William	Fireman	Rescued

NAME	POSITION	RESCUED/LOST
Cochrane, A	Engineer's Boy	Lost
Cody, M	Trimmer	Lost
Connor, James	Donkeyman	Rescued
Connor, John	Greaser	Lost
Cooke, Thomas	Assistant Steward	Rescued
Coombs, Charles	2nd Saloon Pantryman	Rescued
Cooper, Walter	Assistant Steward	Lost
Cope, Hector	Assistant Steward	Lost
Cope, John	Assistant Pantryman	Rescued
Copplin, George	Assistant Pantryman	Rescued
Corfe, John Eustace	Scullion	Lost
Corrigan, Thomas	Seaman	Lost
Cottle, S	Trimmer	Rescued
Cox, S Alan	Writer	Lost
Crabb, Joseph	Assistant Steward	Lost
Craik, Alexander Christopher	Second Steward	Lost
Crayton, Robert	Seaman	Lost
Crellin, Robert William	Assistant Steward	Lost
Crowther, John George	Leading Fireman	Lost
Cunningham, James J	Cook	Rescued
Cure, A	Assistant Steward	Rescued
D'Arcy, Patrick	Greaser	Rescued
Davidson, George	Storekeeper	Rescued
Davies, John	Trimmer	Rescued
Davies, John	Barman	Rescued
Davis, John	Fireman	Rescued
Davis, P	Fireman	Rescued
Dawson, Alfred	Butcher	Rescued
Dawson, Edward	Assistant Steward	Lost
Dehnel, H	Interpreter	Lost
Delaney, Austin	Assistant Saloon Steward	Lost
Dennehy, E	Seaman	Rescued
Dennis, T	Seaman	Rescued
Derbyshire, Anthony	Bedroom Steward	Lost
Dewey, J	Trimmer	Lost
Dinwoodie, Agnes Ethel	Stewardess	Lost
Disley, J	Seaman	Rescued
Dixon, A H	Assistant Steward	Rescued
Dixon, Harold	Bedroom Steward	Lost
Dolan, Paul	Trimmer	Rescued

NAME	POSITION	RESCUED/LOST
Donaldson, John	Trimmer	Rescued
Donegan, James	Assistant Steward	Rescued
Douglas, Thomas	Baker	Rescued
Downey, Thomas Shawn	Seaman	Rescued
Duckworth, William Barrett	Electrician	Rescued
Duffy, J	Fireman	Rescued
Duggan, John	Assistant Printer	Rescued
Duggan, P	Greaser	Rescued
Dumbell, Thomas	Assistant Steward	Rescued
Dunn, J	Trimmer	Rescued
Durkin, John	Café Steward	Lost
Eliott, Alfred	Baker	Rescued
Evans, A	Seaman	Rescued
Evans, John	Seaman	Rescued
Faulkner, Reginald	Assistant Pantryman	Lost
Fawcett, W	Seaman	Rescued
Fayle, R R	Asst. Saloon Steward	Rescued
Fereday, Arthur	Assistant Steward	Rescued
Ferguson, Ronald	Marconi Operator	Rescued
File, O	Ex 2nd Officer	Rescued
Fisher, Samuel	Bell Boy	Lost
Fitzgerald, H	Seaman	Rescued
Fitzpatrick, A	Assistant Steward	Lost
Fitzpatrick, J	Seaman	Rescued
Flagel, J	Seaman	Lost
Flinn, Roy	Assistant Steward	Rescued
Flood, Thomas	Leading Fireman	Rescued
Foster, E	Trimmer	Rescued
Gaade, Augustus William	Chief Steward	Rescued
Gale, Thomas John	Assistant Steward	Lost
Gallagher, W	Deck Boy	Lost
Galway, James Francis	Quarter Master	Rescued
Gardiner, William	Scullion	Lost
Gavigan, Bernard	Assistant Steward	Lost
Gee, Percy	Asst. Saloon Steward	Rescued
Gerrard, Thomas	Smoke Room Steward	Lost
Gibson, John	Assistant Steward	Rescued
Gill, Henry	Saloon Pantryman	Rescued
Gill, James Philip	Bedroom Steward	Lost
Gillespie, Robert Walls	Senior 4th Engineer	Lost

NAME	POSITION	RESCUED/LOST
Glasberg, Rudolph	Barber	Rescued
Glover, Thomas	Cook	Lost
Grant, E	Trimmer	Lost
Grant, John	Electrician	Rescued
Grant, James Frederic	Surgeon	Rescued
Gratwick, T	Seaman	Rescued
Gray, Arthur	Asst. Saloon Steward	Rescued
Gray, Whit W	Assistant Steward	Rescued
Green, Frederick	Assistant Steward	Rescued
Gregory, Frederick	Assistant Steward	Rescued
Greives, G	Assistant Steward	Rescued
Gutcher, James Duncan	Quarter Master	Lost
Hadfield, William James	Asst. Saloon Steward	Lost
Haigh, Samuel	Assistant Steward	Rescued
Hamilton, James Alfred	Bell Boy	Lost
Hamilton, Frank W	Ticket Agent	Lost
Hampton, William	Junior 2nd Engineer	Rescued
Haran, Patrick	Cook	Rescued
Harford, N	Seaman	Rescued
Harrison, Frank	Bedroom Steward	Rescued
Harrison, F	Grill Cook	Lost
Harrold, W	Bedroom Steward	Lost
Hayes, Ernest C	1st Assistant Purser	Rescued
Hayes, E	Trimmer	Rescued
Hayes, Joseph A	Assistant Steward	Rescued
Healey, J	Greaser	Lost
Hepburn, J	Fireman	Lost
Herbert, William	Assistant Steward	Rescued
Highfield, William Duncan Cameron	Printer	Lost
Hird, William	Steward	Rescued
Hobson, Francis Sydney	Assistant Steward	Rescued
Holden, S	Greaser	Rescued
Hollies, Helena	Stewardess	Rescued
Holt, Robert A	Bedroom Steward	Rescued
Hopwood, William	Assistant Steward	Lost
Houghton, Thomas	Trimmer	Rescued
Hudson, John	Seaman	Rescued
Hudson, William Daniel	Barman	Lost
Hughes, Hugh	Bedroom Steward	Rescued
Hughes, William H	Assistant Steward	Rescued

NAME	POSITION	RESCUED/LOST
Hughes, William Lawrence	Assistant Steward	Rescued
Hunt, Thomas	Assistant Steward	Lost
Hutchinson, A	Fireman	Rescued
Jackson, Charles E	Fireman	Rescued
Jacob, Alfred Henry	Bedroom Steward	Lost
Jaques, Henry	Assistant Steward	Rescued
Jeffries, Joseph F	Seaman	Rescued
Johnson, James	Cook	Lost
Johnson, K	Cook	Lost
Johnston, J A B	8th Engineer	Rescued
Jones, C	Assistant Steward	Rescued
Jones, Daniel H	Seaman	Rescued
Jones, Ellen	Stewardess	Lost
Jones, Edward John	First Officer	Rescued
Jones, Hugh	Assistant Steward	Lost
Jones, Henry	Barber	Lost
Jones, Harold	Bedroom Steward	Lost .
Jones, Henry Andrew	Saloon Steward	Lost
Jones, John Jameson	Assistant Steward	Lost
Jones, John Mackenzie	Senior 2nd Engineer	Lost
Jones, Miriam	Matron	Lost
Jones, Owen	Assistant Steward	Rescued
Jones, Percy Reginald	Bell Boy	Lost
Jump, Joseph	Fireman	Lost
Jump, John Thomas	Trimmer	Lost
Kane, T	Trimmer	Lost
Keegan, J	Trimmer	Rescued
Kendall, Henry George	Ship's Captain	Rescued
Kerwin, James H	Trimmer	Lost
King, J	Trimmer	Rescued
Knight, Robert	Butcher	Rescued
Knill, Arthur	Cook	Rescued
Lally, James	Fireman	Lost
Lang, B	Seaman	Rescued
Lappin, W H	Cook	Lost
Lawrie, James	Assistant Steward	Lost
Learmonth, George Seaton	Seaman	Lost
Leary, C	Cook	Lost
Leders, Elizabeth	Stewardess	Lost
Lee, Sydney	Cook	Rescued

NAME	POSITION	RESCUED/LOST
Lennon, George	Assistant Steward	Lost
Leonard, Thomas	Seaman	Lost
Leonard, W	Seaman	Lost
Lewis, Charles	Chief 3rd Class Steward	Lost
Lewis, Henry	Assistant Steward	Lost
Lewis, John	Assistant Cook	Rescued
Liddell, Robert R	Junior 2nd Engineer	Rescued
Lightfoot, George	Officers Steward	Lost
Lyons, William H	Seaman	Lost
MacDonald, L A	Assistant Steward	Rescued
Madden, Bertha Brown	Stewardess	Lost
Madden, Frank	Assistant Steward	Lost
Maguire, Joseph	Fireman	Rescued
Maguire, James	Trimmer	Rescued
Maguire, J	Seaman	Rescued
Maher, Patrick	Greaser	Rescued
Malone, B	Fireman	Rescued
Malone, Peter	Fireman	Rescued
Manderson, Walter George	Assistant Saloon Steward	Lost
Mathews, John	Chef	Rescued
Matthews, J	Trimmer	Rescued
McAdam, William	Greaser	Rescued
McAleavey, Michael	Greaser	Rescued
McAleavey, Patrick	Scullion	Rescued
McBride, William	Trimmer	Lost
McCabe, James	Fireman	Rescued
McCabe, Richard	Trimmer	Rescued
McCabe, Thomas	Trimmer	Rescued
McCowan, J	Fireman	Rescued
McCoy, John William	Seaman	Rescued
McCoy, R L	Assistant Pantryman	Lost
McCready, Thomas	Fireman	Rescued
McDonald, Alexander Betteley	Purser	Lost
McDonald, Charles K	Junior 4th Engineer	Rescued
McDonnell, Michael J	Butcher	Rescued
McDougall, Duncan	Seaman	Rescued
McEnroe, Edward	Trimmer	Lost
McEwan, James	Junior 4th Engineer	Rescued
McEwan, John	Seaman	Rescued
McGuinness, John	Trimmer	Rescued

NAME	POSITION	RESCUED/LOST
McGuinness, Michael	Leading Fireman	Lost
McGuinness. R	Fireman	Lost
McGuinness, T	Leading Fireman	Rescued
McGrath, John	Assistant Steward	Lost
McMahon, Peter	Fireman	Lost
McManus, Henry	Fireman	Lost
McOnie, George Randolph	Junior 3rd Engineer	Rescued
McSherry, James	Assistant Steward	Rescued
McWilliams, Robert	Asst. Saloon Steward	Rescued
Megson, John	Greaser	Rescued
Mellor, Herbert	Deck Steward	Rescued
Metcalfe, George	Asst.Saloon Steward	Rescued
Metcalfe, Thomas	Assistant Steward	Rescued
Mitchell, James	Trimmer	Rescued
Mitchell, Robert	Bedroom Steward	Lost
Mohring, Guy	Assistant Pantryman	Lost
Moore, Charles Alwyn	3rd Officer	Lost
Moran, James	Seaman	Rescued
Morgan, James	Trimmer	Rescued
Morl, William	Boots	Rescued
Morland, H R	Assistant Steward	Rescued
Mountain, Thomas	Fireman	Rescued
Muir, Charles William	Assistant Steward	Lost
Mulvaney, William	Trimmer	Lost
Munroe, William Anderson	2nd Class Pantryman	Lost
Murden, Reuben	Trimmer	Lost
Murphy, Jack	Assistant Steward	Lost
Murphy, John	Quartermaster	Rescued
Murphy, Patrick	Leading Fireman	Rescued
Murphy, W	Trimmer	Rescued
Murray, Peter	Trimmer	Rescued
Murtagh, Matthew	Bedroom Steward	Rescued
Murtagh, William	Bell Boy	Lost
Myers, Frank	Assistant Steward	Lost
Myers, John	Asst. Saloon Steward	Rescued
Neale, H	Trimmer	Rescued
Negus, Matilda	Stewardess	Lost
Nelson, C	Greaser	Rescued
Nelson, George	Assistant Steward	Lost
Newham, Henry	Assistant Saloon Steward	Lost

NAME	POSITION	RESCUED/LOST
Nugent, William J	Bedroom Steward	Rescued
O'Connell, David	Trimmer	Lost
O'Donnell, D	Greaser	Rescued
O'Donovan, George	Junior 3rd Engineer	Rescued
O'Neill, H	Fireman	Lost
Orford, George Leonard	Assistant Steward	Lost
O'Sullivan, James	Seaman	Lost
Owen, Robert	Pantryman	Rescued
Owen, William Salisbury	Assistant Steward	Rescued
Page, Clarrie May	Stewardess	Lost
Parkinson, Charles R	Assistant Steward	Rescued
Parkinson, Frederick	Assistant Steward	Lost
Parry, D	Assistant Steward	Rescued
Passmore, Charles Joseph	Bedroom Steward	Lost
Paterson, John	Butcher	Rescued
Pearson, Sophia Jane	Stewardess	Lost
Pelton, Benjamin David J	Assistant Steward	Lost
Perry, Harold	Assistant Steward	Lost
Peterson, Victor T	Carpenter	Lost
Phenna, Frederick	Assistant Steward	Lost
Pierce, Augustus	Cook	Lost
Pinner, C	Assistant Steward	Rescued
Pitts, William H	Assistant Steward	Rescued
Powell, Leonard	Assistant Boots	Rescued
Preston, John Edwin	Inspector	Lost
Price, J H	Seaman	Rescued
Price, William	Assistant Pantryman	Rescued
Prince, Thomas	Asst. Saloon Steward	Rescued
Pritchard, Ernest	Assistant Cook	Lost
Pritchard, John	Assistant Steward	Rescued
Pritchard, Oliver	Assistant Steward	Rescued
Prowse, James B	Assistant Steward	Rescued
Quinn, J	Trimmer	Rescued
Quinn, W	Trimmer	Rescued
Radley, Alec C	Boatswain's Mate	Rescued
Rankin, Alexander Carmichael	Second Writer	Lost
Ratcliffe, Jack	Assistant Steward	Lost
Reardon, D	Greaser	Rescued
Regan, Michael	Fireman	Lost
Reich, Joseph	Assistant Steward	Lost

NAME	POSITION	RESCUED/LOST
Reid, H	Fireman	Lost
Reid, James	Trimmer	Lost
Reid, James	Fireman	Lost
Rice, Edward	Fireman	Rescued
Richards, Edward	Steward	Lost
Riddell, Alice	Stewardess	Lost
Riley, J	Seaman	Lost
Roberts, James	Engineer's Steward	Rescued
Roberts, William	Assistant Steward	Lost
Robertson, John	2nd Class Steward	Rescued
Robinson, W	Trimmer	Rescued
Rockford, Michael	Fireman	Rescued
Rohr, Arnold	Confectioner	Rescued
Ross, W	Greaser	Lost
Rowan, William	Assistant Steward	Rescued
Rowlands, T	Fireman	Rescued
Rushton, Joseph Albert	Assistant Steward	Lost
Ryan, John	Fireman	Rescued
Ryan, Thomas	Trimmer	Rescued
Sampson, William	Chief Engineer	Rescued
Saunders, Robert	Master At Arms	Rescued
Shannon, Edward	Fireman	Rescued
Shannon, Francis J	Assistant Steward	Rescued
Sharkey, Martin	Cook	Rescued
Sharples, W H	Quartermaster	Lost
Shaw, Henry Edward	Baker	Rescued
Sheridan, R	Greaser	Rescued
Simms, J	Seaman	Rescued
Simon, Albert	Assistant Cook	Rescued
Singer, Joseph	Assistant Steward	Lost
Skarratt, Leonard	Assistant Steward	Lost
Smith, Albert E	Assistant Steward	Rescued
Smith, Alfred E	6th Engineer	Rescued
Smith, C	Assistant Steward	Rescued
Smith, Harry	Assistant Saloon Steward	Lost
Smith, Henry K	Assistant Steward	Rescued
Smith, James	Trimmer	Rescued
Smith, Joseph	Assistant Steward	Rescued
Smith, Thomas J	Baker	Rescued
Smith, Walter Beaumont	Bedroom Steward	Lost

NAME	POSITION	RESCUED/LOST
Smythe, James	Fireman	Rescued
Snowdon, John	Assistant Steward	Lost
Somers, Matthew	Fireman	Rescued
Spencer, Charles	Bell Boy	Rescued
Sprague, Thomas	Boatswain	Rescued
Stair, Edmund	Greaser	Lost
Steede, Mansfield Richard	Chief Officer	Lost
Stephens, John	Fireman	Rescued
Stephens, John	Greaser	Rescued
Stratton, Lucilla	Stewardess	Lost
Summers, John	Greaser	Lost
Swan, John H	10th Engineer	Rescued
Swinton, Alexander	Chief Baker	Lost
Taylor, Walter	Carpenter's Mate	Lost
Terry, John	Assistant Steward	Lost
Thomas, W	Assistant Steward	Lost
Thompson, Gerrard Joseph	Plumber	Lost
Thomson, Archibald	Assistant Steward	Rescued
Toole, John	Fireman	Rescued
O'Toole, Patrick	Trimmer	Rescued
Trainor, Nicholas	Boots	Lost
Tumilty, Bernard	Fireman	Lost
Tunstall, B	4th Officer	Lost
Tunstall, Harry	Assistant Steward	Lost
Turner, Joseph	Assistant Cook	Rescued
Ventre, Joseph	Cook	Rescued
Vivian, Bertie Adams	Assistant Steward	Lost
Wakeford, C	Assistant Purser	Rescued
Walden, David Heron	Fireman	Lost
Walker, Thomas Lyle	Bedroom Steward	Lost
Welsh, Thomas	Trimmer	Lost
White, H	Trimmer	Rescued
White, John Bell	7th Engineer	Rescued
Whitty, John	Leading Fireman	Rescued
Whitty, James	Fireman	Rescued
Wildman, James Alison	Storekeeper	Lost
Williams, Arthur Clement	Saloon Steward	Rescued
Williams, David	Cook	Rescued
Williams, G C	Assistant Steward	Lost
Williams, Joseph	Assistant Steward	Rescued

NAME	POSITION	RESCUED/LOST
Williams, Richard	Bedroom Steward	Rescued
Williams, Roger	2nd Officer	Lost
Williams, Thomas	Chief 2nd Cabin Steward	Rescued
Williams, William	Greaser	Rescued
Williams, William	Lamp Trimmer	Lost
Williamson, Percy Robert	Senior 5th Engineer	Lost
Willis, George Oswald	Smokeroom Steward	Lost
Wilson, F	Assistant Steward	Lost
Wilson, J	Trimmer	Rescued
Wilson, John	Trimmer	Lost
Worthington, P	Fireman	Lost
Wright, Alfred	Assistant Steward	Lost
Wynne, Thomas	Scullion	Rescued

Reader input on both the passenger manifest and the crew list is welcome and may be forwarded to:

Geoffrey Whitfield, P.O. Box 401, Hope Carr Way, Leigh, Lancashire WN7 3WW, United Kingdom.

Some unidentified members of the crew of the Empress of Ireland *aboard the* Storstad, *after being picked up by that vessel.*

A detailed cross section of the Empress of Ireland which illustrates her massive carrying capacity.

SUNK IN COLLISION: THE LINER WHICH MET DISASTER OFF FATHER POINT, AT THE MOUTH OF THE RIVER ST. LAWRENCE

APPENDIX D

INVENTORY OF THE PURSER'S SAFE - RMS EMPRESS OF IRELAND

BANK NOTES

68 Bank of England £5 notes

2 Bank of England £10 notes

Sundry Bank & Dominion notes $250 Roll of bills amounting to $80

4 Canadian Bank of Commerce $100 notes

2 Canadian Bank of Commerce $50 notes

An envelope (No. 8) containing a statement showing $425.20 and in which was found $43 in Canadian and American bills; nineteen foreign notes; and two 2 June *London Mail* Great Derby Sweep tickets Nos. ZA29250 and ZA29245

GOLD AND COIN

57 sovereigns and 7 half-sovereigns

2 silver coins and a half-penny contained in a common black leather purse along with Envelope No. 2 containing £99-12 shillings-6 pence in silver coin

British gold amounting to £1233 and 12 shillings

Small bag of sundry odd foreign silver and copper coins (uncounted) about $5

£173-6 shillings-10 pence in British silver and copper

$19 and thirty cents in Canadian silver

$6 and five cents in American silver

20 francs in gold (Envelope No. 8)

PASSENGER ENVELOPES

Clark, Charles

Safety envelope No. 992, with signature 'Chas.R. Clark' containing $48 in American bills.

Cunningham, R.A.

Safety envelope No. 989 marked 'Cunningham' containing Union Bank of Canada, Portage & Garry Branch, Winnipeg draft for £53-4-10 to the order of R. A. Cunningham; and a U.S. bank note for $20.

Goldthorpe, C.

Safety envelope No. 993 with signature 'C. Goldthorpe' found open and empty.

Herxheimer, W

International Mercantile Marine travellers' cheques in the name of Walter Herxheimer 10 each at $50 and a separate book of 5 each at $50.

Johnston, David

One Windsor Hotel, Montreal, envelope containing three drafts issued by the Fredericton Branch of the Bank of Montreal on the London, England, branch. All payable at sight to the order of David Johnston: No 125 for £500; No. 126 for £1000; and No. 127 for £315-11 shillings-7 pence.

Kavalesky, Ivan

Safety envelope No. 986 marked 'Kavalske' containing 11 Bank of England £5 notes; 1 Bank of England £10 note; and 1 Bank of England £20 note.

Lindsay, M.A.

Safety envelope No. 995 with signature 'M. A. Lindsay' containing 9 Royal Bank of Canada $10 notes; 2 Bank of England £10 notes; and 12 Bank of England £5 notes.

Richards, George

Safety envelope No. 991 marked 'Geo. C. Richards' containing 7 K.N. & K. travellers' cheques $10 each, 19 of same for $20 each, and 1 for $50; 5 American $20 bills; a letter dated 30 September 1911 at Sheffield with envelope plus an empty envelope unaddressed bearing 'Return in five days to Richards & Sons, Miners and Shippers of Coal, Terre Haute, Ind.'

Reilley, John

Safety envelope No. 987 signed by John Reilley found open and empty.

Schongutt, H.

Safety envelope No. 994 signed 'Josephine Schongutt' containing $30 in Canadian notes; four sovereigns; another white envelope within marked 'Mathilde' containing 1 Bank of England £5 note plus four sovereigns.

Yates, H.

Safety envelope No. 988 signed 'Harry Yates' containing 2 Bank of England £5 notes; two sovereigns; and two half-sovereigns.

Wakeford, A.J.

One paper-covered package bound with a shawl strap and metal handle, bearing two tags, one marked 'From Windsor Hotel, Montreal, Room 138, No. of pieces 5, *Empress* Special'; and one marked 'A. J. Wakeford, *Empress of Ireland*, Quebec, May 28th, 1914' which upon being opened was found to contain one lump of quartz.

Unidentified -Safety envelope, signature illegible, containing $175 in notes.

SILVER BULLION

One canvas bag to which was attached an unaddressed tag of the Canadian Express Company, which upon being opened was found to contain custom papers and way bills for a shipment of silver bullion to Mocalta & Co, London, England.

One Bill of Lading for one hundred and sixty-three bars of silver bullion dated at Quebec, 28 May 1914.

One Bill of Lading for forty-nine bars of silver bullion dated at Quebec, 28 May 1914.

FREIGHT FORWARDING

One canvas bag to which is attached a tag marked 'Agent Dominion Express Company, Liverpool, England sealed by M.E.P. Quebec 28 May 1914' containing two sealed packages numbered 239 and 242; and a bundle of 13 Dominion Express envelopes unopened.

One bundle of Dominion Express papers including way bills and way bill statements.

OFFICE AND PURSER

One Bank of Montreal signatures book.

Two Canadian Pacific Railway remittance books, Form E35.

One CPR S.S. Co. Requisition Book, Form S.S. E2036, partly used.

Agents Requisition Book, Form S.S. 2036; and stubs numbered 2 through 111.

Three Purser's cash books: one completed January 1911; one completed November 1913; another continuing through 23 May 1914, with receipts and vouchers.

One Remittance Book: last entry £1900 on 23 May 1914.

One package of private papers and five books apparently belonging to Purser McDonald.

Part of a memo book used to balance cash and two small red memo books.

Two Masonic charts bearing the name of Ernest Hayes.

A cigar box containing private letters and papers apparently belonging to Ernest Hayes.

TRAVELLERS' CHEQUES

Dominion Express travellers' cheques: Nos. 552930 to 552969 at $10 each; Nos. 345850 to 345869 at $20 each; Nos. 127170 to 127229 at $50 each; Nos. 32170 to 32199 at $100 each; and seven empty leather covers for Dominion Express travellers' cheques.

Dominion Express Money Orders: Series AA Nos. 99010 to 99049; Series BB Nos. 678500 to 678549; and a package of eleven stubs for Dominion Express Money Orders and one separate stub.

Dominion Express Foreign Limited Cheques: Nos. 556731 to 556749.

STAMPS

Several sheets of Canadian One and Two Cent stamps which could not be counted due to their condition.

A package containing Insurance Stamps 'National Health Insurance' value shown on cover as £37-14-6.

A package of English Penny and Half-penny stamps value shown on cover as £51-9-0.

MISCELLANEOUS

Certificate of British Registry for SS *Empress of Ireland* with documents attached.

One Private Cypher Code, 6th edition No. 188 which was sealed without having been opened.

One badly damaged automatic revolver (.22) and a box of cartridges (No. 38).

One package of Officers Certificates.

Shipping Master's Receipt for cleaning the ship.

One badly damaged small marine print of *Empress* and sailing vessel.

About two dozen packages of patent medicines which on account of their condition were destroyed.

Two books *Peru To-day*, October and November 1913.

One tin cash box, containing several miscellaneous keys.

Seven wooden cash cups, and one black leather cash bag.

A package of miscellaneous letters and papers of no apparent value.

One small tin lifeboat-shaped bank marked 'Contributions for the Royal National Life Boat Association', the bow of which was slightly damaged.

Certified on 22 August and 24 August 1914, before Reginald Meredith, Notary Public, City of Quebec.

Recertified on 22 January 1997, by Stuart Wright, Notary Public, City of Quebec.

(The original document was handwritten and contained additional detail in some cases. For example, the serial numbers of 66 Bank of England £5 notes were written out. Money found in the centre compartment of the safe and not otherwise marked as the property of individuals was presumed to belong to Canadian Pacific Railway. The Bank of Montreal maintained custody of all valuables until properly turned over to owners and heirs.)

The Purser's safe is raised on August 20th 1914.

Bibliography

BOOKS

Adams, John, *Ocean Steamers*. New Cavendish Books, London, 1993

Archbold, Rick & Ballard, Dr Robert D., *Lost Liners*. Hyperion/Madison Press, Toronto, 1997

Ballard, Dr. Robert D., *The Discovery of* Titanic. Madison Press Books, Toronto, 1987

Ballard, Dr. Robert D., *Exploring the* Titanic. Madison Press Books, Toronto, 1988

Baarslag, Karl, *SOS To The Rescue*. Oxford University Press, New York, 1935

Baker III, Elijah, *Introduction to Shipbuilding*. McGraw-Hill Book Company, Inc., New York, 1943

Barnaby, O.B.E., K. C., *Some Ship Disasters and Their Causes*. Hutchinson & Co. Ltd, London, 1968

Berton, Pierre, *The Last Spike*. McClelland and Stewart Ltd, Toronto, 1972

Biel, Steven, *Down With the Old Canoe*. W W. Norton & Company, New York, 1996

Boar, Roger & Blundell, Nigel, *The World's Most Infamous Murders*. Octopus Books Ltd, London, 1983

Bonsall, Thomas E., *Great Shipwrecks of the 20th Century*. Gallery Books, New York, 1987

Bonsor, N.R.P., *North Atlantic Seaway*. Prescot, Lancashire, 1955

Bowen, Frank C., *A Century of Atlantic Travel*. Sampson Low, Marston & Company, London, 1933

Bowen, Frank C., *History of the Canadian Pacific Line*. Sampson Low, Marston & Co., Ltd, London, 1928

Brinnin, John, Malcolm, *The Sway of the Grand Saloon*. Delacorte Press, New York, 1971

Brown, Rustie, *The* Titanic, *The Psychic and the Sea*. Blue Harbour Press, Lomita, 1981

Chapman, Lawrence B., *The Marine Power Plant*. McGraw Hill Book Company, Inc., New York, 1942

Choko, Marc & Jones, David, *Canadian Pacific Posters* 1883-1963. Meridian Press, Ottawa, 1995

Corson, F. Reid, *The Atlantic Ferry in the Twentieth Century*. Sampson Low, Marston & Co., Ltd, London, 1931

Croall, James, *Fourteen Minutes*. Stein & Day, New York, 1978

Cullen, Tom A., *The Mild Murderer*. Houghton Mifflin Company, Boston, 1977

Ellsberg, Edward, *Men Under the Sea*. Dodd, Mead & Company, New York, 1939

Gibbon, John Murray, *The Romantic History of the Canadian Pacific*. Tudor, New York, 1935

Goss, Michael and Behe, George, *Lost At Sea*. Prometheus Books, Amherst, New York, 1994

Harris, John, *Lost at Sea, True Stories of Disaster*. Guild Publishing, London, 1990

Hoehling, A.A. and Hoehling, M., *The Last Voyage of the Lusitania*. Holt, New York, 1956

Hoehling, A. A., *They Sailed Into Oblivion*. Thomas Yoseloff, Ltd, New York, 1959

Homer, A.N., *Imperial Highway*. Sir Joseph Caustons, London, 1912

Kendall, Capt. H. G., *Adventures on the High Sea*. Hurst & Blacken, Ltd, London, 1939

Longbottom, Ken, *Liverpool and the Mersey Vol. 1: Gladstone Dock and the Great Liners*. Silver Link Publishing, Ltd, Peterborough, Great Britain, 1995

Lotz, Jim & McKenzie, Keith, *Railways of Canada*. Bison Books, Ltd, London, 1988

Luckin, Richard, *Dining on the Rails*, RK Publishing, Golden, Colorado, 1990

Manning, George C., *Manual of Ship Construction*. D. Van Nostrand Company, Inc., New York, 1942

Marshall, Logan, *The Tragic Story of the* Empress of Ireland *and Other Great Sea Disasters*. LT. Myers, New York, 1914

Martin, Simon, *The Other* Titanic. David & Charles, Inc., North Pomfret, Vermont, 1980

Meadley, Robert, *Classics in Murder*. Xanadu Publications Ltd, London, 1984

Mitchell, W H., *Canadian Pacific and Southampton*. World Ship Society, Southampton, 1991

Moscow, Alvin, *Collision Course*. Blackie & Son, Ltd, Glasgow, 1959

Moss, Michael, *The Clyde, A Portrait of a River*. Cannongate Books Ltd., Edinburgh, 1997

Moss, Michael S. and Hume, John R., *Clyde Shipbuilding from Old Photography*. B. T. Batsford, Ltd, London, 1975

Moss, Michael S. and Hume, John R., *Workshop of the British Empire, Engineering and Shipbuilding in West of Scotland.* Heinemann Educational Books, Ltd., London, 1977

Musk, George, *Canadian Pacific: The Story of the Famous Shipping Line.* Holt, Toronto, 1981

Padfield, Peter, *An Agony of Collisions*, Hodder and Stoughton, London,1966

Rasky, Frank, *Great Canadian Disasters.* Longmans, Green & Company, Toronto, 1961

Riddell, John F., *Clyde Navigation.* John Donald Publishers, Ltd, Edinburgh, 1979

Rushton, Gerald A., *Whistle Up the Inlet*, The Union Steamship Story. J. J. Douglas Ltd., Vancouver, 1974

Smith, Eugene W., *Passenger Ships of the World Past and Present.* George H. Dean Company, Boston, 1978

Tantum IV, William H., Editor, *The Tragic Story of the* Empress of Ireland by Logan Marshall, Patrick Stephens, Ltd, London,1972

Turner, Robert D., *The Pacific Empresses.* Sono Nis Press, Victoria, 1981

Walker, Fred M., *Song of the Clyde.* W W. Norton & Company, New York, 1985

Warren, Mark D., Lusitania. Patrick Stephens, Ltd., London 1986

Warren, Mark D., *The Shipbuilder* 1906-1914 Vol. 1. Blue Riband Publications, Inc., New York, 1995

Watson, Milton, H., *Disasters At Sea.* Patrick Stephens Ltd, London, 1987

Whale, Derek, M., *The Liners of Liverpool (Part II).* Countyvise Ltd, Merseyside, 1987

Whale, Derek, M., *The Liners of Liverpool (Part Ill).* Countyvise Ltd, Merseyside, 1988

Wood, Herbert P., *Till We Meet Again: The Sinking of the* Empress of Ireland. Image Publishing, Inc., Toronto, 1982

Woon, Basil, *The Frantic Atlantic: An Intimate Guide to the Well-Known Deep.* Alfred A. Knopf, Inc., New York, 1927

MISCELLANEOUS SOURCES

'The Fairfield Shipbuilding and Engineering Works: History of the Company; Review of its Productions; and Description of the Works'. Souvenir Volume, *Engineering*, London, 1909

The Journal of Commerce, British Shipbuilding, Royal Souvenir Edition, July 1913

'Report and Evidence of the Commission of Inquiry into the Loss of the British Steamship *'Empress of Ireland'* of Liverpool (No. 123972) Through Collision with Norwegian Steamship *'Storstad.'* Quebec, June, 1914.' Printed by Order of Parliament by J. De L. Tache, Printer To The King's Most Excellent Majesty 1914.

Burggraf, Marjorie L., *The* Empress of Ireland, *A Canadian Marine Monument to Twentieth Century Immigrant History.* Marine Museum of the Great Lakes at Kingston, Ontario, 1996

Beaulieu, Nicole, and Normandeau, Anne, *The Forgotten Tragedy.* Souvenir booklet produced by Musée de la Mer, Pointe-au-Pére, Quebec

Musée de la Mer, booklet, La tragédie oubliée... Le naufrage de l'*Empress of Ireland.* Pointe-au-Pére, Quebec, 1995

Reid, John, Esq., 'Notes from a Collision Investigation'. Paper presented to the Institution of Naval Architects, April 13, 1916

Denver Social Record and Club Annual (1913-1914), Denver, Colorado

Letter of J. McSherry to family of Mansfield R. Steede, June 1914

Fairfield Shipbuilding & Engineering Company records, Mitchell Library, Glasgow

Miscellaneous records, National Archives of Canada, Ottawa, Ontario

Saloon and crew lists, miscellaneous records, Canadian Pacific Archives, Windsor Station, Montreal

Exchequer Court of Canada, Quebec Admiralty District, Decision of April 27, 1915

Privy Council Appeal, Supreme Court of Canada, December 5, 1919

Letter of David R. Kennedy, son of CPR passenger agent, July 1997

Letters of Mary A. Shepherd, daughter of Fred Cullen, July 1997

Lloyd's Register of Shipping

Diary of Salvation Army Officer Gideon Miller

Letters of Stuart Wright, February 1997

Note of Protest, Frank Corey, Master, July 9, 1906

Note of Protest, John Forster, Master, October 15, 1909

Inventory of the contents of Purser's safe, August 24, 1914; certified copy furnished by Stuart Wright, Notary, City of Quebec

Letter of William Hughes to A. Veronica Williams, June 1914

The Empress of Ireland, *Lost Not Forgotten,* SeaView Imaging video, 1996

St Lawrence, Stairway to the Sea, Cousteau Video Library, Time Life video distributors, 1982

Empress of Ireland Deck Plans, Ship Reproductions, 1995

NEWSPAPERS AND PERIODICALS

Atlantic Daily Bulletin

Canadian Churchman

Canadian Gazette

Canadian Medical Assoc. Journal

Christian Herald

Chicago Daily News

Chicago Tribune

Daily Colonist (Victoria)

Daily Gleaner (New Brunswick)

Daily Dispatch

Daily Sketch

Daily Telegraph (Montreal)

Denver Post

Detroit Free Press

Detroit News

Diver Magazine

Engineering

Glasgow Herald

Graphic

Halifax Herald

Harbour & Shipping

Hartford Courant

International Marine Engineering

Irish News

La Tribune (Sherbrooke)

Liverpool Echo

London Illustrated News

London Times

Los Angeles Times

Marine Review

Milwaukee Journal

Milwaukee Sentinel

Montreal Daily Star

Montreal Gazette

Nassau Guardian

Nautical Magazine

New York Maritime Register

New York Times

New York World

New Zealand Herald

Ocean Liner Gazette

Provost News (Alberta)

Quebec Chronicle

Reader's Digest

Regina Morning Leader

Rochester Daily Bulletin

Rochester Post & Record

Rocky Mountain News

San Francisco Chronicle

Sea Breezes

Sea Classics

Seattle Daily Times

Seattle Post Intelligencer

Sherbrooke Daily Record

Shipbuilding & Shipping Record

Shipping World

Spectator

Steamboat Bill

Sphere

Toronto Daily Star

Toronto Globe & Mail

Toronto Mail & Empire

Toronto World

Vancouver Daily Province

Vancouver Sun

Verdun Guardian

War Cry

Who's Who in Canada

FOR RELATED READING IN FICTION ON THE EMPRESS OF IRELAND:
Cussler, Clive, *Night Probe*. Bantam Books, New York, N.Y, 1981

FOR RELATED READING IN FICTION ABOUT DR. CRIPPEN:
Williams, Emlyn, *Dr. Crippen's Diary*. Robson Books, Ltd, London, 1987

INDEX

Also Published by Avid Publications
Garth Boulevard, Bebington, Wirral, Merseyside UK. CH63 5LS
Tel / Fax (44) 0151 645 2047
e-mail info@avidpublications.co.uk
website http//www.AvidPublications.co.uk

THETIS - THE ADMIRALTY REGRETS
–THE DISASTER IN LIVERPOOL BAY

by C.Warren & J.Benson

The definitive minute by minute account of this terrible tragedy in 1939 when 99 men lost their lives as HM Submarine *Thetis* undertook her first and only dive. With new photographs and documents as well as a new foreword by Derek Arnold, a survivors son, and a new postscript by maritime historian David Roberts. Why didn't anyone cut open the submarine? Why was there no urgency in the Admiralty's rescue system? Did the Admiralty really regret?

ISBN 0 9521020 8 0   £9.50 + £1.50 p&p

HMS THETIS – SECRETS AND SCANDAL
– AFTERMATH OF A DISASTER.

by David Roberts

The sinking of *Thetis* cost 99 men their lives and is still today the worst submarine disaster in British History. This latest book contains interviews with relatives of victims; sons, daughters, brothers, sisters and those very rare ladies, living widows. Also here are never before seen documents from the time; Offers of outside help, Secret Navy reports and even descriptions of bodies for identification. Why did the Official Inquiry blame nobody, explaining it away as 'an unfortunate sequence of events'? Why did the civil action on behalf of the widow's fail? Did the Admiralty cover it up? How much did Churchill know? How were those left behind treated? A huge publicly subscribed disaster fund was collected for the relatives. How was this managed and distributed? Who got what and why? What ever happened to the money that was left?

'a book that shocks...tells the hidden story of those left behind'   - Sea Breezes.
' now known as the Hillsborough of its day... a disaster surrounded by injustice' - Liverpool Echo

ISBN 0 9521020 0 5   £8.99 + £1.50 p&p

LUSITANIA - UPDATED MERSEYSIDE EDITION
by Colin Simpson

THE definitive work on the real story surrounding this still mysterious ship. On the 7th of May 1915 the Cunard vessel Lusitania was torpedoed by a German submarine off the Old Head of Kinsale on the south west coast of Ireland resulting in the loss of the vessel itself and 1,201 men, women and children. It also ultimately resulted in the United States entry to the First World War. More than eighty five years on the story of the *Lusitania* continues to be shrouded in mystery and suspicion. What was her real cargo? Why wasn't she protected? Why did she sink so quickly? Containing rare photographs from Germany and elsewhere; it is a truly intriguing and fascinating tale.

ISBN 0 95201020 6 4 £9.50 + £1.50 p&p

LUSITANIA AND BEYOND
- THE STORY OF CAPTAIN WILLIAM THOMAS TURNER
by Mitch Peeke & Kevin Walsh- Johnson. Illustrated by John Gray

There are many accounts of the great maritime disasters, but very few portraits of the people at the centre of these vast, tragic events. William Thomas Turner was captain of the RMS *Lusitania* when the giant liner was sunk by a German submarine attack in May 1915, with the loss of more than 1,200 passengers and crew. Turner survived, and this is his story.

A Merseyside man, he came from Victorian seafaring stock and his sole ambition was always to go to sea. Turner became the outstanding seaman of his time, who had learned his craft the hard way- by experience.

The loss of the *Lusitania*, bound for Liverpool from New York, shattered his world and over the years he has been accused of treachery, stubbornness, ignorance and much worse. This book gives the true, remarkable story of Captain William Thomas Turner, the last Master of the doomed *Lusitania*.

'...the Admiralty made 'thoroughly discreditable attempts to blame Turner for the loss'
'...clears Captain Turner's name once and for all'...   Liverpool Echo

ISBN   0 902964 14 4   £7.99 + £1.25 p&p

CAMMELL LAIRD - THE GOLDEN YEARS
by David Roberts.
Foreword by Frank Field MP

Looks back at the world famous shipyard's history with particular focus upon the 1960s and 70s when Lairds were engaged in the building of Polaris Nuclear submarines. A unique look at the history of this yard that contains many photographs and references.
'Captures life in the prosperous years of the historic Birkenhead shipyard'- Liverpool Echo
'Puts into perspective...the strikes...the Polaris contract...and those who worked at the yard'- Sea Breezes
ISBN 09521020 2 1 £5.99 + £0.80 p&p

LIFE AT LAIRDS
- MEMORIES OF WORKING SHIPYARD MEN
by David Roberts
When Cammell Lairds has gone and we are a generation or two down the line who will answer the questions 'What did they do there?' 'What was it like?' This book answers the questions. - Sea Breezes
A Piece of Social History – Liverpool Echo

Life at Lairds is a book of more than 120 pages about what life was like for the thousands of ordinary people that worked in the world famous Birkenhead shipyard. Contains many rare photographs of Lairds, its' ships and its' surroundings.
ISBN 0 9521020 1 3 £6.99 + £1.50 p&p

FASTER THAN THE WIND
- A HISTORY GUIDE TO THE LIVERPOOL TO HOLYHEAD TELEGRAPH.
by Frank Large

Take a journey along the one of most spectacular coastlines in Britain, the beautiful hills and countryside of North Wales and Wirral. On a clear day it is possible to see just how signals were sent along the coast to and from Liverpool. This book contains full details of the intriguing and little known sites of the substantial remains of the Liverpool to Holyhead Telegraph Stations. A second journey can then be taken into the fascinating workings of such a telegraph and those people involved in creating and using the signalling system and what life was really like living and working at the telegraph stations more than 100 years ago.
ISBN 0 9521020 9 9 £8.95 + £1.50 p&p

IRON CLIPPER – 'TAYLEUR'
– THE WHITE STAR LINE'S 'FIRST TITANIC'

by H.F. Starkey

'Iron Clipper' is subtitled 'The First Titanic' for it tells the story of the first White Star liner to be lost on her maiden voyage. Built on the Upper Mersey at Warrington, the 'Tayleur' tragedy of 1854 and the 'Titanic' catastrophe of 1912 are disasters which have so much in common that the many coincidences make this factual book appear to be a work which is stranger than fiction.

ISBN 1 902964 00 4   £7.50+ £1.40 p&p

SCHOONER PORT
– TWO CENTURIES OF UPPER MERSEY SAIL

by H.F. Starkey

Schooner Port tells the story of the part Runcorn and navigation of the upper Mersey played in the Industrial Revolution and of the contribution of merchants, the shipbuilders, and the crews in making Britain 'The Workshop of the World'. Also recounted is something of the courage and tragedy, which was the lot of many flatmen and seamen who helped build British industry on the strength of the shipping fleet.

'Recognised as the only authoritative work on this particular subject '- Sea Breezes
'Packed with hard facts and illustrated with some rare old photographs, this rare book should command a wide readership'. - Liverpool Echo

ISBN 0 9521020 5 6   £8.95 + £1.50 p&p

ALL at SEA
– Memories of Maritime Merseyside

Compiled by Ev Draper.
Foreword by Radio Merseyside's Linda McDermott
Introduction by David Roberts - Maritime Historian

A new book in conjunction with BBC Radio Merseyside's programme of the same name brings the voices of Merseyside seafarers and their lives to the printed page. Here are the stories of brave men, now pensioners, who survived horrendous incidents in the last two wars; stories of luxury liners, from Captains to cabin crew, of young lads forging their identity cards to get away to sea, and of their first eye-opening voyages.

ALL at SEA brings back the sounds and the smells of the docks, which remain vivid in so many people's minds, of busy tugs up and down the river, of men lost at sea; of women serving their country in different ways, and of those who provided guiding lights home. But through all the stories, there's one shining thread, the pride of Merseysiders in their seagoing traditions.

If you want real stories of the sea, told from the heart, by real people about real times and places, then this is a book for you.

ISBN 1 902964 12 8   £5.99 + £1.25 p&p

THE GOLDEN WRECK
- THE TRAGEDY OF THE *ROYAL CHARTER*

by Alexander McKee

The effects great of the great hurricane of October 1859 were to shock the nation. 133 ships were sunk, 90 were badly damaged and almost 800 people lost their lives.

More than half of those that perished were on one ship - The *Royal Charter*.

The *Royal Charter* has a special place in maritime history as one of the greatest ever peacetime disasters. She was built at Sandycroft on the River Dee, the next-door neighbour to the river that was to become her home...the River Mersey. Soon after she was launched...sideways because of her great size for the day, she perhaps seemed ill starred in that whilst being towed down the river she grounded upon a sandbank off Flint, North Wales, and suffered serious damage to her main keel.

She eventually completed her maiden voyage to Melbourne in record time and her owners were able to boast about their new service 'England to Australia in under 60 days'.

Just a few short years later she was returning home and was hours away from disembarking her charges in Liverpool... until, when rounding Anglesey on the northern coast of Wales...disaster struck in the form of a Force 12 hurricane.

The people of the small village of Moelfre, Anglesey, came to the aid of the vessel and those from the ship who tried to escape the lashing waves and the deadly rocks. News of the wreck soon spread and the *Royal Charter's* other cargo, gold, became the focus of people's attention. Was all of it ever recovered? If not where did it go? The *Royal Charter's* gold still has the power to attract the adventurous and this book also explores attempts at salvage and treasure hunting more than 140 years on.

ISBN 1 9029640 2 0   £9.50 & 1.50 p&p

UNION CASTLE
- THE FORGOTTEN NAVY

by Peter Abbott - (author - the Lavender Hull Mob)

The Union - Castle Shipping Company was rightly famed for the Mailships of the line such as the *Pendennis Castle* and the *Windsor Castle* but there is much more to Union Castle than just these well-known liners.

'Union-Castle - the Forgotten Navy' features the Intermediate liners, The Royal East Africa Service, Round Africa vessels, coasters, general cargo ships and reefers. It also covers the Zulu War, Boer War, World War I and World War II.

Using records from company archives, contemporary South African newspapers, the author's own and others private collections of Union-Castle ephemera, this new book about *'the Forgotten Navy'* brings the reader a significant amount of hitherto little known material about the ships, the people and the Union-Castle Company.

ISBN 1 902964 00 15   £10.00 + £2.00 p&p

FROM BATTLEFIELD TO BLIGHTY

The History of Frodsham Military Hospital 1915-1919

by Arthur R Smith

The horrors of the first 'Great War' are well known, but the stories of those sent back from the 'Battlefield to Blighty' tend to be overlooked. This is the little known story of one of the largest auxiliary military hospitals in the country that was established at Frodsham in Cheshire during the First World War.

The men who fought in the trenches suffered horrendous casualty rates and for many of them the hospital at Frodsham provided treatment as well as a haven, however temporary, from the carnage.

Not for these men the modern diagnosis of Post Traumatic Stress Disorder or Stress Counselling after their ordeal... simply the green fields and fresh air of Cheshire and lots of TLC.

The injured and the 'bomb happy' were all welcomed with open arms by the predominantly volunteer staff, while the institution itself received a significant amount of its running costs from the donations of local people and businessmen.

Over the period of the hostilities more than 3,000 patients were cared for at Frodsham Auxiliary Military Hospital and using a recently discovered set of contemporary photographs, '*From Battlefield to Blighty*' tells the stories of the doctors, the nurses, the patients and the local people who were involved in the Auxiliary Military Hospital at Frodsham.

ISBN 1 902964 16 0 £7.99 +1.50 p&p

A WELCOME IN THE HILLSIDES?

- The Merseyside and North Wales Experience of Evacuation 1939-1945

by Jill Wallis

In the first week of September 1939 some 130,000 people left Merseyside for the safety of North Wales during World War II. Many were young children who had never been away from home before. Some didn't know why they were going, most didn't know where they were going. As they peered through train windows at unfamiliar hills and rolling countryside some youngsters thought they'd entered 'indian territory'; hearing a foreign language, others imagined they were 'in Germany'! Actually they had arrived in Wales.

A Welcome in the Hillsides? is an account of the Merseyside/NorthWales experience of the Second World War evacuation scheme. As hundreds of thousands poured into north and mid-Wales how did the authorities cope? - and how did the evacuees fare?

To produce a carefully balanced history the author has made an extensive search of official records and has also spoken to many of those who were involved in the scheme - former billeting officers, teachers, host families and, of course, the evacuees themselves! What emerges is an intensely human story - sometimes hilarious, sometimes painfully sad.

ISBN 1 902964 13 6 £9.95 + £1.90 p&p

JUST NUISANCE AB - His full story

by Terence Sisson

The amazing but true story of the only dog that was officially enlisted into British Royal Navy, a Great Dane whose name was Nuisance, his official rank and name was AB Just Nuisance.

Famed for his preference for the company of navy ratings (he wasn't too keen on Officers) in and around the famous World War II naval base of Simonstown, South Africa, Nuisance helped many a sailor rejoin his ship after a night on the town.

Today his own statue overlooking the bay off the Cape of Good Hope commemorates AB Just Nuisance.

£7.50 & £1.20 p&p

Avid Publications specialises in maritime titles, though other titles of interest are also published, as you can see from the previous few pages.

We welcome new authors.

V I D E O S

CAMMELL LAIRD - OLD SHIPS AND HARDSHIPS
- the story of a shipyard.

After an extensive search for moving footage of this world famous shipyard at work a video of the history of this shipyard has at last been compiled. How Cammell Laird served the nation through two World Wars, building world famous vessels like the *Rodney*, *Hood*, *Mauritania*, *Ark Royal*, *Windsor Castle* and many more, up to the tragic day in 1993 when Lairds was shut down.

The story of the yard is also told through the voices of the men who worked at Lairds; Welders, cranedrivers, electricians and plumbers, they tell of the hardships of building ships in all weathers and the lighter moments that came from some of the 'characters' of the yard.

'ALL IN A DAY'S WORK.' Volumes I & II
— a look at working lives on the River Mersey.

Just when you might have thought that the River Mersey was dead and buried the biggest surprise of all comes along. There is life in the old dog yet! The River Mersey is alive and well. Liverpool, Birkenhead, Tranmere, Eastham and Runcorn are still places that enjoy marine traffic and employ people working on the river.

There are interviews with River Pilots, shipbuilders, shiprepairers, tugmen and dredgermen that show that the age-old crafts and seamanship itself are still as strong as they ever were. There is also archive footage of working life on the river.

Features Rock Boats, Mersey Ferries, the Bunker boats & crews on the Mersey, the Vessel Tracking System for river traffic, new vessels on the river, lockmasters and much more.

All videos are priced at £14.99 including post and packaging in UK.
Videos are also available in international formats price £17.99 + P&P £3.50.